CareerTransitions

Career Transitions provides immediate access to the most important career exploration and employment preparation activities. If you are college bound, on a vocational track, or preparing to enter the workforce, you will find an intuitive user experience designed to engage and guide you through practical learning activities and important education and career decisions.

Engaging, Interactive, and Focused

CT provides you with Personal Learning Experiences (PLEs) that are interactive and engaging. These include:

- Identify career inclinations through an engaging and eye-opening career interest assessment
- Browse through the Department of Education's 16 Career Clusters as well as spotlight career categories (including Green, New Economy, and High-Growth careers)
- Engage in a practice ride through real job situations with a customized, interactive interview simulation
- Create beginning resumes and cover letters with realistic samples and in-context tips and examples, and get practical guidance in the form of videos and short how-to articles
- Use a job and internship search to seek real opportunities for today and the future

Guiding Careers from Start to Finish

Career Transitions provides an intuitive user experience with direct access to a span of activities and information encompassing the entire career exploration and employment preparation arc.

SOUTH-WESTERN
CENGAGE Learning·

FIRST-TIME REGISTRATION

1. Go to: http://login.cengage.com/cb/
2. Click "**Create My Account**"
3. Click "**Student**"
4. Enter your **ACCESS CODE** and click "**continue**"

> access code
> ## PP91W9SP5NTJ68
> duration: 1 year

5. Enter account information
6. Select your institution (school name)
7. Begin accessing **Career Transitions**

CareerTransitions

RETURNING USER

1. Go to: http://login.cengage.com/cb/
2. Enter your email address and password and click "**Sign In**"
3. Click "**Go**"
4. Click on "**Career Transitions**" to access

Enter your email and password in the spaces below and save this card for future reference. To access this resource you will ALWAYS need to return to **http://login.cengage.com/cb/** and enter your email address and password to sign in.

> Email

> Password

8e

Your
Career
How to Make It **Happen**

Lauri Harwood

Business Consultant and Trainer
Cincinnati, Ohio

SOUTH-WESTERN
CENGAGE Learning·

Australia • Brazil • Japan • Korea • Mexico • Singapore • Spain • United Kingdom • United States

**Your Career: How to Make It Happen,
Eighth Edition**
Lauri Harwood

Vice President of Editorial, Business:
Jack W. Calhoun

Vice President/Editor-in-Chief: Karen Schmohe

Associate Acquisitions Editor: Michael
Guendelsberger

Senior Developmental Editor: Penny Shank

Editorial Assistant: Anne Kelly

Associate Marketing Manager: Shanna Shelton

Marketing Communications Manager:
Megan Faletra

Media Editor: Lysa Kosins

Manufacturing Planner: Kevin Kluck

Design Direction, Production Management,
and Composition: PreMediaGlobal

Senior Art Director: Michelle Kunkler

Cover Designer: Lou Ann Thesing

Cover Images: ©Yuri Arcurs, Shutterstock;
©kali9, ©LdF, iStock

Rights Acquisition Director: Audrey Pettingill

Rights Acquisition Specialist, Text and Image:
Amber Hosea

The Twitter mark is a trademark of Twitter, Inc.

The FACEBOOK mark and the Facebook F Logo
are a trademark of Facebook, Inc.

All model documents: ©Cengage Learning

For product information and technology assistance, contact us at
Cengage Learning Customer & Sales Support, 1-800-354-9706

For permission to use material from this text or product,
submit all requests online at **www.cengage.com/permissions**
Further permissions questions can be emailed to
permissionrequest@cengage.com

The Career Clusters icons are being used with permission of the:

States' Career Clusters Initiative, 2007, www.careerclusters.org

Library of Congress Control Number: 2011939724

ISBN-13: 978-1-111-57231-0

ISBN-10: 1-111-57231-3

Student Edition ISBN 13: 978-1-133-31925-2

Student Edition ISBN 10: 1-133-31925-4

South-Western
5191 Natorp Boulevard
Mason, OH 45040
USA

Cengage Learning products are represented in Canada by
Nelson Education, Ltd.

For your course and learning solutions, visit www.cengage.com
Visit our company website at www.cengage.com

Printed in the United States of America
2 3 4 5 15 14 13

BRIEF TABLE OF CONTENTS

TABLE OF CONTENTS

Introducing *YOUR CAREER: HOW TO MAKE IT HAPPEN, 8e ...*

YOUR GUIDE TO EXPLORING, CONNECTING, SUCCEEDING!

Packed with innovative resources readers can apply now and throughout their careers, best-selling YOUR CAREER: HOW TO MAKE IT HAPPEN, 8e delivers a comprehensive, step-by-step guide to finding and keeping a job—turning job seekers into job finders.

Part Opener ...

Each section of the book *showcases* the real-life perspective of two experts—one who sits behind the desk and one who is a jobseeker or a newly hired employee. Includes a planner for organizing class assignments and outside commitments in the coming weeks.

Readers plan their assignments and other commitments for the coming weeks.

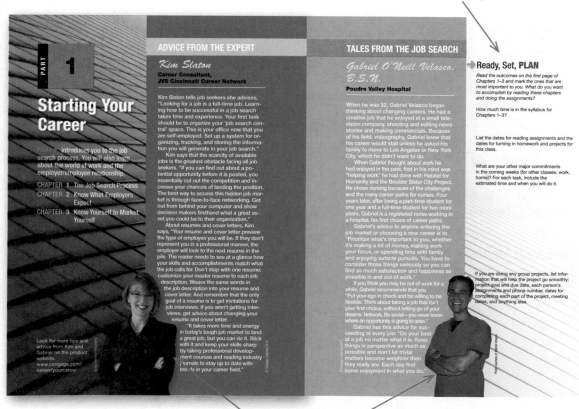

Hiring professionals and jobseekers give timely advice about finding a job.

GETTING STARTED
Chapter Opener ...

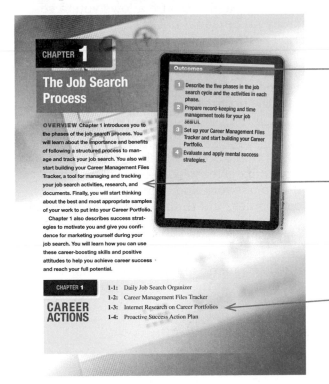

Outcomes—a quick review of core concepts tied to content throughout the chapter.

Overview—summary of achievement expectations of the chapter.

BEYOND THE CLASSROOM ...

Career Actions—an at-a-glance list of the chapter Career Action assignments, which take students beyond the classroom and into the business world.

CAREER FOCUSED FEATURES

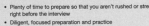

Make It a Habit provides information about job etiquette, manners, and behavior.

Watch Out warns about career taboos and mistakes to avoid.

Jump Start challenges students to analyze careers of interest and questions associated with them and to conduct research to get the answers.

GET CONNECTED

Find Job Leads with Twitter

Unlike many other social networking sites, Twitter users commonly chat and connect with complete strangers. This is great news for job seekers who are willing to be outgoing to meet others in their industry. A simple search can yield hundreds of people and businesses that hold the same interests and are willing to talk with you.

- Create a free Twitter profile, if you haven't already, and complete your profile indicating interest in your industry and career fields.
- Search for people and businesses that are interested and active in your field and "follow" them.
- Read tweets sent out by select companies to learn what's new with them and whether they're hiring. More and more companies tweet out current job openings.
- Follow experts who are active in your industry; read the articles and information they are twittering, and ask them for advice.
- Send out tweets about your job-seeking interests.

Twitter users share information and links in real time, so you can often find the most up-to-date information on the Web. Search engines have to play catch-up because they need more time to find and index articles.

NEW! Social Media Feature allows you to go beyond your personal network and tap into the best job search resources available on the Internet. YOUR CAREER: HOW TO MAKE IT HAPPEN, 8e emphasizes the importance of being socially active and responsible to make YOU stand out and get the best results.

NEW! Using Social Media in Your Job Search Appendix gives job seekers advice and tips to network and connect with experts, companies, and their peers. The top social media sites are free, are easy to use, and will help you gain an advantage among job-seekers. This Appendix focuses on social media etiquette and common sense to keep candidates at the top of the list.

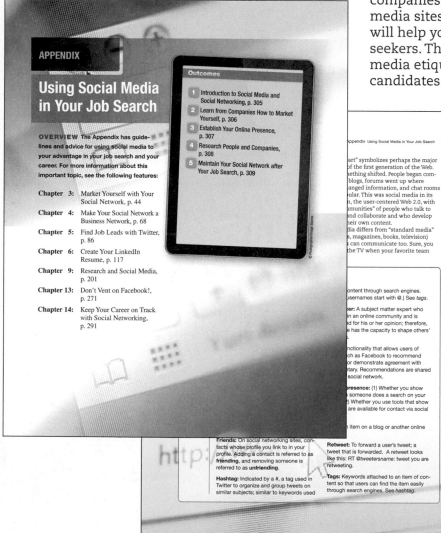

APPLICATIONS FOR SUCCESS
End of the Chapter ...

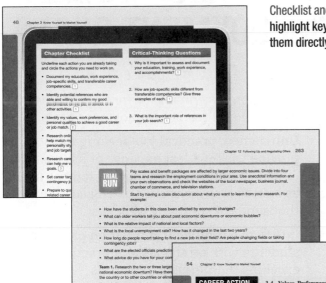

Checklist and Critical-Thinking Questions highlight key chapter concepts and apply them directly to students' career goals.

Trial Run interactive or role-playing activities model the desired outcomes of the chapter. Each activity requires peer or self-evaluation.

For Your Career Management Files Tracker reminds students of documents that should be placed in their employment portfolio.

Career Action assignments take students beyond the classroom to make real-world connections with businesses in their field, investigate current business practices, and stimulate the action necessary in the job search process.

ADDED VALUE AND GREATER CONVENIENCE

Job Search Quick Reference ...

A removable guide at the back of every text for use in interviewing and networking situations:

- Quick access to the job seeker's frequently used information
- Space for vital information and qualifications
- Common and tricky interview questions
- Resume and job action verbs

CENGAGE brain.com

Student Resources available only at CengageBrain

- Gain access to FREE book companion resources, including Critical-Thinking Questions, Career Action Worksheets, Glossary, Web Links, Model Resumes and Letters, PLUS MORE!
- Try a demo chapter or access free content within CourseMate
- Study smarter, not harder

CAREER TRANSITIONS: EXPLORE CAREER INTERESTS. ACHIEVE EMPLOYMENT GOALS.

Give students instant access to the most valuable, complete career exploration and job-seeking resources available online with this one-of-a-kind application. *Career Transitions* guides students through the entire career process—from individualized assessment of personal strengths and corresponding career opportunities to focused, expert guidance and practical, results-driven job-seeking tools.

Effective Career Exploration

- **Students define and determine ideal career paths** using intuitive, engaging activities.

- **Individualized assessments** help students candidly evaluate personal abilities, test skill sets, and determine career opportunities that most closely align with their distinctive strengths.

- **Clear, reliable information** highlights green, new economy, and high-growth occupations.

- **Candid videos** provide realistic glimpses into daily job and career choices.

Practical Job-Seeking Expertise

- **Expert, professional guidance** helps students establish and realize employment goals.

- **Unmatched, practical job-seeking tools** provide the broadest expanse of job postings online and drawn from reliable sources such as *indeed®.com, monster®, CareerBuilder®,* and thousands of company websites.

- **Interactive interview simulation** provides students with strategies and practice for excelling in interview situations.

- **Useful tracking tools** keep job searches organized, efficient, and focused.

- **Professional resources help perfect presentations,** from resumes and cover letters to interview techniques for employment success.

Help today's students transition to success with the unique *Career Transitions.*

COURSEMATE: ENGAGING. TRACKABLE. AFFORDABLE.

Interested in a simple way to complement your text and course content with study and practice materials?

Cengage Learning's Career CourseMate brings course concepts to life with interactive learning, study, and exam preparation tools that support the printed textbook. Watch student comprehension soar as your class works with the printed textbook and the textbook-specific website. CourseMate for Your Career goes beyond the book to deliver what you need!

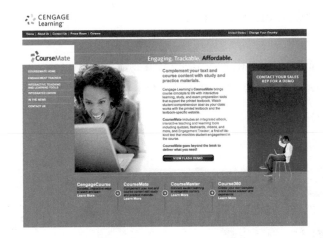

CENGAGE brain.com

BUY. RENT. ACCESS.

On CengageBrain.com, students will be able to save up to 60% on their course materials through our full spectrum of options. Students will have the option to rent their textbooks or purchase print textbooks, e-textbooks, or individual e-chapters and audio books all for substantial savings over average retail prices. CengageBrain.com also includes access to Cengage Learning's broad range of homework and study tools and features a selection of free content.

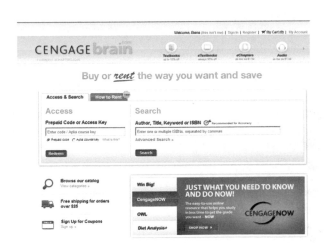

TEACHING RESOURCES

Online Companion Site or Instructor's Resource CD ...

Offers complete and customizable content:

- Instructor's Guide
- Career Action Worksheets
- PowerPoint® Presentations
- Exam*View*® Testbanks and Solutions
- List of Social Media Features from the text
- Instructor Course Management Forms
- And more!

Robust Companion Website ...

Includes flash cards, crossword puzzles, Career Action forms, Web links, sample resumes and cover letters, and more.

www.cengage.com/career/yourcareer

REVIEWERS

Renee Albrecht
Business Education Teacher
Greendale High School
Greendale, Wisconsin

Holly Bales
Instructor
International Business College
Indianapolis, Indiana

Angele Blackshear-Brown
Academic Affairs Department
   Chairperson
Brown Mackie College
Ft. Mitchell, Kentucky

Sharon Dayton
Allied Health Instructor
Processional Skills Institute
Toledo, Ohio

Amanda Hardin
BOT Department Instructor
Mississippi Delta Community College
Moorhead, Mississippi

Terrance J. Hunter
Lead CAD Instructor
Virginia College
Mobile, Alabama

Anne Landon, CPRW
Internship Coordinator and Assistant
   Director
Lycoming College
Williamsport, Pennsylvania

Gloria H. Longakit
Office of Academic Affairs Director
ASA Institute
Brooklyn, New York

Dr. Jean A. Lutz
English Professor
Miami University
Oxford, Ohio

Amie L. Mayhall
Media Office Careers Lead Instructor
Olney Central College
Olney, Illinois

Dr. Byron Lynn Morgan
Management Department Lecturer
Texas State University – San Marcos
San Marcos, Texas

Kim Slaton
Career Consultant
Jewish Vocational Service
Cincinnati Career Network
Cincinnati, Ohio

LaToya Smith
Office Administration Instructor
Piedmont Community College
Roxboro, North Carolina

Helen W. Spain
Office Administration and Medical Office
   Administration Instructor
Wake Technical Community College
Raleigh, North Carolina

Marci Stone
Fortis College
Salt Lake City, Utah

MESSAGE FROM THE AUTHOR

Among the good things in life, a good job doing work you enjoy is one of the best. The single purpose of this book is to help you achieve this goal. You'll find practical, useful, and realistic advice to help you get interviews and job offers and become a valued employee.

Here's some advice to make this class helpful and meaningful to *you*: where you are now and where you want to go.

- Aim for a career, not a series of jobs. Plan for your entire working life and for your retirement.
- **Finish your degree or certificate.** A degree is an extremely valuable asset for nearly every aspect of your work and life. Employers who see a degree and/or certificate on your resume know that you finish what you start.
- Count yourself lucky to be taking this class. Use the class to get a head start on your job search so that you can act fast when you need to find a job.
- You are your own boss when you look for a job. Like any savvy business owner, set high standards, set realistic and challenging goals, and get expert advice and help.
- Evaluate your skills, work traits, and preferences so that you can concentrate on career fields that you will enjoy and will do well in.
- Use the class to practice excelling in your job. Do the things required in the real world to keep your job and to advance in your career. Do your best work and complete it on time. Don't be the employee (or student) who just goes through the motions.
- During class or afterwards, meet with a professional job counselor for tips about job leads, an expert review of your resume, a practice interview, and so much more.
- Use the class resources wisely.
  - Read the book, complete the assignments, make time for group activities, and network with your classmates and instructors. No single book has all of the advice that applies to every situation, so use other resources too.
  - Take your Career Management Files Tracker and Career Portfolio seriously (see page 8). Set them up thoughtfully and update them throughout your career.
  - Set goals for getting the most out of each chapter—for your situation. Use the online study guides to record the advice that applies to you.
  - Use the *Your Career* website and the *Career Transitions* website. They contain valuable tools and advice that other job seekers don't have access to.
  - Read Chapter 14, Take Charge of Your Career, while you read the rest of the book, not at the end of the course. Start applying the advice from day one.

Your working life will last about 55 years, maybe longer, so **get serious and get started!** Believe in yourself to meet your goals, and decide today to become a *job finder*, not a job seeker.

Starting Your Career

PART 1 introduces you to the job search process. You will also learn about the world of work and the employer/employee relationship.

Look for more tips and advice from Kim and Gabriel on the product website. www.cengage.com/ career/yourcareer

©Jim Calloway Photography

ADVICE FROM THE EXPERT

Kim Slaton
Career Consultant, JVS Cincinnati Career Network

Kim Slaton tells job seekers she advises, "Looking for a job is a full-time job. Learning how to be successful in a job search takes time and experience. Your first task should be to organize your 'job search central' space. This is your office now that you are self-employed. Set up a system for organizing, tracking, and storing the information you will generate in your job search."

Kim says that the scarcity of available jobs is the greatest obstacle facing all job seekers. "If you can find out about a potential opportunity before it is posted, you essentially cut out the competition and increase your chances of landing the position. The best way to access this hidden job market is through face-to-face networking. Get out from behind your computer and show decision makers firsthand what a great asset you could be to their organization."

About resumes and cover letters, Kim says, "Your resume and cover letter preview the type of employee you will be. If they don't represent you in a professional manner, the employer will look to the next resume in the pile. The reader needs to see at a glance how your skills and accomplishments match what the job calls for. Don't stop with one resume; customize your master resume to each job description. Weave the same words in the job description into your resume and cover letter. And remember that the only goal of a resume is to get invitations for job interviews. If you aren't getting interviews, get advice about changing your resume and cover letter.

"It takes more time and energy in today's tough job market to land a great job, but you can do it. Stick with it and keep your skills sharp by taking professional development courses and reading industry journals to stay up to date with trends in your career field."

© Cengage Learning 2013

Gabriel O'Neill Velasco, B.S.N.

Poudre Valley Hospital

When he was 32, Gabriel Velasco began thinking about changing careers. He had a creative job that he enjoyed at a small television company, shooting and editing news stories and making commercials. Because of his field, videography, Gabriel knew that his career would stall unless he asked his family to move to Los Angeles or New York City, which he didn't want to do.

When Gabriel thought about work he had enjoyed in the past, first in his mind was "helping work" he had done with Habitat for Humanity and the Boulder Sister City Project. He chose nursing because of the challenges and the many career paths for nurses. Four years later, after being a part-time student for one year and a full-time student for two more years, Gabriel is a registered nurse working in a hospital, his first choice of career paths.

Gabriel's advice to anyone entering the job market or choosing a new career is to "Prioritize what's important to you, whether it's making a lot of money, making work your focus, or spending time with family and enjoying outside pursuits. You have to consider those things seriously so you can find as much satisfaction and happiness as possible in and out of work."

If you think you may be out of work for a while, Gabriel recommends that you "Put your ego in check and be willing to be flexible. Think about taking a job that isn't your first choice, without letting go of your dreams. Network. Be social—you never know where an opportunity is going to arise."

Gabriel has this advice for succeeding at every job: "Do your best at a job no matter what it is. Keep things in perspective as much as possible and don't let trivial matters become weightier than they really are. Each day find some enjoyment in what you do."

→ Ready, Set, PLAN

Read the outcomes on the first page of Chapters 1–3 and mark the ones that are most important to you. What do you want to accomplish by reading these chapters and doing the assignments?

How much time is in the syllabus for Chapters 1–3?

List the dates for reading assignments and the dates for turning in homework and projects for this class.

What are your other major commitments in the coming weeks (for other classes, work, home)? For each task, include the estimated time and when you will do it.

If you are doing any group projects, list information that will help the project go smoothly: project goal and due date, each person's assignments and phone number, dates for completing each part of the project, meeting dates, and anything else.

The Job Search Process

Outcomes

1 Describe the five phases in the job search cycle and the activities in each phase.

2 Prepare record-keeping and time management tools for your job search.

3 Set up your Career Management Files Tracker and start building your Career Portfolio.

4 Evaluate and apply mental success strategies.

OVERVIEW Chapter 1 introduces you to the phases of the job search process. You will learn about the importance and benefits of following a structured process to manage and track your job search. You also will start building your Career Management Files Tracker, a tool for managing and tracking your job search activities, research, and documents. Finally, you will start thinking about the best and most appropriate samples of your work to put into your Career Portfolio.

Chapter 1 also describes success strategies to motivate you and give you confidence for marketing yourself during your job search. You will learn how you can use these career-boosting skills and positive attitudes to help you achieve career success and reach your full potential.

CHAPTER 1

CAREER ACTIONS

1-1: Daily Job Search Organizer

1-2: Career Management Files Tracker

1-3: Internet Research on Career Portfolios

1-4: Proactive Success Action Plan

JUMP START
Your Job Search Knowledge

Think about your current job or a job you had in the past. If you haven't had a full-time job, think about a part-time job or volunteer work. Answer these questions about how you handled the job search process.

- Why did you want the job?
- Why did you think you were suited for the job?
- How did you learn about the job opening? How did you apply for the job?
- Why do you think you were hired'?
- Did the work match what you learned about the job during the hiring process?
- Do you still have this job? Why or why not?
- What will you do differently when you apply for other jobs?

The Job Search Cycle: Where to Start?

Outcome 1

The process of finding a job can be daunting and difficult to navigate, even for someone with plenty of work experience. It helps to think of the process as an ongoing cycle rather than a series of steps.

The cycle of exploring career fields and opportunities, assessing your skills and qualifications, finding job leads, writing resumes and cover letters, interviewing for jobs, and following up with prospective employers is an important part of your work life not only for your first job, but also for your entire career. Revisiting these phases to stay current with your job goals, qualifications, and career documents will save you time and help you manage your career.

The job search cycle has five phases with specific activities. The five Parts of this book correspond to these phases. In each Part, you will practice the job search activities for that phase, building your experience, learning new skills, and creating documents that will help you succeed in your job search.

PHASE 1: Prepare For Your Job Search Learn about the workplace and employer expectations, plan for your career, assess your skills and characteristics, and determine your career target(s).

PHASE 2: Find Job Leads Network; search for job leads; and conduct research using a variety of job sources, including the Internet, your contacts, and print resources.

PHASE 3: Apply for Jobs Market yourself by preparing effective resumes and cover letters. Know how to fill out printed applications and how to apply for jobs online.

PHASE 4: Interview for Jobs Use strategies for getting interviews, prepare and practice for different types of interviews and interview questions, practice effective interviewing techniques, and write effective thank-you letters.

PHASE 5: Follow Up and Evaluate Follow up with employers and evaluate and consider job offers. During this phase, a job seeker accepts a job offer or returns to an earlier phase to look for a different job or to explore other opportunities.

Managing Your Job Search

Outcome **2**

The job market is not always organized. Employers have different hiring processes and requirements. Their processes may be simple or complex, well organized or poorly organized, short or long.

To enter the job market, you—the job applicant—must be well organized even though the job market is not. You need a system to organize, manage, and track your job search. The information, advice, and activities in *Your Career: How to Make It Happen* will help you organize an efficient, successful job-seeking campaign.

Set Up Your Job Search Headquarters

The planning and energy you put into organizing your job search directly affects the speed and success of your search; so take the time now to set up a system that will maximize your efforts.

Organize a space for keeping your job search records and documents so that you can easily find what you need and follow up on leads quickly and effectively.

- If you work best with printed documents, use labeled file folders or an expanding folder with pockets you can label.

- If you own a computer or have reliable access to one and do most of your work online, create a logical system of folders and subfolders for storing your work.

Track Your Progress

One of the most useful tasks you can do as a job seeker is to keep a record of everything you undertake in your job search. Because you may be applying for several jobs at the same time, this can become a challenge.

Prepare a Weekly Schedule

Use a monthly calendar to schedule your activities a week or more in advance. Record the hours you will spend on your search each day.

Prepare a Daily Plan

Establish a routine and work on your job search every day. Keep a daily log of your activities. Write down employer contacts and research sources (including log-in information for websites). Keep track of job leads, resumes, completed or submitted applications, telephone calls, emails, and other activities. To get started, use the form in Career Action 1-1 at the end of this chapter.

The Job Search Cycle

Anastasios Kandris/Shutterstock.com

Phase 1: Prepare for Your Job Search
- Career Planning
- Self-Assessment

Phase 2: Find Job Leads
- Research
- Networking

Phase 3: Apply for Jobs
- Resumes
- Job Applications
- Cover Letters

Phase 4: Interview for Jobs
- Preparation and Practice
- Interview Questions
- Pre-employment Tests

Phase 5: Follow Up and Evaluate
- Follow Up with Employers
- Accept a Job Offer or Restart the Job Search Cycle

"**You are your own boss** while you look for a job. Hold yourself accountable and report for work every day."

 COMPLETE **CAREER ACTION 1-1**

Daily Job Search Organizer, p. 16

Outcome 3 Your Job Search Files and Career Portfolio

Keeping good records is an essential skill for job seekers (and everyone who works). This section introduces two tools to help you manage your work and reach your full career potential: your Career Management Files Tracker and your Career Portfolio. A third tool, your Interview Marketing Kit, is introduced in Chapter 8, page 189.

Career Management Files Tracker

To help you assess your learning and prepare for success in your job search and career, you will develop a **Career Management Files Tracker**, a three-ring binder for collecting, organizing, and updating your career information. The binder is for storing the career development and job search information you record in the Career Action activities at the end of each chapter, such as self-assessments, records of experience and skills, networking lists, drafts of resumes and cover letters, and job search aids. The pages in this book are perforated so that you can save pages in the binder and refer to them later. (The entire book is an excellent resource after the course ends, of course.) You can also print and keep information you find on the Internet.

Your Career Management Files Tracker will become a personal record of your job search

experience and a resource you can use when seeking a promotion, a new job, or a career change. The time you spend making the binder a personalized, useful collection of career information will be time well spent. Career Action 1-2 is the first step in organizing this essential career tool.

1. **Set up your Career Management Files Tracker.** Use a three-ring binder with divider tabs labeled Chapter 1 through Chapter 14, with several extra sections for notes, examples, etc. You can also use tabs with topic labels such as "network contacts," "resumes," "cover letters," and "references."

2. **File your completed Career Actions.** Put these worksheets and other documents, such as drafts of your resume, behind the appropriate tab. Use the Career Action worksheets in the book or the worksheets at www.cengage.com/career/yourcareer.

3. **Back up your work.** If you use the online PDF forms to complete the Career Action worksheets, back up these files and the other documents you create.

While you are taking this class, it may be convenient to keep your daily plan and weekly schedule in your Career Management Files Tracker. When the class is over, keep your Career Management Files Tracker and backup files. This "career to go" tool will come in handy when you need to revise and update your career documents and reference data.

 COMPLETE **CAREER ACTION 1-2**

Career Management Files Tracker, p. 17

Career Portfolio

Your **Career Portfolio** is an organized collection of documents and other items that demonstrate your skills, abilities, achievements, experience, and qualifications.

This portfolio will contain items such as your final resume, a list of references, letters of recommendation, awards, and samples of your best work. These items showcase your talents and demonstrate that you have the organizational skills all employers are looking for, such as critical thinking, planning, preparation, and attention to detail.

The items in your portfolio can be from paid or volunteer work, classes, internships, clubs, and community activities. Use items that demonstrate your qualifications for the jobs and career fields you are interested in.

For example, to demonstrate your computer skills, you could include transcripts listing related course work and a DVD with multimedia presentations or applications you developed. To demonstrate your fluency in another language, you could include printed or spoken examples, such as a document you have written or an audio or video clip.

Select Items for Your Portfolio

Begin by deciding which of your skills and experiences relate most directly to your job target. Then think about what you have done or accomplished that best demonstrates your qualifications.

The first two pages in your portfolio should include your contact information and a list of the contents.

Figure 1-1 is a list of items and ideas for building your portfolio. Be sure to remove all confidential information from the work samples in your portfolio.

Assemble Your Portfolio

For a portfolio with 8½- by 11-inch pages, use a professional-looking folder or a three-ring binder with labeled divider tabs. Larger portfolios are appropriate for artists, journalists, and others who have oversized work samples. Use sheet protectors and CD inserts to protect and display the items in your portfolio.

File the original documents, such as letters of recommendation, in your Career Management Files Tracker and make copies for your portfolio.

Career Management Files Tracker and Career Portfolio

Your **Career Management Files Tracker** is a tool for organizing the information you use to look for jobs and to manage your career throughout your working life. Your **Career Portfolio** contains documents that you can show to prospective employers.

You will not take your entire Career Portfolio to job interviews. For each interview, you select the most appropriate samples of your work for that position and put them in a professional-looking folder or binder that becomes part of your Interview Marketing Kit. Chapter 8, Interview Essentials, explains how to use samples from your Career Portfolio in interviews.

Career Management Files Tracker	Career Portfolio
For personal use in keeping records and organizing your job search	Select appropriate documents from your portfolio to show to prospective employers during interviews
Documents your job search progress and learning and serves as a reference tool	Showcases your skills and qualifications through high-quality documents and work samples
Includes all research, notes, document drafts, contacts, and other items you have used in your job search	Is a collection of your best work that represents your accomplishments and qualifications (including cover letter, resume, references, and work samples)

Sample Portfolio Items

Examples of items for your portfolio include the following:

- [ ] Paper documents (beginning with a professional-looking cover sheet with contact information and a content list)
- [ ] Artwork and photographs
- [ ] DVD, CD, or flash drive with text documents, audio and/or video files, artwork, and similar items
- [ ] Other work-related items that demonstrate your qualifications and experience

Use your imagination and aim for a close match with your target job.

Work Experience, Work Performance, and Credentials

- **Resume:** Error-free copies of your resume printed on quality paper. Your resume should be the first item in your portfolio (after the cover sheet and content list). Include a CD or flash drive with a resume file.
- **Employer or Internship Performance Reviews:** Copies of all favorable performance reviews.
- **Licenses:** Copies of licenses for professions requiring a license to work in the field.
- **List of References:** References' names, addresses, and phone numbers and their association to you. Past employers, direct supervisors, and instructors are good references.
- **Letters of Recommendation/Commendation:** Include these letters; they speak for themselves.

Education, Training, Degrees, and Certificates

- **Diploma/Degree:** Copies of your diploma(s) or degree(s). Place originals in your Career Management Files Tracker (or frame them).
- **Transcripts:** If your academic performance was good, keep copies of transcripts to demonstrate this strength. Place original transcripts in your Career Management Files Tracker.
- **Certificates:** Professional certification (for example, CPS, CET, PE, and teaching certificates) and certificates of completion for continuing education, specialized training, workshops, and/or seminars.
- **Awards:** For perfect attendance on the job and in school, academic accomplishments, employee of the month, etc. Awards are proof of accomplishments and are of interest to employers.

Samples of Work, Use of Technology, and Information

IMPORTANT: On a case-by-case basis, verify that you can share work you did for your employer and delete or black out all confidential information. A prospective employer will not trust you if you share confidential information from other jobs.

- **Design Work:** Computer or manual drawings to prove technical ability in mechanical, architectural, structural, or electrical designs.
- **Artwork:** Sketches, drawings, and paintings; photographs or video footage; computer-generated artwork.
- **Writing Samples:** Many jobs involve a fair amount of writing. Include samples of presentations, text for websites, technical writing, reports, articles, business plans, and training materials, for example. Strong communication skills indicate that you possess other important skills, such as critical-thinking and organizational skills.
- **Software-Generated Documents:** Include your best examples from school if you lack related job experience (for example, spreadsheets, presentation documents, and newsletters).
- **Software Applications:** Screenshots of websites, multimedia presentations, and applications; DVD or CD with actual work or links to work.

Other Items

- **Military Records:** Your military service with awards and badges.
- **Community Service:** Materials that demonstrate active involvement in community service.
- **Forms of Identification:** Front and back photocopies of a valid driver's license or photo ID. Many employers request at least two forms of identification to process your application.
- **Proof of Citizenship:** Copies of your birth certificate, passport, visas, and/or immigration forms. These documents show that you are eligible to work. Black out your social security number.

Figure 1-1 Sample Portfolio Items

MAKE IT A HABIT

Give Yourself a Pep Talk

Repeat each of the following sentences aloud and think about how the words apply to you and your life. If it helps you get started, substitute the word *you* the first time and imagine that the person you admire most in your life is saying these things to you.

- I have the power to succeed.
- I deserve happiness and success.
- I can make my own choices and decisions.
- I can choose to make changes in every area of my life.
- I am worthy of being loved.
- My family and friends are glad that I am part of their lives.
- I am satisfied that I have done my best.
- I have a plan for the future, and my plan is open to change.
- I will not give up on myself.
- I have the power to succeed. (End your pep talk by repeating the first sentence—it says it all.)

Don't be shy about starting your day with a pep talk. Add your own sentences and repeat them to yourself throughout the day.

hfng/Shutterstock.com

Create an Online Career Portfolio

The Internet is *the* essential tool for both parties involved in a job search. Many companies rely solely on the Internet to find job candidates to

interview. Consider posting a professional-looking portfolio and putting a link to it on your business card, resume, cover letter, and online applications. Prospective employers can review your work at their convenience, and they will know that you can use the tools needed to create an online portfolio.

COMPLETE | **CAREER ACTION 1-3**

Internet Research on Career Portfolios, p. 17

Outcome 4 Success Strategies for Marketing Yourself

Looking for a job is hard work and can be overwhelming. A positive outlook and positive behaviors can help you develop confidence, stay focused, and improve your performance so that you can effectively market yourself to prospective employers.

Maintain a Positive Outlook

Research has shown that a positive outlook can have a powerful effect on personal performance, confidence, and even health. This section has some tips for using the power of positive thinking to enhance your job search performance and career development.

Positive Thinking and Behavior

Positive thinking is making a conscious effort to be optimistic and to anticipate positive outcomes. **Positive behavior** is purposely acting with energy and enthusiasm. When you think and behave positively, you guide your mind toward your goals and generate matching mental and physical energy.

Positive thinking actually causes changes in the brain that boost your ability to perform and to project enthusiasm, energy, competence, and confidence—qualities that companies look for when they hire and promote employees.

Positive Visualization

Positive visualization is purposely forming a mental picture of your successful performance and recalling the image frequently. The act of visualizing the successful performance of a skill or an activity in detail increases learning and skill development.

To strengthen your performance, practice visualizing yourself achieving your career goals with confidence and ease.

Positive Self-Talk

Positive self-talk is purposely giving yourself positive reinforcement, motivation, and recognition—just as you would do for a friend. What you habitually say to yourself can have a profound impact on your self-image, your self-esteem, and your performance and success.

Make this work for you by keeping your self-talk positive—for example, "I did a good job on that report" or "I can do this." Avoid sabotaging your attitude with self-critical or uncertain language such as "I'm too nervous" or "I'll try."

Congratulate yourself when you do well and remind yourself of your abilities, strengths, accomplishments, and skills.

Strong Self-Esteem

Projecting confidence requires healthy **self-esteem**, a belief in your abilities and your worth. Think about how easy it is to project a confident, competent image when you feel good about yourself. Because life experiences may change your level of self-esteem, work consciously on strengthening and maintaining your self-esteem. Negative self-esteem and a fear of failure can keep you from meeting your full potential.

To feel good about yourself and to maintain your self-esteem, surround yourself with a positive environment (positive people and positive reading, viewing, and audio materials). Taking care of your body, mind, and spirit also boosts your self-esteem. Looking your best boosts your confidence, and others respond positively to your appearance.

WATCH OUT!

Take Charge of Your Career Right Now

Many factors in your job search are not under your control, but one thing certainly is—the effort you make to stand out from the crowd every step of the way. To get an edge over other job seekers, do the following: (1) set personal goals for this class and for your job search, (2) believe in your drive and commitment to achieve your goals, and (3) use this class and textbook to succeed. Don't cheat yourself by just going through the motions in class.

The book is filled with practical, useful, and realistic advice and actions. When you read each chapter, think about how you can apply the information and advice to your goals and situation. Complete all of the assignments and maintain your Career Management Files Tracker and Career Portfolio.

You owe it to yourself and your family to be committed to your job search. Set a goal today to become a *job finder*, not a job seeker.

Set Goals for Your Job Search

Organizations stay in business by setting and achieving goals (for example, increased sales, new product development, and lower production costs). Sucessful job seekers also set goals and work to achieve them. Follow these steps to focus your efforts on achieving your goals.

- **Set long-term and short-term goals.** More ambitious goals such as earning your college degree require more time and are called **long-term goals**. Your **short-term goals** are accomplishments you want to achieve more quickly, such as assembling your Career Management Files Tracker. Short-term goals are also the steps you need to take to achieve a long-term goal.

- **Define your goals clearly in writing.** Experts say that writing down your goals strongly increases your likelihood of achieving them. Written goals increase your sense of commitment, clarify the steps you need to take, and help you remember important details. Use short, specific statements ("turn in my college application by August 15") that you can aim for. Avoid vague goal statements such as "I will earn more money this year."

- **Define the purpose and benefit of your goals.** Link your goals to a realistic, practical, and specific purpose that benefits you. But also aim high. To boost your motivation, base your goals on inspiration, not just logic.

- **Develop an action plan, set deadlines, and act.** Divide each goal into logical, progressive steps. Set deadlines and priorities for completing each step. Complete the steps on time.

- **Identify your support system.** Examples include your instructors, books that motivate you, and the people who want you to succeed and will encourage you to persevere. Share your goals with others to ensure that you have someone to ask for help when you need it and to increase your sense of responsibility.

- **Record your progress.** It may seem simplistic, but a long series of check marks on a list can motivate you by providing a sense of accomplishment. Don't get discouraged by missing an occasional daily goal—stay focused on your long-term goal.

- **Reward yourself.** Rewards are motivators. Do something nice for yourself as you progress toward achieving your goals.

- **Evaluate your goals and adjust as necessary.** Evaluate your progress toward achieving your goals. Experiment with new methods if you're not getting the results you want and if circumstances or priorities change your goals.

Manage Your Time

Time management is an important personal and professional skill. Everyone has 24 hours in every day, but successful people learn to make the most of their time by setting priorities and using organizational strategies and tools. Try some of these basic time management tips:

- Decide which activities are important and make sure they get done. Plan ahead to avoid doing everything at the last minute.

- Break large projects into small, manageable steps.

- Practice using small amounts of time productively.

- Try new ways to take care of necessary but unrewarding activities in less time.

- Use a calendar or daily planner.

- Decide which activities are not important. Cut back on your commitments or free time.

Be Proactive

In his world-acclaimed book *7 Habits of Highly Successful People*, Stephen Covey emphasizes that the way people typically approach challenging situations and tasks is a major determinant of their career success.

People who use a **proactive approach** to situations boost their careers by focusing on solving problems, taking positive actions, and taking responsibility for their actions. People who use a **reactive approach** sabotage their success by focusing on problems instead of solutions and by avoiding difficult situations. Using proactive skills leads to many career benefits, such as positive work relationships, improved work performance, better problem-solving skills, increased motivation, and enhanced self-esteem.

 COMPLETE **CAREER ACTION 1-4**

Proactive Success Action Plan, p. 18

Act Assertively

Assertive behavior—the ability to express yourself and to stand up for your point of view without disrespecting others—is critical in your job search because it conveys self-esteem and capability. Employers avoid hiring people who lack confidence and have difficulty expressing themselves. They also avoid aggressive people who are overly confident, pushy, and controlling.

Employers hire people who project confidence and who can discuss their job qualifications clearly. They want employees who project competence in the workplace through their assertive behavior. These employees strengthen human relations with coworkers and clients and and present a positive image of the organization to outsiders. Employers hire applicants who demonstrate assertiveness in their resume, cover letter, and interviews.

To reach your full career potential, be assertive and tactful in expressing yourself and respect the rights of others.

Career**Transitions**

Career Transitions provides immediate access to the most important career exploration and employment preparation activities. Whether you are college-bound, are on a vocational track, or are preparing to enter the workforce, you will find an intuitive user experience designed to engage and guide you through practical learning activities and important education and career decisions.

Engaging, Interactive, and Focused

Career Transitions provides you with Personal Learning Experiences (PLEs) that are interactive and engaging.

- Identify career inclinations through an engaging and eye-opening career interest assessment.
- Browse the Department of Education's 16 Career Clusters as well as spotlight career categories (including Green, New Economy, and High-Growth careers).
- Engage in a practice ride through real-world job situations with a customized, interactive interview simulation.
- Create beginning resumes and cover letters with realistic samples and in-context tips and examples. Get practical guidance in the form of videos and short how-to articles.
- Use a job and an internship to seek opportunities for today and the future.

Many of the Career Actions in *Your Career: How to Make It Happen* use the functionality of *Career Transitions*. Watch for opportunities to apply what you've learned in the book to real-world, career-focused results.

http://careertransitions.cengage.com

Chapter Checklist

Underline each action you are already taking and circle the actions you need to work on.

- Plan and organize my job search and spend time on my job search every day. [2]

- Collect and file documents and other items that will help me organize my job search and demonstrate my qualifications. [3]

- Develop a portfolio of my best work to demonstrate my job qualifications to prospective employers. [3]

- Think and act positively and develop my self-esteem. [4]

- Set clear long-term and short-term goals, define concrete steps to achieve each goal, and follow through. [4]

- Practice proactive skills that demonstrate responsibility and a focus on solving problems. [4]

- Practice assertive behaviors that show my confidence and capabilities. [4]

Critical-Thinking Questions

1. Why is the job search process a cycle rather than a series of steps? [1]

2. Why is it important to set up a system to organize, manage, and track your job search? What tools will you use? How will you get started? [2]

3. How will your Career Management Files Tracker help you organize your job search? Why should you keep your tracker up to date throughout your career? [3]

4. How is a Career Portfolio different from a Career Management Files Tracker? What items should you put in your Career Portfolio? [3]

5. How can projecting enthusiasm and a positive attitude help in your job search? [4]

6. What effects do positive and negative thoughts, images, and self-talk have on performance? [4]

7. Would you rate your assertiveness skills as excellent, good, or needing improvement? If you need to improve, what specific actions can you take to strengthen these skills? [4]

Want access to career resources, study tools, activities, and job information links? Get started at www.cengage.com/career/yourcareer.

TRIAL RUN

The beginning of your job search is a good time to make a thorough and honest evaluation of the organizational skills and success attitudes you will need to market yourself effectively in a job search. Read these statements and rate yourself using the following scale:

Rating Scale: 1 to 4 (1 = not really; 2 = sometimes/somewhat; 3 = usually; 4 = definitely)

_____ 1. I understand the phases of the job search and the main activities in each phase.

_____ 2. I understand why it is important to track the progress on my job search and to manage my time effectively.

_____ 3. I use charts and spreadsheets to record my job search activities.

_____ 4. I spend time on job search activities every day.

_____ 5. I use time management strategies to increase my productivity, and I rarely procrastinate.

_____ 6. I know what materials to store in my Career Management Files.

_____ 7. I understand the difference between my Career Management Files Tracker and my Career Portfolio.

_____ 8. I understand the importance of positive thinking and behavior for my job search.

_____ 9. I use success strategies to motivate myself.

_____ 10. I know how to visualize my success.

_____ 11. I practice positive self-talk to increase my confidence.

_____ 12. I know how to increase my self-esteem.

_____ 13. I write down my goals and develop action plans for meeting those goals.

_____ 14. I understand the difference between being assertive and being aggressive.

_____ 15. I practice proactive skills that focus on finding solutions, taking responsibility, and building relationships.

On which items did you give yourself the highest score? Why did you give yourself a high score?

On which items did you give yourself a low score? Why did you give yourself a low score?

Select one or more of the low-scoring statements and write a goal for improving in that area. Set a time frame and write the steps you will take to achieve the goal.

CAREER ACTION   1-1 Daily Job Search Organizer ②

Make several copies of this page or use the worksheet on the product website. Record your job search activities every day and complete the last four sections at the end of the day. Use the Find Jobs tool in *Career Transitions* to implement your strategies.

Date _____ Number of hours spent on my job search _____ From _____ To _____

Contacts

Employer, Name of Contact, and Job Target (include contact information)	Form of Contact (personal visit, phone call, letter, email)	Purpose of Contact	Purpose Achieved?

Job Research Sources

Name of Website or Resource	Information Found	Log-in Information	Useful Source?

Other Job Search Activities:

Summary of Progress Made Today:

New Job Leads:

Follow-up/Next Steps/Goals for Tomorrow:

CAREER ACTION 1-2 **Career Management Files Tracker** 3

Follow the instructions on page 7 to set up your Career Management Files Tracker. Use the three-ring binder to store your completed Career Action assignments, important pages from the textbook, printouts from the product website and other sites, and other helpful documents. You can turn your Career Management Files Tracker into a valuable collection of information and documents to use throughout your career: records of your education and work experience, summaries of job- and career-related values and skills, resumes, cover letters, and more. Use the space below to plan how you will create your Career Management Files Tracker.

CAREER ACTION 1-3 **Internet Research on Career Portfolios** 3

Search for examples of items to include in a Career Portfolio. Think about the specific career area that interests you and list at least five job-specific items you could include in a portfolio to demonstrate your work skills and qualifications. (For example, if you want to work as a cook or chef, you might include a sample menu, recipes, and a nutritional analysis.) The Find Jobs tool in *Career Transitions* can aid you in your research. Record your findings and ideas below.

Search for articles and advice on portfolios, samples of online career portfolios, and information on online services that can host portfolios and that provide portfolio templates. Record your findings below.

CAREER ACTION 1-4 Proactive Success Action Plan [4]

Complete this Proactive Success Action Plan form or use the form on the product website.

Name:

Goal I Consider Most Important in My Life:

Benefits of Achieving This Goal (to myself and others):

Steps I Plan to Take to Achieve This Goal:

Action Steps	Date
1.	
2.	
3.	
4.	
5.	

Positive Thinking Strategies I Will Use to Motivate Myself to Achieve This Goal:

For Your Career Management Files Tracker

File your completed Career Action worksheets in your Career Management Files Tracker.

CA 1-1   Daily Job Search Organizer (make multiple copies or use the file on the product website)

CA 1-2   Organization plan for my Career Management Files Tracker (sections, tabs, etc.)

CA 1-3   Internet research findings about traditional and online career portfolios

CA 1-4   Completed Proactive Success Action Plan

Outcomes

1 Describe the basic skills, knowledge, values, and traits that employers expect of job applicants and employees.

2 Describe ethical standards and expectations in the workplace.

3 Examine growing industries and in-demand occupations; research the requirements for different careers.

© Photographer/Image Source

Know What Employers Expect

OVERVIEW Chapter 2 introduces you to the world of work and explores the relationship in the workplace between employers and employees. You will learn about the skills, knowledge, work values, and personal traits of successful employees.

You will learn about growth industries and in-demand occupations and will research the skill qualifications for careers that interest you. The chapter activities will guide you through a self-assessment from the employer's perspective, identifying your most important qualifications. You will also start to think about careers that may interest you and consider how your skills and talents match up with the careers.

CHAPTER 2

CAREER ACTIONS

2-1: Employer/Employee Relationship and Expectations
2-2: Workplace Skills and Competencies Profile
2-3: Career Competencies Inventory
2-4: Internet Research on Corporate Codes of Ethics
2-5: Internet Research on In-Demand Careers

JUMP START

Your Workplace Knowledge

akva/Shutterstock.com

How much do you know about the world of work? Even if you have never held a job, you have probably had plenty of opportunities to observe people in different workplaces. After all, nearly every place you go is a workplace for someone.

Think of three workplaces you visited last week: stores, medical and business offices, restaurants, child care centers, hair and nail salons, movie theaters, train stations, schools, etc. Think about the job duties, activities, appearance, attitude, and other traits you noticed about the employees you interacted with. Make a two-column list. In the left column, list the qualities the employees in the three work-places had in common, and in the right column, list the qualities that were different among the employees.

Imagine that in one day, you interacted with a salesclerk in a skate-board shop, a nurse in a doctor's office, and a manicurist in a nail salon. In what ways would you expect these employees to be alike? In what ways would you expect them to be different?

Outcome 1 — The World of Work: Basic Expectations

If you are like most students who use this book, one of your goals for being in school is to get the training and skills that you will use in the workplace. Your classes are an essential part of your preparation for working, and it is essential to know the requirements and expectations of the workplace.

In today's tight labor market, employers can be very selective during the hiring process. One of your first steps as a successful job seeker is to make sure you understand what employers expect of their employees.

The Employer/Employee Relationship

In the workplace, you will be expected to understand the relationship between employers and employees. This important two-way relationship is a big commitment for both parties.

- Employers rely on employees to operate their business, produce high-quality products or services, meet the needs of customers, and help make a profit. Employers invest a great deal of money in training and paying workers.

- Employees invest considerable time and energy in performing their job duties every day. They expect to be paid for their work and to have a safe, healthy work environment and the equipment and supplies they need to do their jobs.

Both parties in the relationship must make a good match—with employers hiring workers who meet their needs and employees finding a workplace that fits their career goals.

For the relationship to be successful, the expectations of the employer and the employee must be met. The employee must be satisfied with the pay scale, job duties, work environment, benefits, and future opportunities. The employer must be satisfied with the employee's job performance, standards of conduct, quality of work, reliability, personal qualities, and potential for taking on more responsibilities.

Employer Expectations

Employees make or break a business, and employers want to hire people who will make their businesses more successful. The most desirable employees have the skills, knowledge, work values, and personal qualities necessary to be successful in the employer's organization. Sometimes called **career competencies**, these are the skills and traits that employers look for during job interviews and expect employees to demonstrate on the job. They include the following:

- Academic skills
- Technical skills
- Thinking skills
- Interpersonal skills
- Teamwork skills
- Communication skills
- Job performance and productivity
- Proper workplace behavior and conduct
- A strong work ethic
- Adherence to ethical standards and laws

As you read this section, think about how you can improve your own workplace competencies and how you can demonstrate them in your job search.

Academic Skills

Employers look for employees who have the required education and qualifications for the job. Basic academic skills—especially a good foundation in math, science, and English—are required, and employers expect workers to be able to read, write, listen, and speak well. Employers also expect employees to be able to apply their academic knowledge to on-the-job tasks.

Technical Skills

Employers expect new employees to possess technical skills and apply these skills in their jobs. Employers expect employees to stay current with regard to their computer and other technical skills so that the employers don't have to provide as much training. When technology changes, employers expect employees to be able to use and adjust to new technology quickly.

Specialized industries that require specific work skills, such as healthcare, hospitality, construction, and transportation, also require specialized education and certification. Employers assume that employees have learned the required work skills in their training and education. Employers may require updated certification or retraining as proof that the employee's skills are current.

Thinking Skills

Employees in most jobs are expected to be able to solve problems and learn new tasks. These thinking skills are important to employers because they indicate that an employee can think things through, make effective decisions, and learn new tasks quickly without needing to be retrained.

Interpersonal Skills

One of the most important personal traits expected in the workplace is the ability to get along with other people. Strong interpersonal skills require taking a positive attitude toward work as demonstrated by a pleasant demeanor; good manners; a cooperative, can-do attitude; and a willingness to try.

Employees who have good interpersonal skills contribute to a postive, pleasant work environment. They send a positive message to customers and do a good job representing the organization to the public.

COMPLETE **CAREER ACTION 2-1**

Employer/Employee Relationship and Expectations, p. 31

Teamwork Skills

Many tasks in today's workplace are carried out by teams or groups. Employees collaborate with each other and work on teams to share information, solve problems, and perform assignments.

Employers expect employees to be productive team members who can be counted on to do their share of the work and help the team complete its assignment and meet the organization's goals.

> **COMPLETE** **CAREER ACTION 2-2**
>
> Workplace Skills and Competencies Profile, p. 32

Communication Skills

Effective communication skills are absolutely essential in a smooth-running, successful workplace. During the hiring process, employers form their impression of job applicants by how well the applicants communicate the following:

- Written communication skills: the cover letter and resume
- Verbal communication and listening skills: the interview

Employers hire people who demonstrate that they can get their message across—and understand what others mean—accurately and efficiently.

Job Performance and Productivity

Job performance and productivity are closely related concepts that describe how well an employee does his or her job. **Performance** refers to how an employee carries out work assignments, and **productivity** refers to the effectiveness of the employee's work.

A job well done is critical to the success of the business and to the employee's future with the organization. Productive employees take pride in their job performance. They accept responsibility for completing their assignments accurately and thoroughly and on time.

Why Teams Work

kali9/iStockphoto.com

Teamwork leads to a more productive and pleasant work environment and to benefits for employees and employers.

- **Collaboration.** People want to work well together and support one another because they identify with the team.
- **Communication.** Coworkers realize the importance of sharing information that others need to operate more effectively.
- **More efficient application of resources and strengths.** Team members apply themselves willingly. When one member lacks certain skills, another team member is there to fill the gap.
- **Sound decisions and solutions made simultaneously.** A team can generate more discussion, ideas, and solutions than a single individual can.
- **Quality.** Team members take pride in the team effort and ensure that each member gets what he or she needs from other team members to turn out the best possible work.

Proper Workplace Behavior and Conduct

At the most basic level, proper conduct means following the workplace rules. This means working hard, following health and safety rules, maintaining a clean and orderly work area, and being punctual and reliable.

Business etiquette is the expected professional behavior in the workplace and is based on courtesy, manners, and customs. Etiquette requires respect, which means treating others the way you want to be treated and making them feel at ease. It also includes following the social customs and rules for interactions with coworkers and customers. For example, to avoid creating an uncomfortable work environment, many workplaces have rules against employees dating.

Etiquette also involves unwritten rules, which are sometimes tricky to navigate in the workplace. In some restaurant kitchens, for example, the senior cook prefers to be addressed as "chef," but this is not always the case. New employees learn the unwritten rules by observing their coworkers and seeking the advice of trusted coworkers.

Strong Work Ethic

The most successful employees in every workplace have one trait in common: a strong work ethic. These workers have an inner drive to do their jobs well.

- They set goals and are persistent in meeting those goals.
- They make sure they understand assignments and stick with tasks until they are finished.
- They develop efficient work processes and check their work before they turn it in.
- They complete their work with little supervision.
- They maintain their self-control in difficult or rushed situations.
- They are loyal to their organization and represent it well to outsiders.

COMPLETE **CAREER ACTION 2-3**

Career Competencies Inventory, p. 34

MAKE IT A HABIT

Dealing with Ethical Dilemmas

Effective problem solving and critical thinking at work sometimes involve dealing with an ethical dilemma. If you are not sure what to do in a situation, start by asking yourself these questions:

- Would I be violating any laws or policies?
- Do I have the proper consent?
- Will my decision be fair and respectful?
- What are the consequences of my actions? Will anyone benefit or suffer from my actions?
- How will my decision make me feel about myself? Will I be proud of my actions?

Think about the situation carefully and gather as much information as you can. If you have any reservations about an action, don't let yourself be talked into doing it. If you do something unethical, you are the one who must live with the loss of your reputation and with the consequences.

Protect your long-term career by demonstrating your personal integrity and ethics. Nothing will damage your career as drastically as losing your reputation for being ethical.

Yuri Arcurs/Shutterstock.com

Outcome 2 # Ethical Expectations in the Workplace

Ethics are guidelines or accepted standards about what is right or wrong. **Business ethics** is the application of ethical principles in a business environment. The principles apply to individual employees and to the entire organization.

The Ethical Employer

Employers and employees expect one another to show integrity in the workplace. Among other things, employees can expect employers to:

- Provide a safe, healthful, reasonably comfortable workplace.

- Provide the tools, equipment, and supplies employees need to do their jobs properly and safely.

- Treat employees equally without regard for their sex, age, ethnicity, race, religion, physical ability, or lifestyle.

- Base raises, bonuses, and promotions on merit and productivity, not on personal relationships.

- Conduct an honest, responsible business. If the company produces products, they should be safe and effective and the advertisements for the products should be honest. If the business provides a service, the best interests of customers and clients should be the driving force behind the way business is done.

- Keep accurate, honest records and accounts.

- Respect the environment.

- Follow local, state, and federal laws.

Many companies and professions have an official **code of ethics**, which provides written guidelines for workers to follow based on specific ethical standards and values. The official code of ethics and business conduct is often available on a company's website and may be mailed to customers and shareholders as a normal practice.

A portion of The Hershey Company's Code of Ethical Business Conduct is shown in Figure 2-1.[1] The Hershey Company's entire code of conduct is 44 pages in English. It is available in the languages of the other countries in which the company does business.

Everyone connected with Hershey is expected to follow the code: "All employees, officers, and directors must act according to the principles set forth in our Code. We expect everyone working on our Company's behalf, including consultants, agents, suppliers, and business partners, to adhere to our ethical standards. We may never ask a third party to engage in any activity that violates these standards."[2]

[1]The Hershey Company. "Code of Ethical Business Conduct," page iii. Web. Accessed 28 April 2011. http://www.thehersheycompany.com/about/conduct.asp

[2]Ibid., page 1.

Code of Ethical Business Conduct

At its website, The Hershey Company posts its Code of Conduct in the language of every country in which it does business. Here is the high-level overview:

OUR COMMITMENT TO FELLOW EMPLOYEES. We treat one another fairly and with respect, valuing the talents, experiences and strengths of our diverse workforce.

OUR COMMITMENT TO CONSUMERS. We maintain the trust consumers place in our brands, providing the best products on the market and adhering to honest marketing practices.

OUR COMMITMENT TO THE MARKETPLACE. We deal fairly with our business partners, competitors and suppliers, acting ethically and upholding the law in everything we do.

OUR COMMITMENT TO STOCKHOLDERS. We act honestly and transparently at all times, maintaining the trust our stockholders have placed in us.

OUR COMMITMENT TO THE GLOBAL COMMUNITY. We comply with all global trade laws, protecting our natural resources and supporting the communities where we live, work and do business.

Figure 2-1 The Hershey Company's Code of Conduct (overview)

The Ethical Employee

Employers want to hire people who have integrity—people who can be trusted to keep their word and who are honest, fair, law-abiding, and trustworthy.

Act Honestly and with Integrity

Honesty and integrity are signs of a dependable and reliable employee and a trusted coworker. Working with honesty means working a full day, not being late or taking long breaks, not stealing or borrowing from the employer (including not texting your friends instead of working), and being trusted with merchandise and business finances.

Employees who are known for their honesty and integrity are trusted to follow directions, make smart business decisions, and keep business information confidential. They demonstrate responsibility through their actions and are given more opportunities because they are trustworthy.

Managing money honestly and well is essential for achieving career success. Even employees who do not handle cash in a job may have to report expenses or manage a budget in some way.

Many employers run credit checks on job applicants. A good personal credit rating is a sign that an employee knows how to manage money. A poor credit score is a sign that an employee is financially irresponsible or takes financial risks.

COMPLETE **CAREER ACTION 2-4**

Internet Research on Corporate Codes of Ethics, p. 36

Be Fair to Everyone

A sure-fire way to antagonize your coworkers is to take credit for someone else's ideas or work. This extends to letting a supervisor assume that you did the work. Fairness also means fulfilling your commitments and doing your share of the assigned work. Never, ever shirk your responsibilities to your team, your work group, your supervisor—or the mail clerk or janitorial staff.

Vladmir Wrangel/Shutterstock.com

WATCH OUT!

Be Careful with Sensitive Information

At one time or another, every employee has access to sensitive company information or knows things about the company that are not intended to be made public. Be as careful with company information as you are with your personal information.

- Consider the information your boss shares with you to be confidential and do not divulge it to anyone.
- Password-protect confidential documents.
- Do not leave your computer with open documents on the monitor. Close the files before you leave your station.
- Never leave the office unattended. If you go on break and your boss is not in, leave a note on the door and lock it.
- Never leave sensitive documents on your desk.
- When you leave work for the day, store sensitive documents in a locked file cabinet.

If you use a laptop, password-protect the system. Do not leave your laptop someplace where it might be stolen.

If the shredder bag breaks because you let it get too full, clean up the mess; don't leave it for the night crew even if you seldom see them. Through your actions, show that you respect everyone, and you will earn their respect.

Obey the Law

What would you think if, during a job interview with a car rental agency, the interviewer asks if you are married or have children? If the answers have nothing to do with your ability to do the job, the questions are inappropriate (and perhaps illegal) and you may think twice about wanting to work for the organization.

Employees also must obey the law, of course. An ethical employee who is injured playing softball on Friday night would not consider filing a worker's compensation claim to cover medical expenses. Similar situations will arise in every workplace, and an ethical employee will know how to act. Take a moment now to review "Dealing with Ethical Dilemmas" on page 23.

Be Trustworthy

Show your coworkers that you can be trusted in all situations. Like the other ethical qualities covered in this section, trustworthiness is good business sense as well as a good principle to live by.

If you have any doubts about the wisdom of this advice, consider the story of a job applicant who indicated on her resume that she was fluent in Spanish. Imagine her dismay when the interviewer, Nasim Yousef, spoke to her in Spanish until he realized that she didn't understand what he was saying.

In every situation in the workplace, do what you know is right.

Outcome 3 In-Demand Industries and Occupations

A good way to start thinking about prospective employers that might be right for you is to consider growing industries and in-demand occupations—career fields that may have better wages, more job openings, and a more promising future. As a job seeker, you will be in demand if you are able to target growing career areas that are going to need more workers and if you understand the expectations and requirements of those jobs.

Since the 1990s, the U.S. economy has undergone a shift from a goods-producing economy to an economy based in service occupations. The U.S. Bureau of Labor Statistics (BLS) employment projections show a continued decline in jobs in goods-producing industries such as construction, agriculture, mining and oil and gas extraction, and manufacturing. Service-providing industries are expected to add approximately 14.5 million new jobs by 2018.

Figure 2-2 shows the BLS projections of the fastest-growing occupations through 2018. Figure 2-3 shows the occupations that will add the largest number of jobs through 2018. Here are some of the key facts to learn from these figures.

- Figure 2-2 shows that half of the fastest-growing occupations are related to healthcare.
- Many of the occupations listed in Figure 2-3 are very large and will create more jobs than the fastest-growing occupations shown in Figure 2-2.

If you can demonstrate grace under pressure—by projecting a positive attitude and working toward the goal when things get tough—you are a valuable employee.

Occupations	Percent Change	Number of New Jobs	Median Wage (May 2008)	Education/Training
Biomedical engineers	72	116,000	$77,400	Bachelor's degree
Network systems and data communication analysts	53	1,558,000	71,000	Bachelor's degree
Personal and home health care aides	48	8,367,000	19,820	Short-term on-the-job training
Financial examiners	41	1,100,000	70,930	Bachelor's degree
Physician assistants	39	292,000	81,230	Master's degree
Skin care specialists	38	147,000	28,730	Postsecondary vocational award
Athletic trainers	37	6,000	39,640	Bachelor's degree
Physical therapy aides	36	167,000	23,760	Short-term on-the-job training
Dental hygienists	36	629,000	66,750	Associate degree
Veterinarian technicians	36	285,000	28,900	Associate degree
Dental assistants	36	1,056,000	32,380	Moderate-term on-the-job training
Software engineers	34	1,751,000	85,430	Bachelor's degree
Medical assistants	34	1,639,000	28,300	Moderate-term on-the-job training
Physical therapy assistants	33	212,000	46,140	Associate degree
Self-enrichment teachers	32	813,000	35,720	Experience in related occupation
Compliance officers[1]	31	808,000	48,890	Long-term on-the-job training

Figure 2-2 Occupations with Fastest Growth

Occupations	Number of New Jobs	Percent Change	Median Wage (May 2008)	Education/Training
Registered nurses	5,815,000	22	$62,450	Associate degree
Home health aides	4,609,000	50	20,460	Short-term on-the-job training
Customer service reps	3,995,000	18	29,860	Moderate-term on-the-job training
Food preparation and serving workers	3,943,000	15	16,430	Short-term on-the-job training
Personal and home health care aides	3,758,000	46	19,180	Short-term on-the-job training
Retail salespersons	3,747,000	8	20,510	Short-term on-the-job training
Office clerks, general	3,587,000	12	23,320	Short-term on-the-job training
Accountants and auditors	2,794,000	22	59,430	Bachelor's degree
Nursing aides, orderlies, and attendants	2,760,000	19	23,850	Postsecondary vocational award
Construction laborers	2,559,000	20	28,520	Moderate-term on-the-job training
Elementary school teachers, except special education	2,442,000	16	49,330	Bachelor's degree
Truck drivers	2,329,000	13	37,270	Short-term on-the-job training
Landscaping workers	2,171,000	18	23,150	Short-term on-the-job training
Bookkeeping, accounting, and auditing clerks	2,124,000	10	32,510	Moderate-term on-the-job training
Executive secretaries and administrative assistants	2,044,000	13	40,030	Experience in related occupation
Management analysts	1,783,000	24	73,570	Bachelor's or higher degree in addition to work experience
Software engineers	1,751,000	34	85,430	Bachelor's degree
Receptionists; info. clerks	1,729,000	15	24,550	Short-term on-the-job training
Carpenters	1,654,000	13	38,940	Short-term on-the-job training

Figure 2-3 Occupations with Largest Number of New Jobs

[1]Except agriculture, construction, health and safety, and transportation

Source: "Overview of the 2008–2018 Projections," *BLS Occupational Outlook Handbook, 2010–11 Edition.* http://www.bls.gov/oco2003.htm#industry

- The 20 fastest-growing occupations in Figure 2-3 are projected to add more than one-third of all new jobs—5.8 million—through 2018.

- Figure 2-3 also shows that office and administrative support services occupations are projected to add about one-fifth of all new jobs—about 1.3 million jobs.

Online Resources for In-Demand Careers

The U.S. Departments of Education and Labor have developed extensive online and print resources for exploring careers, with additional information about in-demand industries and fast-growing occupations.

These resources—the most comprehensive guides on the Internet—should be a destination for every job seeker who is actively exploring career information.

CareerOneStop

To help promote fast-growing industries and help job seekers research careers, the U.S. Department of Labor maintains the CareerOneStop website. This site is designed to provide information on high-growth, in-demand occupations, including average wages and information on the skills and education needed to attain those jobs.

CareerOneStop is updated annually to ensure that it reflects current hiring trends.

Career Guide to Industries and *Occupational Outlook Handbook*

The BLS publishes two essential resources for exploring industries and occupations, the *Career Guide to Industries* and the *Occupational Outlook Handbook*. If you are still exploring your career goals, spend some time using these essential resources. You can listen to people who work in fast-growing careers and industries talk about their jobs.

Printed copies are available at libraries, and online versions are on the BLS website. Using these resources, you will find information on dozens of industries and hundred of occupations, including the following details:

- Occupations in the career field
- Training and advancement
- Earnings
- Working conditions
- Expected job prospects

COMPLETE | **CAREER ACTION 2-5**

Internet Research on In-Demand Careers, p. 37

Digital Vision/Getty Images

Respect Diversity

An ethical organization is committed to diversity. So, too, is the ethical employee.

- The ethical employee understands that the world is diverse and that it will continue to grow more diverse in the future.

- The ethical employee accepts and respects diversity in all people—whether that diversity pertains to ethnicity, race, gender, age, physical ability, or lifestyle.

- The ethical employee understands that there is no place in the office for telling jokes that have racial, ethnic, gender, or lifestyle overtones.

The workplace should be an inclusive space. Diversity is about learning from others and showing respect for everyone.

Chapter Checklist

Underline each action you are already taking and circle the actions you need to work on.

- Understand the relationship between employers and employees. 1

- Learn about basic employer expectations, including academic, technology-related, thinking, interpersonal, teamwork, and communication skills; job performance and productivity; proper workplace behavior and conduct; and a strong work ethic. 1

- Understand the importance of ethical behavior on the part of organizations. 2

- Understand employees' ethical obligations to the organization and to each other. 2

- Explore growth industries and in-demand occupations. 3

- Use the Internet to research the occupational requirements of in-demand careers. 3

Critical-Thinking Questions

1. What are an employer's responsibilities to employees? Brainstorm some responsibilities the chapter did not list. 1

2. Why do a person's interpersonal skills depend on him or her having a good attitude toward work? 1

3. What are thinking skills? Why do employers care how employees think? 1

4. Why are interpersonal skills and teamwork skills so important in the workplace? 1

5. Why do employers have an obligation to employees to maintain an ethical organization and work environment? 2

6. Besides employees, who else is affected when an organization acts unethically? List at least three groups and explain how each group is affected. 2

7. Why is it important to consider growth industries when exploring careers and thinking about your job prospects? 3

Want access to career resources, study tools, activities, and job information links? Get started at www.cengage.com/career/yourcareer.

TRIAL RUN

Working alone or with a partner, watch a movie or television show centered around a workplace (such as a hospital, an office, a police station, a laboratory, a restaurant, a television station, a hair salon, a coffee shop, a school, or another workplace). Identify and discuss the employee/employer relationships in the movie or TV show that you watched. Then select one character who is an employee. Evaluate that employee on the expectations and skills listed below. For each item, provide an example to explain how the character earned the score.

Rating Scale: 1 to 4 (1 = poor; 2 = mediocre; 3 = adequate; 4 = strong)

Meeting employer's expectations:

Example:

Reliability and promptness:

Example:

Work performance:

Example:

Interpersonal skills and positive attitude:

Example:

Workplace behavior and conduct:

Example:

Thinking and problem-solving skills:

Example:

Communication and teamwork skills:

Example:

Technology-related skills (for example, using technology, equipment, and medical skills):

Example:

Strong work ethic:

Example:

Professional appearance and grooming:

Example:

What advice would you give the character to improve his or her score in any areas of weakness? How could the person improve workplace competencies to be successful on the job and in the future?

CAREER ACTION   2-1 Employer/Employee Relationship and Expectations [1]

Think about a successful employer/employee relationship you have experienced or observed. Explain the workplace expectations for the job.

Why was it a successful relationship?

Now think of an unsuccessful employer/employee relationship you have experienced or witnessed. Explain the workplace expectations for this job.

Why was it not a good match?

How could the situation have been improved or avoided?

CAREER ACTION   2-2   Workplace Skills and Competencies Profile [1]

Review the following skill categories and related career competencies. For each skill category:

- Check the box to the left of the skill category that applies to you in any way.
- Highlight the career competencies you have developed. Think of each skill from an employer's perspective and imagine how the skill could be useful on the job.
- In another color, highlight the career competencies you could develop that would be useful on the job.
- Use "Other" for your notes about the skills category, such as additional competencies you have in the category.

Skill Category | Related Career Competencies

❏ **Art**

Drawing, designing, painting, sculpting, computer graphics design
Other: _____
_____

❏ **Athletics**

Physical strength, physical ability, physical coordination, coaching, physical development, agility, team sports, individual sports
Other: _____
_____

❏ **Communication**

Explaining/persuading, strong grammar/vocabulary, organizing thoughts clearly, communicating logically, listening, speaking, good telephone/reception skills, writing, knowledge of foreign languages
Other: _____
_____

❏ **Computer Technology**

Computer operation, researching, training, testing, workflow analysis, evaluating, writing instructions, programming
Other: _____
_____

❏ **Creativity**

Creative, innovative, imaginative, "idea" person, bold
Other: _____
_____

❏ **Engineering**

Researching, testing, designing, constructing, analyzing, evaluating, controlling, electronic technology
Other: _____
_____

❏ **Human Relations**

Counseling, diplomacy, negotiating, patience, outgoing, teamwork ability, understanding, resolving conflict, handling complaints
Other: _____
_____

❏ **Management**

Analyzing data, directing, delegating, evaluating performance, organizing people/data/things, leading, making decisions, managing time, motivating self/others, planning, budgeting money/resources, solving problems, supervising, interviewing/hiring people, owning/operating a business
Other: _____
_____

☐ **Manual/ Mechanical**   Good manual dexterity, building, operating, maintaining/repairing, assembling, installing, carrying, loading, lifting, cooking, driving/ operating vehicles, performing precision work, assessing spatial relationships, operating heavy equipment
Other: _____
_____

☐ **Mathematical**   Mathematical computations, accuracy, analyzing data, mathematical reasoning, statistical problem solving, analyzing cost effectiveness, budgeting, applying formulas, collecting money, calculating
Other: _____
_____

☐ **Office**   Keyboarding, data entry, computer operation, text processing, data processing, office equipment operation, filing/retrieving records, recording data, computing data, record keeping, telephone skills, business writing
Other: _____
_____

☐ **Outdoor Activities**   Animal care, farming, landscaping, grounds care, boating, navigating, oceanographic studies, forestry, logging, mining, fishing, horticulture
Other: _____
_____

☐ **Performing**   Speaking, acting, dancing, singing, musical ability, comedy, conducting
Other: _____
_____

☐ **Sales/Promotion**   Persuading, negotiating, promoting, influencing, selling, projecting enthusiasm, organizing, handling rejection, following up
Other: _____
_____

☐ **Scientific Activities**   Investigating, researching, analyzing, systematizing, observing, diagnosing
Other: _____
_____

☐ **Service/General**   Serving, referring, receiving, billing, handling complaints, good customer relations, good listening skills, patience, managing difficult people, helping others, relating to others
Other: _____
_____

☐ **Service/Medical**   Nursing, diagnosing, treating, rehabilitating, counseling, consoling, sympathizing, managing stress/emergencies, good interpersonal skills
Other: _____
_____

☐ **Training/Teaching**   Teaching skills/knowledge, tutoring, researching instructional content, organizing/developing content, explaining logically/clearly, demonstrating clearly, coaching others, evaluating learning, addressing all learning styles, using instructional technology
Other: _____
_____

CAREER ACTION

2-3 Career Competencies Inventory [1]

Read the following list of workplace competencies from the U.S. Department of Labor's SCANS Report on Necessary Work Skills. As you read about each competency, check the box for each skill or quality you have developed and circle the portions of the detailed descriptions that apply to you.

Workplace Competencies

Resources: Identifies, organizes, plans, and manages resources

☐ **Manages Time:** Selects relevant, goal-related activities; ranks activities in order of importance; allocates time to activities; and understands, prepares, and follows schedules

☐ **Manages Money:** Uses budgets, keeps records, and makes adjustments to meet objectives

☐ **Manages Materials and Facilities:** Acquires, stores, allocates, and uses materials and/or space efficiently

☐ **Manages Human Resources:** Assesses skills and distributes work accordingly, uses coaching/ mentoring skills with peers and subordinates, evaluates performance, and provides feedback

Interpersonal: Works well with others

☐ **Participates as Team Member:** Contributes to group effort

☐ **Teaches Others New Skills**

☐ **Serves Clients/Customers:** Works to satisfy customers' expectations

☐ **Exercises Leadership:** Communicates ideas to justify position and persuades/convinces

☐ **Negotiates Decisions:** Works toward agreements involving exchange of resources and resolves divergent interests

☐ **Respects Cultural Diversity:** Works well with people from diverse backgrounds

Information: Acquires, organizes, interprets, and uses information

☐ **Acquires/Evaluates Information**

☐ **Organizes/Maintains Information**

☐ **Interprets/Communicates Information**

☐ **Uses Computers to Process Information**

Systems: Understands complex social, organizational, and technological systems and interrelationships

☐ **Understands Systems:** Knows how social, organizational, and technological systems work and operates effectively with them

☐ **Monitors/Corrects Performance:** Distinguishes trends, predicts impacts on system operations, diagnoses deviations in systems' performance, and corrects malfunctions

☐ **Improves/Designs Systems:** Suggests modifications to existing systems and develops new or alternative systems to improve performance

Technology: Works with a variety of technologies

❒ **Selects Technology:** Chooses procedures, tools, or equipment, including computers and related technologies

❒ **Applies Technology to Task:** Understands overall intent and proper procedures for setup and operation of equipment

❒ **Maintains/Troubleshoots Technology:** Prevents, identifies, or solves problems with equipment, including computers and other technologies

Foundation Skills and Personal Qualities

Basic Skills: Reads, writes, performs arithmetic/mathematical operations, listens, and speaks

❒ **Reading:** Locates, understands, and interprets written information, including material in documents such as manuals, graphs, and schedules

❒ **Writing:** Communicates thoughts, ideas, information, and messages in writing and creates documents such as letters, directions, manuals, reports, graphs, and flowcharts

❒ **Arithmetic/Mathematics:** Performs basic computations and approaches practical problems by choosing appropriately from a variety of mathematical techniques

❒ **Listening:** Receives, attends to, interprets, and responds to verbal messages and other cues

❒ **Speaking:** Organizes ideas and communicates orally

Thinking Skills: Thinks creatively, makes decisions, solves problems, visualizes, knows how to learn, and reasons

❒ **Creative Thinking:** Generates new ideas

❒ **Decision Making:** Specifies goals and constraints, generates alternatives, considers risks, facilitates group decision-making processes, and evaluates and chooses best alternative

❒ **Problem Solving:** Recognizes problems, devises and implements plan of action, and facilitates problem-solving and brainstorming discussions

❒ **Knowing How to Learn:** Uses efficient learning techniques to acquire and apply new knowledge and skills

❒ **Reasoning:** Discovers a rule or principle underlying the relationship between two or more objects and applies it when solving a problem

Personal Qualities: Displays responsibility, self-esteem, sociability, self-management, integrity, and honesty

❒ **Responsibility:** Exerts a high level of effort, perseveres toward goal attainment, and multitasks effectively

❒ **Self-Esteem:** Believes in own self-worth and maintains a positive view of self

❒ **Sociability:** Demonstrates understanding, friendliness, adaptability, and empathy; manages conflict effectively; is polite

❒ **Self-Management:** Assesses self accurately, sets personal goals, monitors progress, works well under pressure, and exhibits self-control

❒ **Integrity/Honesty:** Chooses ethical courses

Select three skills you identified in the checklist and write a description of tasks you have completed where you used or developed that skill. Use tasks from current or past jobs or school or community activities.

Skill 1:

Skill 2:

Skill 3:

CAREER ACTION

2-4 Internet Research on Corporate Codes of Ethics 2

Use the *Internet* site to find and report on two organizations in your career field that have posted their code of ethics on their website.

Career Field: _____

Organization 1: _____

What are the key issues covered in the code of ethics?

Does the organization provide a list of values? If so, list them.

Does the organization outline an ethics policy with respect to hiring, the environment, social responsibility, or other ethics issues? If so, summarize the policies.

Organization 2: _____

What are the key issues covered in the code of ethics?

Does the organization provide a list of values? If so, list them.

Does the organization outline an ethics policy with respect to hiring, the environment, social responsibility, or other ethics issues? If so, summarize the policies.

Both Companies

How are the codes of ethics different? Are the differences significant? Explain.

Summarize the code of ethics for this career field.

Based on its codes of ethics, which organization would you rather work for? Why?

CAREER ACTION   2-5   **Internet Research on In-Demand Careers** 3

Use the *Career Transitions* website or CareerOneStop website to research two in-demand jobs that interest you. Write a brief summary of your findings in the areas provided here.

Occupation 1

Job Title:

Description:

Tasks:

Skills:

Median salary:

Education required:

Technology skills required:

Occupation 2

Job Title:

Description:

Tasks:

Skills:

Median salary:

Education required:

Technology skills required:

For Your Career Management Files Tracker

File your completed Career Action worksheets in your Career Management Files Tracker.

CA 2-1   Notes and examples of employee/employer relationships

CA 2-2   Workplace Skills and Competencies Profile checklist

CA 2-3   Career Competencies Inventory checklist

CA 2-4   Internet research findings about corporate codes of ethics

CA 2-5   Internet research findings about in-demand careers

Know Yourself to Market Yourself

Outcomes

1 Document your education, work experience, activities, and career-related skills. Identify people who can be your references.

2 Identify your values, preferences, and personal qualities so that you can choose the best possible career match.

3 Research online self-assessment tools and career planning resources.

4 Identify your career target.

5 Develop your Job Qualifications Profile to help you market your skills.

OVERVIEW To achieve each step throughout your career—your first job, a promotion, a job or career change—you must sell the product: you. You must know your qualifications and be able to communicate them clearly to employers. In this chapter, you will complete a self-inventory to evaluate your skills and learn how well they qualify you for specific jobs. You will prepare an inventory of your education, training, experience, accomplishments, values, work preferences, and performance traits. You will use this inventory to explore careers or confirm your career target and create your Job Qualifications Profile.

CHAPTER 3

CAREER ACTIONS

JUMP START
Your Workplace Knowledge

Would you hire you? Imagine that you are a manager in a field that interests you (e.g., a nursing supervisor, an office manager, a restaurant owner, a transportation supervisor), and you must hire a new employee. What are you looking for in an employee? What type of person would you want to hire? What will the person need to know and do?

Make a list of at least ten education requirements, skills, and personality characteristics you will require and explain why these requirements are important for success on the job. How well would *you* qualify for these requirements?

Finally, brainstorm several other resources you could use to locate this information. Use at least one of these sources to try to find the answers to your questions.

akva/Shutterstock.com

Take a Personal Inventory
Outcome 1

The information you compile about yourself through the Career Action assignments will form your **personal career inventory**. Your inventory will be an important source of information when you develop your resumes, cover letters, and job applications and when you prepare for interviews.

Employers may want this information when considering you for a job. Included in your career inventory are basic personal data and information about the following:

- Education and professional training
- Work experience, skills, and accomplishments
- People who can vouch for your work and recommend you

Your Education and Training

The first step in compiling your personal career inventory is to use Career Action 3-1 to document your education and training, including dates, places, career-relevant courses and activities, skills, and accomplishments. You will also document your membership and achievements in organizations related to your job and career targets. This information will help you identify or confirm your career choice, develop resumes and cover letters, and prepare for job interviews.

Complete this section of your personal career inventory thoroughly and accurately. Put yourself under a microscope and look at every detail carefully. Ask people who know you well to help you document your accomplishments. Consider scholarships, honors, and awards you have received and competitions in which you have participated.

In describing your accomplishments, be as specific as possible (for example, "Member of winning team in math competition" or "Voted treasurer of the senior class").

COMPLETE   **CAREER ACTION 3-1**

Education, Training, and Activities Inventory, p. 50

Your Work Experience and Skills

In Career Action 3-2, you will document your work and other pertinent experience and record the dates and places of these experiences.

Know your strengths and weaknesses. Practice describing real situations where you used your strengths and overcame your weaknesses.

You will also list the skills and knowledge you developed and any accomplishments, achievements, or recognition you received. Include internships, cooperative education placements, and paid or volunteer work such as community service projects and fund-raising. Be specific about the contributions you made (for example, "Raised 20 percent more in contributions over previous year").

When identifying the skills and accomplishments you achieved through your education, training, and organizational activities, consider two kinds of skills (or competencies) that employers are seeking: job-specific skills and transferable competencies.

> COMPLETE **CAREER ACTION 3-2**
>
> Experience and Skills Inventory, p. 52

Job-Specific Skills

Job-specific skills are the skills and technical abilities that relate to a particular job. For example, using accounting software to prepare a customized balance sheet for a client is a job-specific skill. Relining brakes is a job-specific skill for an auto mechanic. Operating medical diagnostic equipment is another job-specific skill.

Employers often require employees to have certain job-specific skills so that they do not have to provide as much training. For example, job applicants might be required to show that they know how to use specialized tools and equipment or use specific software.

Job applicants must be able to prove to an employer that they have these skills. When you develop your resume and career portfolio and interview for jobs, you will be expected to provide proof through examples, demonstrations, tests, grades, degrees, or certifications.

Transferable Competencies

Transferable competencies are abilities that can be applied in more than one work environment. Employers need workers who have transferable career competencies because these are the basic skills and attitudes that are important for all types of work. These skills make workers highly marketable because the skills are needed for a wide variety of jobs and can be transferred from one task, job, or workplace to another. Consider, for example, a construction supervisor and a bookkeeper. Both must work well with others, manage time, solve problems, read, and communicate effectively. All of these are transferable competencies. Both professionals must be competent in these areas even though framing a house and balancing a set of books (a job-specific skill for each field) are not related.

Transferable skills are especially important to job seekers who have limited work experience. Students who seek entry-level jobs are often able to develop transferable competencies through course work, volunteer activities, and part-time jobs. Think hard about your school and volunteer experiences. They may seem to be unrelated to your job goals, but in reality, they are helping you build valuable transferable workplace skills that you can use to market yourself to employers. See the examples in Figure 3-1 on the next page.

Your Connections

The final step in completing your personal career inventory is identifying job references. A **job reference** is a person who can and will vouch for your capabilities, skills, and suitability for a job. References are typically people who have been your instructors and coaches in school or your supervisors or coworkers in volunteer and paid work environments.

School/Volunteer Activity or Part-Time Job	Transferable Competency for Marketing Yourself
Receiving an A in a business writing course . . .	Shows workplace writing skills
Being elected Treasurer of the Student Government . . .	Shows that the candidate is trusted and has financial skills
Selling the most advertisements for a soccer tournament program . . .	Shows that the candidate has marketing skills and perseveres at tasks
Receiving a perfect attendance award . . .	Shows that the candidate is dedicated and reliable
Receiving a positive comment card from a customer in a restaurant . . .	Shows that the candidate has customer service skills
Participating in a committee to solve a campus parking problem . . .	Shows that the candidate has experience working with others to solve problems
Working on a school or community newspaper . . .	Shows that the candidate is accustomed to deadline pressures

Figure 3-1 Demonstrating Transferable Competencies

In every occupation, transferable competencies are as important as technical expertise and job-specific skills. Strong transferable career skills are the keys to showing prospective employers that you have the skills to be successful in a variety of jobs. See the examples in Figure 3-2.

Job-Specific Skills	Transferable Competencies
• Taking a patient's blood pressure	• Managing budgets
• Using specific software	• Research skills
• Operating a forklift	• Public speaking skills
• Framing a house	• Writing skills
• Driving a truck or vehicle	• Problem-solving skills
• Creating a balance sheet	• Human relations and interpersonal skills
• Giving a customer a manicure	• Interviewing skills
• Calculating a store's cash receipts	• Management skills
• Applying makeup on a television actor	• Negotiating and resolving conflicts
• Training a police dog	• Planning and managing multiple tasks
• Roasting vegetables	• Coping with deadline pressure
• Using email to respond to a customer	• Maintaining a positive attitude
• Repairing a dented bumper on a car	• Teaching others
• Cleaning a hotel room	• Time management
• Teaching a toddler the alphabet	• Using resources wisely

Figure 3-2 Examples of Job-Specific Skills and Transferable Competencies

Identify people with whom you have a good relationship and who can confirm (from first-hand observation) your performance on the job, in school, or in other activities. *Relatives and classmates are not appropriate references.*

The more references you have available, the better prepared you will be for current and future job campaigns. Many employers will ask job candidates who get an interview to provide three references they can contact before making a job offer. With a large list of references, you can use the most helpful references for each job you apply for. For example, if one of your references knows someone at a company you are targeting, you can use that person as a reference when you apply for a job there. If you are qualified to work in two career fields, such as retail sales and accounting, ask people in each field to be your references.

Do not assume that a person will agree to be a reference for you. Always ask (and get) permission before using anyone as a reference. The product website (www.cengage.com/career/yourcareer) has a model reference sheet.

> **COMPLETE** **CAREER ACTION 3-3**
>
> Potential Job References, p. 53

Potential Job References, p. 53

Know What Is Important to You

Outcome 2

Equally important in knowing yourself is an accurate assessment of your personal values, work preferences, and job-related performance traits. Understanding the personal factors that influence your performance and job satisfaction will help you make good choices when you set your job and career targets and consider job offers.

Personal Values

Values are deeply held beliefs about the importance of different personal qualities and traits. Your values are influenced by everything that has happened in your life and by the people and institutions you are closest to and that have

MAKE IT A HABIT

Get Effective Recommendation Letters

Written letters of recommendation are an impressive addition to your list of references. Ask the people who agree to be a reference for you and who are most enthusiastic about your job performance, qualifications, skills, and/or abilities if they are willing to write a recommendation letter.

You are more likely to get a positive answer if you can give the person written starter information for the letter. Use the data in Career Actions 3-1 and 3-2 to make a short, bulleted list of the key facts about you. Give the person your resume and the list so that they have concrete information to work with.

File your recommendation letters in your Career Portfolio (Chapter 1) and in your Interview Marketing Kit (Chapter 8).

track5/iStockphoto.com

shaped you: your parents and family, friends and peers, neighborhood, religious affiliation, ethnic background, education, and even the entertainment you were exposed to growing up and your current entertainment preferences.

Your values affect every area of your life—your behavior, decisions, goals, relationships, priorities, and accomplishments. Thinking about your personal values at this early stage in your job search will help you focus on career fields that match your values. When you know what is important to you, you greatly increase your chances of enjoying your work and succeeding in the jobs you hold.

Work Environment

Most adults spend a great deal of time in their work environment. For that reason, it is important to know where you feel most comfortable and where you perform best. For example, if you are an extrovert who gets energized by working around other people, you probably won't enjoy a job where you spend most of your time in an isolated environment.

Personal Qualities and Work Performance Traits

To get the job you want, you must be able to sell to prospective employers your personal qualities, positive job performance traits, and enthusiasm. Identifying your personal qualities and work performance traits will also help you decide what type of work suits you best.

COMPLETE **CAREER ACTION 3-4**

Values, Preferences, and Personal Qualities Inventory, p. 54

Self-Assessment and Career Planning Resources

Outcome 3

Many self-assessment tools and resources are available to job seekers to speed the process of investigating and selecting career fields. (Some resources may require a fee.)

Review the following resources and mark the ones you could use to improve your career planning and self-assessment.

- **Your school's career services staff and counselors.** These counselors specialize in helping students with career planning. They provide aptitude and interest tests as well as resources for and information about the job market and career fields.

- **The Internet.** A wealth of career planning and job information is available through the Internet. Many sites offer online tools that help you assess your career interests and values and match the results with appropriate careers and jobs. The product website has links to many of these tools.

Market Yourself with Your Social Network

Social media offers a new world of opportunity for job seekers—from networking on LinkedIn to researching companies on Facebook to finding job leads on Twitter.

Social media networking now accounts for one out of every six minutes spent online. While most people log in to their favorite network daily to chat with friends and to enjoy the personal benefits of an online community, many job seekers do not realize how important this network can be in career building.

Everything you do on social media sites is seen by others, including potential employers. Use that visibility to your advantage and create a positive image for yourself on each profile. Whether you use Facebook, Twitter, Foursquare, Reddit, or something else, make sure your profile information is updated. Highlight the qualities and experiences that employers in your field want to see. Keep your comments positive and constructive and your photos clean. Treat your social media profiles as interactive resumes that show the world the best you have to offer. Impress your future employer before you even get to the interview!

You can learn more about social media and career building in the Appendix.

- **Commercial software.** Some commercial software is available on the Internet and through schools' career offices. With these systems, a user completes a computerized questionnaire regarding his or her personal interests and abilities. The program then provides a list of occupations consistent with the user's answers. Check with your school's career counselor or with the state department of education to locate the nearest computerized system.

- **Career planning publications.** Ask your school's career services counselor or librarian for help in locating books, magazines, and articles about your field and current career or job target. (Many of these publications are now available online.) Your school may also have facilities or links through which you can take the Myers-Briggs personality test, which helps you identify your personality and temperament for certain types of work.

- **People you know.** Contact people you have observed or known, people you admire, and people who have jobs just like the one you dream of. Ask them to help you explore your readiness for a similar job or career.

- **Volunteer work.** Volunteer experience can be a big asset when applying for the job you want. It demonstrates initiative and helps you get a feel for a job and a career. You can volunteer on a part-time or temporary basis or ask about arranging an internship through your school.

- **Summer job.** Summer jobs can also offer a taste of the type of work you are interested in. You can get three to four months of work experience that you didn't have before, and you may find that you enjoy this work more than the fields you were interested in before. Try working at a retail job, canvassing for a political cause, tutoring a student, maintaining trails at a national park, walking dogs, or working at a landscaping store. Look online for more ideas—and jobs.

- **City, county, state, and federal employment or human resources departments.** For information about government occupations, contact the employment or human resources department that manages employment in your target field.

> **COMPLETE** **CAREER ACTION 3-5**
>
> Internet Research on Self-Assessments and Career Planning, p. 57

What Do You Value?

mangostock/Shutterstock.com

Because your values began to form when you were an infant, you are not consciously aware of all of the qualities that you value and that influence how you live your life.

Read this list of values and underline the ones that are most important to you: *ambition, competency, individuality, equality, integrity, service, responsibility, accuracy, respect, dedication, diversity, improvement, enjoyment/ fun, loyalty, credibility, honesty, innovativeness, teamwork, excellence, accountability, empowerment, quality, efficiency, dignity, collaboration,* *patience, empathy, accomplishment, courage, wisdom, independence, security, challenge, influence, learning, compassion, friendliness, discipline/order, generosity, persistence, optimism, dependability, flexibility.*

The values you believe in define your character. Putting your values into action and strengthening them—living your values—will help you accomplish your goals and dreams and become the person you want to be.

Adapted from "Identify and Live Your Personal Values" by Susan M. Heathfield, Human Resources Guide, About.com.

Outcome 4 Set Your Career Targets

To know where you would like to go in your career, you must be clear about your career goals and your qualifications. You must know what you would like to achieve, where you want to live and work, and what types of tasks you would like to do. You must also understand if and how your skills and attributes make you a competitive candidate for the jobs you seek.

The thoughtful self-assessments and research you have completed in this chapter have prepared you to select one or two career fields to target. You may want to use the visualization skills from Chapter 1 to help you define your personal career objectives. Together with friends and associates, brainstorm appropriate careers. Think about work, hobbies, and volunteer experiences you have enjoyed in the past. What kind of work do you want to do? Where would you like to do this work? How much do you want to get paid for your work?

Described next are the three types of career targets to set when you start your job search.

Career Target

A **career target** is a job that is ideal for you right now. It suits your current qualifications and interests, matches your salary and work environment preferences, and provides a challenging and interesting work situation. You have a realistic opportunity at being hired for such a job. You will probably have more than one career target.

COMPLETE **CAREER ACTION 3-6**

Career Targets, p. 57

Stretch Job Target

A **stretch job target** is the hard-to-get "dream job" you would like to have in the near future. It might be in a competitive organization or field that does not hire many candidates, it might offer exceptional salary and benefits, or it might offer a desirable location. You may not be fully qualified for the job yet, but reaching for jobs that are higher than you think you can

WATCH OUT!

Don't Lock Yourself In to One Option

Successful career planning requires flexibility. Changing technologies and a global economy cause some careers to become obsolete or vastly changed. Broaden your job options. Prepare to qualify for two or more closely related career targets that require related education, training, and general capabilities.

Which transferable career competencies do you have that qualify you for jobs within and between career fields? Ask a knowledgeable career counselor to help you identify different career fields so that you can set career targets that match your interests and abilities.

To make sure you have plenty of options for success, continue to develop your career flexibility and pursue lifelong learning.

Elena Elisseeva/Shutterstock.com

achieve gives you exposure and experience and helps you along the path to your future career goals.

Contingency Job Target

A **contingency job target** is your backup plan. You could easily get this job because you are overqualified or you have a contact. It is a "safe bet." It is not your first choice because it might lack the salary or work environment that you want or might not be in your preferred career area. It offers security through salary and the opportunity to develop your workplace skills, but it is usually the job you take when you have exhausted other options.

Don't let taking a contingency job be the end of your job search. If you are overqualified or unhappy, you can leave a job for a better one without burning bridges with a contingency employer.

Always be respectful and gracious, remembering that this work is the choice of others. In the long run, you'll be adding skills that you learned at this job to your Job Qualifications Profile.

Outcome 5 Job Qualifications Profile

The Job Qualifications Profile is a snapshot that helps you persuade prospective employers that you are qualified for the jobs you apply for. The profile organizes the qualifications information you have summarized about yourself. It gives a solid description of what your abilities are and how they relate to your job target. This is the evidence employers need to see of a good match between the job and the job applicant— you. Follow these steps to start developing this summary and preparing yourself for a successful job search:

1. **Clearly identify your job target.** If you find this difficult, a career counselor can help. Also refer to the other sources of career planning information and assistance listed in this chapter.

2. **Write a clear description of your targeted job.** Obtain job descriptions from prospective employers. If that isn't feasible, ask your school's career counselor or librarian to help you locate a general description of your job target in the *Dictionary of Occupational Titles,* published by the U.S. Department of Labor. For more complete descriptions of major occupations, use the online or printed edition of the *Occupational Outlook Handbook.*

3. **Look at the Career Action worksheets you completed in Chapters 2 and 3.** This information will help you complete the rest of the Job Qualifications Profile.

4. **Copy or print Career Action Worksheet 3-6 for multiple job targets.** Develop the broadest possible career planning base by including as many options as possible.

Your Job Qualifications Profile will be a valuable resource throughout your career for writing your resume and cover letters and for preparing for interviews for each job you target. As your career progresses, you can update the profile with your expanded skills and experiences. Your Job Qualifications Profile will result in a well-organized summary of the qualifications that relate directly to your current job target. This profile provides a snapshot of the qualifications you need to persuade an employer to hire you for the job you want.

COMPLETE **CAREER ACTION 3-7**

Job Qualifications Profile, p. 58

Chapter Checklist

Underline each action you are already taking and circle the actions you need to work on.

- Document my education, work experience, job-specific skills, and transferable career competencies. [1]

- Identify potential references who are able and willing to confirm my good performance on the job, in school, or in other activities. [1]

- Identify my values, work preferences, and personal qualities to achieve a good career or job match. [2]

- Research online self-assessments to help match my interests, values, and personality style to appropriate career and job targets. [3]

- Research career planning resources that can help me validate my career choices and goals. [3]

- Set career targets, stretch job targets, and contingency job targets. [4]

- Prepare to qualify for two or more closely related career targets that require similar skills and training to increase my career flexibility. [4]

- Develop my Job Qualifications Profile to help market myself to employers. [5]

Critical-Thinking Questions

1. Why is it important to assess and document your education, training, work experience, and accomplishments? [1]

2. How are job-specific skills different from transferable competencies? Give three examples of each. [1]

3. What is the important role of references in your job search? [1]

4. Why is it useful to identify your work performance traits and career-related personal qualities? [2]

5. What career planning resources will be most helpful in your job search and career planning activities? Why? [3]

6. Why is it important to develop a broad base of skills and competencies that is flexible enough to encompass at least two fields? [4]

7. How can you use your Job Qualifications Profile information in your job search and interviews? [5]

Want access to career resources, study tools, activities, and job information links? Get started at www.cengage.com/career/ yourcareer.

TRIAL RUN

Do both parts of this assignment independently or work with a partner who has a job target and background similar to yours.

After you have completed Career Actions 3-6 and 3-7, research your career and job target(s) in more detail. Use the career planning websites listed in Career Action 3-5 and in Chapter 2 to learn education and skill requirements, salary information, work environment, tasks, job outlook, and opportunities for advancement. (You can find links to these sites at the product website.) Summarize your findings in a PowerPoint presentation or in a table in a Word file.

Next, identify the most important job-specific skills (such as word processing skills in an office job) and transferable competencies (such as math and problem-solving skills) for your current career target.

Job Skills:

Transferable Competencies:

Evaluate yourself on how well your qualifications and values match the requirements of the job.

Rating Scale: 1 to 4 (1 = not a match; 2 = mediocre match; 3 = adequate match; 4 = excellent match)

Qualifications and Values	Rating (1–4)
Education	_____
Work Experience	_____
Job Skills	_____
Transferable Competencies	_____
Accomplishments and Recognition	_____
Values	_____
Work Environment Preferences	_____
Personal Traits and Qualities	_____

Overall, how well-suited do you think you are for the job? Explain.

What can you do to improve your ratings and qualifications?

CAREER ACTION   3-1   Education, Training, and Activities Inventory [1]

Complete the sections of this inventory that apply to you: (1) High School Inventory, (2) Post-Secondary Education Inventory, and (3) Seminars and Workshops Inventory. Be thorough in documenting your accomplishments and achievements. Use this information to begin building your resume in *Career Transitions*.

High School Inventory

Name of School _____

Address _____

_____

Dates of Attendance _____ to _____ Date of Diploma _____

Grade Point Average _____

1. **Career-Related Courses.** List the career-related courses you completed.

2. **Career-Related and Organizational Activities.** Describe your involvement in school, extracurricular, community, and other activities (examples: clubs, sports, organizations, and volunteer work).

3. **Career-Related Skills.** List the skills you developed in high school and through other activities. Include both job-specific skills and transferable competencies (examples: operating a computer, calculating numbers, persuading others, using specific tools/equipment, leading others, and working on a team).

4. **Accomplishments, Achievements, and Recognition.** List all special accomplishments, achievements, and recognition you received in high school and through other activities (examples: selected to play lead in musical production, selected to serve on state debate team, and awarded first place in math competition). List any scholarships or honors you earned. Also summarize praise you received from instructors, peers, and others.

Post-Secondary Education Inventory

Complete one form for each post-secondary school you attended. Duplicate the form if you attended more than one post-secondary school.

Name of School _____

Address _____

_____

Dates of Attendance _____ to _____ Date of Diploma _____

Grade Point Average _____

1. **Career-Related Courses.** List the career-related courses you completed.

2. **Career-Related and Organizational Activities.** Describe your involvement in school and extracurricular activities, in professional or other associations or organizations, in community activities, in volunteer work, and in other activities (examples: sports, clubs, offices held, volunteer work, and community projects or programs).

3. **Career-Related Skills.** List the skills you developed through your classes and other activities. Include your *job-specific skills* and *transferable competencies* (examples: operating a computer, using specific software, preparing oral and written communication, marketing, calculating numbers, persuading and leading others, working as a team member, and researching).

4. **Accomplishments, Achievements, and Recognition.** List all special accomplishments, achievements, and recognition you received for school activities. List any scholarships or honors you earned (examples: awarded second place in state business education skills competition, won scholarship, earned service award, prepared lesson plans that were used as model for campus, and restored two-bedroom apartment).

Seminars and Workshops Inventory

List the seminars and workshops you have attended. If necessary, add to the list of seminars and workshops by keying in the additional information (if you are using the Word file for this activity) or by using additional paper (if you are handwriting this activity).

Name of Seminar/Workshop _____

Offered by _____ Date(s) _____

Career-related concepts or skills I learned _____

Name of Seminar/Workshop _____

Offered by _____ Date(s) _____

Career-related concepts or skills I learned _____

Name of Seminar/Workshop _____

Offered by _____ Date(s) _____

Career-related concepts or skills I learned _____

CAREER ACTION   3-2   Experience and Skills Inventory [1]

Complete this form for each position or project you have had (cooperative work experience, internship, volunteer/paid work experience, military experience). Begin with the most recent experience and continue in reverse chronological order. Duplicate the form for additional job experience. Complete each section of the worksheet that applies to you. Be as specific and thorough as possible. Add this information to the resume you are building in *Career Transitions*.

POSITION (or ACTIVITY) TITLE _____

Name of Organization/Committee _____

Address _____

Telephone Number _____ Salary (if paid experience) _____

Circle Type of Experience: (1) Cooperative   (2) Volunteer   (3) Internship   (4) Paid Work

Dates of Employment or Involvement _____

Supervisor Name/Title _____

1. **Career-Related Skills.** List the job-specific skills, transferable competencies, and responsibilities you developed in this position.

   Job-Specific Skills _____

   Transferable Competencies _____

   Responsibilities _____

2. **Accomplishments and Achievements.** List your accomplishments in this position, preferably in measurable terms (examples: reduced order processing time by 15 percent by developing more efficient processing methods, named employee/volunteer of the month, supervised evening shift of five employees).

3. **Praise Received.** Summarize praise received from employers, coworkers, committee members, and customers.

Why did you leave?

Performance rating (circle one):   Excellent   Very Good   Good   Needs Improvement   Poor

CAREER ACTION   3-3   **Potential Job References** [1]

List at least three people who would recommend you to prospective employers. Consider potential job references from your education/training and work experience along with respected people
who can be personal references. Record their names and information below and add them to the
References under Prepare Resume in *Career Transitions*. Plan to contact each reference and ask him
or her to write you a letter of reference. Be sure to get their permission to use them as references
during your job search. Duplicate this form to list more references if possible.

Name _____

Title and Organization _____

Mailing Address _____

How I know this person _____

Telephone Number(s) _____ Permission date to use reference _____

Email Address _____ Twitter Account _____

LinkedIn URL _____ Facebook Account _____

Date of recommendation letter _____ Date of last personal contact _____

Name _____

Title and Organization _____

Mailing Address _____

How I know this person_____

Telephone Number(s) _____ Permission date to use reference _____

Email Address _____ Twitter Account _____

LinkedIn URL _____ Facebook Account _____

Date of recommendation letter _____ Date of last personal contact _____

Name _____

Title and Organization _____

Mailing Address _____

How I know this person _____

Telephone Number(s) _____ Permission date to use reference _____

Email Address _____ Twitter Account _____

LinkedIn URL _____ Facebook Account _____

Date of recommendation letter _____ Date of last personal contact _____

CAREER ACTION

3-4 Values, Preferences, and Personal Qualities Inventory [2]

Use this worksheet to identify and prioritize the values that are important to you. It will help you clarify the kinds of work environments you prefer. Remember, there are no wrong answers in defining what is important to you.

Part 1: Values

Rank the importance of each value as it relates to your career and job goals (H: high; M: medium; L: low).

Value	Ranking (H, M, L)
1. Adventure (risk taking, new challenges)	_____
2. Education/learning/wisdom	_____
3. Social needs (need for relationships with people)	_____
4. Self-respect/integrity/self-discipline	_____
5. Helping/serving	_____
6. Recognition/respect from others	_____
7. Freedom/independence (working independently with minimal supervision)	_____
8. Security (job, family, national, financial)	_____
9. Spiritual needs	_____
10. Expression (creative, artistic)	_____
11. Responsibility (reliability, dependability)	_____
12. Balance in work and personal life	_____

Others (List other values below and rank each one.)

_____   _____

_____   _____

_____   _____

_____   _____

Part 2: Work Environment Preferences

Place a check mark next to each work environment condition you prefer.

Work Environment	Check Those Preferred
1. Indoor work	❑
2. Outdoor work	❑
3. Industrial/manufacturing setting	❑

4. Office setting ☐

5. Working alone ☐

6. Working with people ☐

7. Working with things ☐

8. Working with data ☐

9. Working with ideas ☐

10. Challenging opportunities ☐

11. Predictable, orderly, structured work ☐

12. Pressures at work ☐

13. Problem solving ☐

14. Standing while working ☐

15. Sitting while working ☐

16. Busy surroundings ☐

17. Quiet surroundings ☐

18. Exciting, adventurous conditions ☐

19. Safe working conditions/environment ☐

20. Creative environment ☐

21. Opportunities for professional development and ongoing training/education ☐

22. Flexibility in work structure ☐

23. Teamwork and work groups ☐

24. Opportunities to supervise, lead, advance ☐

25. Opportunities to make a meaningful difference or to help others ☐

26. Use of cutting-edge technology or techniques ☐

27. Integrity and truth in work environment ☐

28. Stability and security ☐

29. High-level earnings potential ☐

30. Opportunities to participate in community affairs ☐

Others (List other conditions you are seeking in your job target.)

_____ ☐

_____ ☐

_____ ☐

_____ ☐

Part 3: Personal Qualities and Work Performance Traits

Rate yourself on the personal qualities and work performance traits listed below using a scale of high (H), average (A), or low (L). Respond to the statements at the end of the form.

Personal Quality or Work Performance Trait	Rating (H, A, L)
1. Initiative/resourcefulness/motivation	_____
2. Dependability	_____
3. Punctuality	_____
4. Flexibility	_____
5. Creativity	_____
6. Patience	_____
7. Perseverance	_____
8. Humor	_____
9. Diplomacy	_____
10. Intelligence	_____
11. High energy level	_____
12. Ability to work well with a team	_____
13. Ability to set and achieve goals	_____
14. Ability to plan, organize, prioritize work	_____
15. Outgoing personality	_____
16. Ability to handle conflict	_____
17. Optimistic attitude	_____
18. Realistic attitude	_____
19. Enthusiastic attitude	_____
20. Willingness to work	_____
21. Orderliness of work	_____
22. Attention to detail	_____
23. Ability to manage time well	_____
24. Honesty and integrity	_____
25. Ability to multitask	_____

List and rank other positive personal qualities and/or work performance traits.

List and describe at least five positive examples of how you have used some of these qualities and traits in the past.

CAREER ACTION   3-5   Internet Research on Self-Assessments and Career Planning ③

Part 1. Use *Career Transitions* to complete the self-assessment. Also use the Internet to locate and complete one or two career-related self-assessment tests that measure your interests, values, and/or personality style. Print the results for your Career Management Files Tracker. Some versions of tests to search for are The Career Key, the mini-Myers-Briggs Type Indicator quiz, and The Keirsey Temperament Sorter. A fee may be required to take some of these assessments, but you can find free assessments.

Part 2. Use several of the resources below to find information about your career and job targets, including descriptions of your targeted fields and jobs, salary information, and employment outlook projections. Prepare a written summary of your findings or print useful information that you find. Links to these sites are on the product website.

- America's Career InfoNet
- CareerOneStop
- The College Board
- JobStar Central
- Occupational Outlook Handbook
- O*NET OnLine (onetonline.org)
- Quintessential Careers
- U.S. Bureau of Labor Statistics

CAREER ACTION   3-6   Career Targets ④

Answer these questions about your current career target.

1. In which career field are you planning to seek employment? (Examples: accounting, office management, healthcare, teaching, administration, construction, computer technology)

2. Which specific job(s) are you targeting in your employment search? (List every job you are qualified for and interested in pursuing. Maximize your options by listing jobs within and between career fields that require transferable competencies that you have.)

3. What specific activities are you most interested in performing in your ideal job? What energizes and excites you most?

4. Describe the stretch job target you aspire to in this career. What additional training, experience, skills, and qualifications will you need to achieve your stretch job target?

5. Describe several contingency job targets that might help you prepare for your career target and stretch job target. What will you learn and do in each job to increase your qualifications for the job you hope to get?

6. Are you willing to travel or relocate for a job in your career target? Explain.

Broaden your possibilities and answer the same questions about a second career target you are interested in.

1. In which career field are you planning to seek employment? (Examples: accounting, office management, healthcare, teaching, administration, construction, computer technology)

2. Which specific job(s) are you targeting in your employment search? (List every job you are qualified for and interested in pursuing. Maximize your options by listing jobs within and between career fields that require transferable competencies that you have.)

3. What specific activities are you most interested in performing in your ideal job? What energizes and excites you most?

4. Describe the stretch job target you aspire to in this career. What additional training, experience, skills, and qualifications will you need to achieve your stretch job target?

5. Describe several contingency job targets that might help you prepare for your career target and stretch job target. What will you learn and do in each job to increase your qualifications for the job you hope to get?

6. Are you willing to travel or relocate for a job in your career target? Explain.

CAREER ACTION   3-7   Job Qualifications Profile ⑤

Complete this Job Qualifications Profile. Refer to your completed Career Action worksheets for this chapter; CA 2-2, Workplace Skills and Competencies Profile; and CA 2-3, Career Competencies Inventory.

Title of Job Target _____

1. Description of job:

2. How my education and training relate to the job target:

3. How my work experience relates to the job target:

4. How my accomplishments relate to the job target:

5. Praise or recognition I have received related to the job target:

6. How my skills and transferable competencies relate to the job target:

7. How my values relate to the job target:

8. How my preferences about my work environment relate to the job target:

9. How my personality traits relate to the job target:

10. What appeals to me about this job:

11. Actions I can take to improve my qualifications (education, training, skills, unpaid work opportunities):

For Your Career Management Files Tracker

File your completed Career Action worksheets in your Career Management Files Tracker.

CA 3-1   Education, Training, and Activities Inventory

CA 3-2   Experience and Skills Inventory

CA 3-3   Contact information for potential job references

CA 3-4   Values, Preferences, and Personal Qualities Inventory

CA 3-5   Internet research findings about self-assessments and career planning

CA 3-6   Career target, stretch job target, and contingency job targets for two career fields

CA 3-7   Job Qualifications Profile

PART

2

Sources of Job Information

©Jim Calloway Photography

Dedra Perlmutter, Certified HR Professional
JVS Cincinnati Career Network

After 13 years in Human Resources helping employees navigate the workplace, Dedra Perlmutter changed direction and decided to help job seekers *become* employees.

The Cincinnati Career Network is not a job placement agency. Clients attend small-group workshops and get one-on-one counseling on any part of their job search. Dedra believes that "It's essential to find a 'go-to person' you feel comfortable with and who will be honest and helpful."

Dedra stresses "the power of networking—everywhere you go!" She emphasizes that networking is about giving and receiving and reminds job seekers to communicate their appreciation to the people they meet. She also promotes "LinkedIn as an important tool for both job seekers and recruiters."

Dedra advises job seekers that "the interview starts in the parking lot, continues with the receptionist, and doesn't end until you send your thank-you note."

Dedra's most heartfelt advice is to keep reminding yourself that "Rejections are not personal! Seek out others who are going through the same thing and share your experiences, disappointments, and successes."

As a free career center, the not-for-profit Cincinnati Career Network has seen an increase in clients since the economic downturn in 2008. "Most communities have an agency like ours. Call the library or United Way to find the one near you—and go!" Dedra knows that every job search is unique and is constantly changing. "Please," she says, "find a counselor who can coach and guide you through the process."

© Cengage Learning 2013

TALES FROM THE JOB SEARCH

Clarissa Cutrell
Web Content Writer

For three years, Clarissa Cutrell had helped companies envision and establish social media campaigns using blogs, Twitter feeds, Facebook Fan Pages, online contests, and other social media networking tools. When the e-marketing company she worked for decided to get out of the social media management business, Clarissa turned to what she knew best to look for new opportunities.

Clarissa updated her personal blog with writing samples and made sure that her LinkedIn profile was polished with her updated resume. She let her friends know she was looking for work via Facebook and received tips on several job lists she could subscribe to for weekly emails of new opportunities in her area.

"I was surprised how much I ended up using social media sites for the application and interview process," Clarissa says. "LinkedIn was great for finding the right person to address my cover letter to. For one application, I discovered I had a common connection with the hiring manager and was able to slip that into the cover letter. Facebook, Twitter, and company blogs were useful for learning more about the companies I interviewed with."

As soon as she left her first interview for her new position, Clarissa knew her research had paid off. "I spent hours learning about the city of Golden, Colorado, and getting to know the website I would be working on. It paid off. The very first question was, 'What do you know about Golden?'

"I knew the city wanted to redesign the website, so I prepared a list of ideas for the project. I truly believe being so well prepared for that interview is what gave me the confidence to sail through it. The interview lasted almost two hours—and I felt prepared for every question they threw my way. I think that confidence is what landed me the job."

→ Ready, Set, PLAN

Read the outcomes on the first page of Chapters 4 and 5 and mark the ones that are most important to you. What do you want to accomplish by reading these chapters and doing the assignments?

How much time is in the syllabus for Chapters 4 and 5?

List the dates for reading assignments and the dates for turning in homework and projects for this class.

What are your other major commitments in the coming weeks (for other classes, work, home)? For each task, include the estimated time and when you will do it.

If you are doing any group projects, list information that will help the project go smoothly: project goal and due date, each person's assignments and phone number, dates for completing each part of the project, meeting dates, and anything else.

CHAPTER 4

Your Winning Network

OVERVIEW In this chapter, you will learn how to build a powerful job search network. This chapter guides you through the development of two important support groups to help you achieve your career goals: a personal support system to motivate you and a network of people to help identify solid job leads. You will learn strategies for networking and learn how to conduct Career Information Surveys with members of your network to get career information and job advice.

Outcomes

1. Explain the benefits and goals of successful networking.
2. Identify the people in your personal support system and your job search network.
3. Describe networking strategies and etiquette, including online networking.
4. Set up career information surveys (informational interviews).

© Photographer/Image Source

JUMP START
Your Network

If possible, work on this activity in small groups with classmates who have similar job goals. Identify a job or career that you think you would like to pursue. Then imagine that you know someone who works in the job. Think of ten questions you could ask the person to help you find out if the job or career matches your qualifications and to learn more about how to find that type of job.

Start by jotting down ten things you want to know about this job or career. Then draft questions you could ask someone to get the information. For example, if you want to know about a job's hours, you might ask, "What time do you start and end your work day?"

Finally, write five more questions you could ask to gain advice about how to find a job (for example, "What is the best strategy for finding a job in this field?").

akva/Shutterstock.com

 ## Networking Pays Off

Outcome 1

Because it is the No. 1 source of finding a good job, smart job seekers focus heavily on **networking**—developing relationships with people who can help in forming job search strategies and in finding strong job leads. Networking is the top source of job leads because employers are more likely to hire people who are referred to them personally—through networking. The larger your network, the more networking contacts you have and the greater your chances of finding someone who knows about a job lead that could be a good fit. So tap into this dynamic source, build your network, and get the word out now.

Many successful job seekers find jobs with the help of friends, family members, and acquaintances. At any time, there are many more job openings than the ones that are advertised. You can increase your chances of being called for an interview by seeking unadvertised jobs that you find through networking. The more people you make aware of your search, the more solid leads you can get. Through networking, you can:

- Seek career advice from many people and make them aware of your qualifications and availability.
- Tap into jobs you would not have access to without networking.
- Get insider information about the industry, trends, and job search and hiring methods in your field.
- Get access to information about specific employers.
- Promote yourself and make a good impression.
- Practice your communication and interviewing skills.
- Seek job leads and obtain referrals to other people who may be able to help you.

 ## Identify Your Networks

Outcome 2

Each job seeker has a two-tiered network: a personal support system—the "inner circle" that can be counted on to encourage and motivate the job seeker—and a job search network—the people who can provide advice, job leads, referrals, etc.

Your Personal Support System

One important reason for networking is to have support, advice, and positive feedback while you undertake the challenge of looking for a job. Networking begins with your **personal support system:** the group of people who can motivate, advise, and encourage you during your job search and throughout your career.

Good choices for your personal support system are people who are willing to provide you with motivational support, such as the following:

- Family
- Friends
- School, work, and social acquaintances
- Former or current employers
- Career services staff
- Instructors and counselors from school

One support system member may help boost your commitment. Another may help soothe your ego after a job rejection. Still another support system member may help you polish your resumes and cover letters. These people sustain and motivate you when you need a push and can help you reach your full potential.

Select your support system members for their ability to do the following:

- Motivate you
- Help you develop effective job search documents
- Help you practice for interviews
- Help you find solid job leads, provide job search advice, and/or share similar experiences

COMPLETE **CAREER ACTION 4-1**

Personal Support System Network, p. 77

Your Job Search Network

The network of people who can help you with job leads and contacts is your **job search network**. This group grows exponentially with each new contact you make. A good contact is someone who can give you career advice, tell you about job openings, arrange an interview, or refer you to people who can. People who have met you in person or who know someone who knows you well are most likely to help you. Your network begins with people you know who can link you to others, increasing your chances of discovering good job prospects.

Starting with the suggestions on the next page, brainstorm a list of possible contacts. Who else do you know? (Don't overlook anyone.) Who do they know? Consider the spouses and family members of people you know. Someone could have a connection exactly where you need it.

COMPLETE **CAREER ACTION 4-2**

Job Search Network List, p. 77

Outcome 3 ## Strategies for Networking

You could easily have 100 acquaintances—maybe many more. Think of the number of job leads you would get if even a quarter of these people gave you referrals. This is why networking is such an important source of job leads. The guidelines in this section will help you get the most from your networking efforts.

Create a Network List and Contact the People on It

Job search networking is a numbers game. The more people who know about your job search goals and qualifications, the greater your chances of getting interviews and finding the ideal job. By focusing your energies on networking to expand your job search reach and to communicate the fact that you are looking for a job, you can maximize your job and career development potential.

- Contact people who can help with your career preparation and job search.

- Discuss your job target with your contacts. In planned meetings, leave a copy of your resume and a brief outline of your job target and qualifications. In spontaneous situations, follow up by sending the person these documents.

- Ask for the names of at least two people you can contact to find job leads and information.

- Contact these people; repeat the process.

- Follow up on every lead. Be persistent.

Update your job search network list periodically to ensure that your original choices were the best ones. Eliminate the contacts who, over time, are reluctant to help or have too many commitments to get involved.

Talk about Your Job Search

Go out of your way to initiate conversations about your job search. Be friendly and outgoing and introduce yourself to people. If people ask how you are doing or what you've been up to, tell them that you've been busy working on your job search. Often that is all it takes for other people to inquire about the type of job you are seeking. You never know—they just might know someone in your field.

When you meet new people in social situations, ask what they do for a living and don't be afraid to ask how they found their job and request their advice. In networking, getting job leads is important. Asking directly is typically not as productive as saying, "I'm looking for a(n) _____ job. Do you have any advice for finding one in _____ (industry) (company) (city)?" This approach focuses on the word *advice* and makes your contacts more inclined to help. Be courteous. Also ask for names of people you can contact to seek additional information.

Demonstrate Your Workplace Savvy

OJO Images/Jupiter Images

The people you meet while networking must decide if you are someone they feel comfortable referring to *their* network.

Networking will most likely take you into some of your contacts' workplaces. You need to demonstrate that you are a professional who understands and follows the rules of the business world. For example, you need to dress appropriately when you meet with your contacts in person, and you need to leave them professional-sounding voice-mail messages.

This chapter introduces several basic workplace expectations that are covered in later chapters. Look carefully at the following list and read

more about anything you are unsure about.

- Chapter 6, list of references
- Chapter 7, business cards
- Chapter 8, professional binder or portfolio
- Chapter 8, dressing appropriately
- Chapter 9, using the telephone effectively
- Chapter 11, interview etiquette
- Chapter 11, thank-you notes

Learn as much as you can about the issues you may encounter during networking—before you encounter them and risk making a poor impression.

Never forget the impression you are making when you talk about your job search. Talk about your efforts in positive terms; do not whine about how long you have been looking for a job or how many bills you need to pay. The people who give you leads are taking a risk with their own reputation, and they expect you to make a good impression on the people they refer you to.

Attend Job Fairs

Job fairs (also called career fairs) are excellent networking opportunities because you can connect with many prospective employers at one time. Check with your school's career center to learn about job fairs and other networking events in your area.

Practice making a good first impression. These types of events call for professional attire and behavior. Pay attention to your appearance and practice good manners. Use positive body language, such as an easygoing smile and eye contact that shows you are interested in what people have to say.

Prepare for events ahead of time. Prepare a few questions you can ask in any networking situation and come with some conversation starters, such as "What brings you here?" or "This location works well for this event." Practice introducing yourself. Set a goal to talk with a certain number of people. If you are shy or uncomfortable talking with strangers, consider volunteering to work at the registration table, hand out material, or help with other tasks that will require you to interact with many people. Job interview are sales calls, and you are your product. Your discomfort in an interview may make the interviewer uncomfortable in turn. That's not the impression you want to make.

Participate in Professional Groups

Join and be active in professional, trade, and other relevant associations or groups. These types of groups actively encourage people to enter their fields and are eager to offer assistance to job seekers. Nearly every career field has such a group, and most can be accessed via their websites.

For example, a college student studying physical therapy in New York could easily find the New York Physical Therapy Association by searching online using the terms *physical therapy* and *New York*. Likewise, a student working on a certificate in nail technology could quickly search for the local chapter of the International Nail Technicians Association.

The websites of professional organizations are worth reviewing carefully. They offer valuable resources for getting job leads and staying informed about industry developments. Many also offer networking opportunities and mentoring programs in which experienced members work with new members to work toward their goals by offering advice and guidance and connecting them to resources and other contacts. You will learn more about these groups in Chapter 5.

Join or Start a Job Club

A **job club** is a group of job seekers who meet regularly to share experiences and advice, set goals, and offer encouragement. Also known as networking or job search clubs, they can be located through newspapers, alumni and employment offices, chambers of commerce, and online (try www.meetup.com). If you can't find a job club that meets your needs, consider starting your own. Recruit members online or in community newspapers.

Use your social network to maintain your people network.

Follow Networking Etiquette

Proper networking etiquette centers around effective communication with the people on your network list. Networking requires effective written communication (letters or email) and effective verbal and listening skills (meetings, interviews, and conversations).

Job seekers need to communicate well to make contacts, request meetings, introduce themselves, participate in conversations, ask questions, and write thank-you notes. Take advantage of these tips:

- **For written communication, follow proper business writing conventions and formatting.** Email is a perfectly acceptable way to network, but make sure your correspondence is professional and error-free. If necessary, have a friend or contact read your work to check for mistakes and to help you improve your clarity and conciseness.

- **If possible, try to contact people in person.** Otherwise, use the telephone or email to update them about your job search status and to get additional assistance. Make notes before you call anyone so that you know what to say if you reach the person or if you need to leave a message. Be professional, respectful, and friendly in all of your communication.

- **Be a resource to others.** Every job hunter can use regular encouragement. If you're asked to help another job seeker, be gracious and willing to do so. Share their information with members of your network and send them leads that aren't a good match for your goals.

- **Be polite and get to the point quickly.** Show your contacts that you respect their authority and expertise. Ask for their opinions and ask them to recommend additional job search strategies or job leads.

- **Treat every networking contact (whether a planned or spontaneous opportunity) with professional respect.** Don't correct your contacts if you think their advice is wrong; just thank them for providing it. The impression you make can help or hinder the outcome.

MAKE IT A HABIT

Respect People's Time

Always arrive on time or early (no more than 5 or 10 minutes) for networking events and meetings. Punctuality is courteous and shows that you are responsible and prepared.

Likewise, respect the time limits that have been set. Busy employers are not able to take much time from their workday.

Effective preparation and focused questions will help you stick to your time limit and respect your contact's time.

Stockbyte/Jupiter Images

- **Be flexible and make it easy for your contacts to meet with you.** Your contacts are doing you a favor by helping you with your job search. Read each situation carefully; for example, don't push to meet in person if they prefer a phone meeting. Don't expect contacts to change their schedule for you. Change your schedule to accommodate their needs.

- **Respect your contacts' time.** Never be late or allow a meeting to run long. Listen and watch for cues that the person wants to end the conversation or meeting.

- **Bring your business card.** Business cards are essential to networking. They look professional and allow people to stay in touch. Exchange business cards when you meet new people. Later, write notes about the encounter on the back of the card. Keep plenty of your own cards on hand in networking situations.

- **Follow through with all referrals and thank contacts in writing.** Professional and error-free emails are appropriate for follow-up communications.

- **Stay in touch throughout your search and let your contacts know when you get a job.** In today's changing work world, you should build and maintain strong networking relationships throughout your career, not just when you are looking for a job.

COMPLETE   **CAREER ACTION 4-3**

Internet Research on Networking Tips and Etiquette, p. 78

Personal References

Be sure to identify people from your network who can act as your **references**. References are people who are willing to vouch for your qualifications and recommend you to prospective employers. These people should be able to attest to your strong performance at work, in school, or elsewhere and to your desirable character traits and values and your suitability for a job. They also should be willing to write letters recommending you to employers. The more references you have available, the better prepared you are for your current and future job campaign. Add their names to the list of references you recorded in Career Action 3-3.

Follow these guidelines for developing your references:

- Use only those references who have given you permission to use their names and thank them for allowing you to do so.

- Use only those references who would recommend you highly from firsthand knowledge and with whom you have a good relationship and regular communication.

Make Your Social Network a Business Network

The next time you log in to Facebook, Twitter, or another social network, count the number of people in your network. Even if you have only a handful, multiply that number by the number of people in each of their networks—that's a powerful resource. Your winning network can easily be an online one.

Don't underestimate the power of your personal network to boost your job search. Most people enjoy facilitating connections between people they know and respect. The more friends who know you're looking for a job, the more likely you are to connect with someone who has a lead for you.

- Tell your network that you're job hunting and be specific about what you're looking for.
- Seek out and befriend or follow people who have jobs you admire and who work in your industry or for the companies you're interested in.
- Subscribe to blog feeds, join industry forums, and stay up to date on changes and advances in your industry.
- Join the conversation by reading what others have to say and by adding your own comments to blog posts and conversation threads.

Continue to use your social network to connect with friends, but don't be afraid to use it as a powerful business networking tool as well. The rise of social media has made it easy to connect with like-minded people—whenever and wherever you want.

- Because legal constraints may restrict your previous employers from giving a reference, ask former coworkers. They may be more willing to give you a recommendation.

- Do not use relatives as references.

- Ask each reference to write a letter of reference that you can provide to potential employers. Keep copies of your reference letters in your Career Portfolio for use during your job search.

- Let your references know when you will be using their names.

- Find both personal references (people who vouch for your good character) and professional references (people who vouch for your work skills and qualities).

It is inappropriate to use someone you have not spoken to in years as a reference. He or she may not have enough information to provide an accurate view of your qualifications. To maintain your references, stay in touch via an occasional email or phone call with regular updates on your job status and career goals.

Prospective employers will check your previous employers and your references. Previous employers might only confirm your dates of employment, but references may be asked to respond to questions about your attitude, work history, job performance, ability to work with others, and work habits. Coach your references accordingly. You can't control what your references will say about you, but you should give them information about the jobs you seek and the skills required so that they will be able to emphasize your qualifications and abilities.

In Chapter 7, you will develop a formal reference list to send with applications and resumes.

Networking Correspondence

Whether in a printed letter or an email message, correspondence with your network should be professional and businesslike. The following sample demonstrates the proper

tone, business writing style, and language for all of your networking correspondence. Page 74 shows a sample thank-you letter.

Example Contact Letter

Dear [Mr./Ms. Contact],

I was recently referred to you by Grace Santana of Springfield Career School. She recommended you as an excellent source of information about the physical therapy field.

I am a student about to begin a search for an entry-level position in physical therapy, and I would welcome the chance to hear your advice about the industry and get your feedback on my qualifications and skills.

Do you have time to talk with me in the next two weeks? I will contact you next week about a convenient time to meet briefly or to talk by phone. Thanks in advance for your insights. I look forward to meeting you.

Sincerely,
[Your name and contact information]

 ## Career Information Survey

One formal form of networking is the **career information survey**. Also known as an *informational interview*, a career information survey is a meeting in which a job seeker interviews a contact about his or her job or career. Using a list of questions prepared in advance, the job seeker makes the appointment and behaves as if this were a job interview. The job seeker's goal is to develop networking contacts and learn about a job or career.

Professionals in your field can provide valuable inside information and advice to help you realize your career goals. Through your meetings, you will gain:

- **Practice.** You will go directly to the business community as you research and network. You will schedule appointments and practice communicating about your career and job targets—terrific preparation for actual interviews.

- **Information.** You will obtain important information about the scope of jobs and the hiring procedures in your field. You may even get valuable job leads.

- **Competitive edge.** You will have the edge over applicants who do not complete these activities.

To complete your Career Information Surveys, you will contact two people who hold jobs that are similar to your job target. You will meet them at their work sites to learn about their jobs and the hiring procedures their employers use. This will help prepare you for a successful job search in your field.

Making an Appointment for a Survey Meeting

To make a survey appointment, contact at least two organizations that employ people in your field. Making the initial contact in person is preferable. If you cannot do that, review the telephone techniques outlined in Chapter 10 before you call the organization.

Ask to speak with someone whose job is similar to your job target. Emphasize that you are carrying out an assignment from your instructor or doing research in your field. Explain that you want to learn about your occupational field as part of your career planning research. Do not say that you are looking for a job. Strangers are more likely to help you with research than with getting a job.

Connecting With Hard-to-Reach Employers

Some organizations are not as accessible for career survey meetings as others. If your target employer is such an organization, follow these guidelines to identify people with whom you can meet for a survey.

- Turn to your network. Ask everyone in your job search network (friends, family, school counselors, etc.) to help you identify someone who works in your targeted employment field—a person you can meet with to gather career information. Your network may provide opportunities or think of options that would not otherwise be available to you.

- Search the Internet. Many firms have computerized hiring processes and provide application and hiring information through their company websites or through third-party

---

Guidelines for Requesting an Appointment

Follow these guidelines when making an appointment for a survey meeting.

- Be clean, neat, and properly dressed if you make an appointment in person. Be prepared by having your binder and questions with you.

- Introduce yourself. Explain your purpose for calling—you are completing an assignment for your class at _____. If you are using this book independently, tell the person that you are conducting career research.

- Request an appointment to ask a few questions (those you prepared in Career Action 4-4) about the person's job and the career field.

- Confirm the date and time. If you are making your initial contact in person, the person may offer to meet with you immediately.

- Thank the person for his or her time and assistance.

job-posting websites. If your target employer falls in this category, obtain the company and/or third-party Internet addresses, search for the application and hiring information, and print your findings or prepare a written summary to submit as your report for Career Action 4-3.

- Confirm the date and time. If you are making your initial contact in person, the person may offer to meet with you immediately.

- Choose a closely related employer target. If you are unable to schedule an appointment to meet with your preferred employer, schedule a meeting with a closely related organization. This will still be an opportunity to learn about the field you are investigating and to decide whether it is right for you. Face-to-face meetings give you the valuable business communication practice necessary to outdistance your competition.

Figure 4-1 page 73 lists some questions to ask during a career information survey meeting.

COMPLETE **CAREER ACTION 4-4**

Career Information Survey Questions, p. 79

During the Survey Meeting

Your attitude, actions, and attentiveness during a career information survey meeting—especially one held in your contact's place of work—will help you gather important information about the work environment. Be professional and friendly; take notes; and most of all, be a good listener to gather as much information as possible.

Maridav/Shutterstock.com

WATCH OUT!

Don't Dress Like an Amateur

Dress professionally for every meeting with a network contact. Good grooming and proper hygiene require cleanliness; tidiness; styled hair; clean clothing; and conservative hair, makeup, and jewelry. Follow these simple "Don'ts" to avoid making a fashion error that could damage your reputation with a contact:

- Don't wear revealing or tight clothing such as tank tops, shorts, or low-rise jeans. Showing skin is never appropriate in the workplace.

- Don't wear athletic wear at work. If you are heading to the gym after work, pack a change of clothing.

- Don't wear T-shirts or buttons with political or religious slogans or advertisements. Such attire is inappropriate and could offend coworkers.

- Don't show body art if you can help it. Only the most creative and casual workplaces will allow visible tattoos, piercings, or excessive jewelry.

- Don't forget about neatness. Even the nicest clothes look unattractive when they are stained or wrinkled. Make sure your clothes are nicely pressed, clean, and always stain-free.

If you are running errands and think you may have a chance to meet a contact, leave the house in "casual Friday" clothes—no flip-flops, jeans, or T-shirts without a collar or with writing or logos on them.

Study the Work Environment

Through careful observation of workplaces, you can learn about the working conditions for the type of job you want. Try to notice these things:

- What type of work area does my contact have? Does my contact work at a desk, share office space, or use some other type of workspace?

- What equipment and software does my contact use?

- Is the environment appropriate for the type of work?

- Is the environment quiet, noisy, slow-paced, or fast-paced?

- Does my contact interact with others? If so, with whom and how often?

- Is the atmosphere formal or informal? What type of dress is appropriate?

Be on the Lookout for Prospects

Be alert to the work atmosphere and listen for revealing comments from your contacts. Employees of desirable workplaces may mention freedom, trust, pride, teamwork, fair pay and benefits, opportunities for growth, recognition, and fairness in management. Ask about and watch for these characteristics during your meetings. Keep these qualities in mind as you select your actual job prospects.

Be Professional

Take your career information survey meetings seriously. By making a strong first impression, you may gain job leads from the meetings. Some people even obtain job offers. Maximize your information-gathering sessions by following these tips:

- Be professional. Be courteous and friendly and dress and act professionally.

- Respect the person's time. Be prompt and respect the time limits of the meeting. You should not take more than 20 or 30 minutes of your contact's time.

- Address the person by name when you meet and when you leave.

- Exchange business cards.

- Start by restating your reason for being there. Ask well-prepared, open-ended questions. Let your questions show that you did your homework.

- Move quickly through your questions and avoid wasting time. Take brief notes; do not try to write complete answers.

- Show that you are interested in the conversation. Listen carefully and ask follow-up questions—without interrupting, of course.

- Pay attention to body language and watch for cues that the person needs to end the meeting.

- Ask for the names of other people you can contact.

- Be alert for job leads and accept help enthusiastically. Do not make a direct bid for a job. (If you do, you risk offending your contact.)

- Apply the success strategies from Chapter 1. Conduct your career information survey meetings with energy, enthusiasm, and attention to detail.

Learn about Your Contact

Most of the people you meet will be glad to talk about their role in the organization, describe their career path, and discuss how they got into the organization. Be careful though: watch the person's body language and look for other cues that show how interested he or she is in the meeting and don't risk being rude by pressing for personal information.

After the Survey Meeting

Within one day of your meeting, write thank-you letters to the people who helped you. Let them know they were helpful and thank them for their time. It is a nice touch to mention something specific the person said and to indicate how helpful that information was. (See the example letter on page 74.)

Sample Career Information Survey Questions

To prepare for your survey meetings, write a list of questions to ask your contacts. Use these sample questions as a guide. Print your questions or write them in a professional-looking notebook. Leave space under each question to take notes during the meeting.

Questions about Job Scope and Career Development

- Is the firm privately owned, a government agency, or a nonprofit organization?
- What are the main goals of the organization? Is it a product or service oriented firm?
- What skills, education, experience, and knowledge are required to qualify for a position such as yours?
- What personal qualities or traits are important in your work?
- What are your specific duties?
- What do you like most/least about your job?
- What is the average starting salary range for a position such as yours?
- What employee benefits are offered in this position (health insurance, retirement savings programs, others)?
- What future changes do you anticipate in this field?
- What additional or ongoing education or training do you need to achieve your career goals?
- Does the employer offer on-the-job training for employees in your position? If so, what does it involve?
- Does the employer encourage continuing education for your position? If so, what kinds of programs are available and does the employer pay the associated fees?
- Would it be possible to get a written description of your job if one is available?
- What professional or other associations would you recommend joining to stay informed about this career field?
- What publications would you recommend (books, journals, etc.)?
- Could you suggest other people to help me with my research?
- What advice can you give me about planning my career and job search?

Questions about Application, Interview, and Hiring Procedures

- What are the general application procedures for positions such as the one I will be seeking?
- Do you have an employment application form I could see, or may I keep a copy of one to review as a reference?
- What are the organization's typical interview procedures (one person interviewing the applicant, team interviewing, multiple interviews, typical length of interviews, testing)?
- What do you think is important to show in a resume for a position such as the one I will be seeking?
- What advice can you give me about preparing and interviewing successfully?

Figure 4-1 Sample Career Information Survey Questions

Ask the person to keep you in mind if he or she can recommend any other people or resources that may help in your career research. Include your phone number and email address under your signature. With any luck, your note will lead to follow-up correspondence or phone calls.

If a contact offers to help you with a job lead, hand-deliver or mail a copy of your resume within a week. This person could become a key part of your job search network.

Finally, take the time to review your notes and to evaluate yourself. Consider what went well and what you can improve for your next meeting.

COMPLETE   **CAREER ACTION 4-5**

Career Information Survey Meeting, p. 80

Example Thank-You Letter

Dear [Mr./Ms. Contact],

Thank you for taking the time to talk with me today about my career objectives. I am grateful for your insights and plan to update my portfolio based on your recommendations. I especially appreciate your offer to connect me with your colleagues, and I have already followed up with _____.

I look forward to reviewing the online resources you suggested and would welcome any additional ideas and resources you may have. Thank you again for your help. I'll be sure to update you on my job search progress.

Best Regards,
[Your name and contact information]

WATCH OUT!

Don't Ask for a Job during a Career Survey Meeting

A career information survey meeting is an informational interview—not a job interview. The purpose of the interview is to gather information and to network. Keep in mind that people who agree to meet with you are making time in their busy workday to help with your career planning.

The employer will trust that you are there to gather information and that you are not going to push for a job. If you do, the employer may feel misled and not trust you or want to help you further if a job opening becomes available.

However, you should be prepared to discuss a job opening if the employer brings up the topic. Sometimes successful informational interviews do lead to job discussions (and even job offers), and you should be ready and willing to consider the options that sound good to you.

Chapter Checklist

Underline each action you are already taking and circle the actions you need to work on.

- Understand the benefits and goals of networking. [1]

- Develop a support system of people who will encourage and motivate me and who can help me with my resume and job search letters. [2]

- Develop a large network of people who can help in my job search by providing career advice, job leads, referrals, and other assistance. [2]

- Increase my networking potential by identifying as many networking prospects as possible and considering many different networking sources. [3]

- Get the most from my networking efforts by approaching as many people as possible, joining professional organizations, attending job fairs, and networking online. [3]

- Prepare for and conduct career information survey meetings with people in the career field I'm interested in. [4]

- After each survey meeting, summarize what I learned and evaluate my performance. Send each person a thank-you note. [4]

Critical-Thinking Questions

1. What is networking? [1]

2. Are neighbors and fellow club members as useful for networking as instructors and coworkers are? Explain your answer. [2]

3. What are five strategies for effective networking? [3]

4. Why is it so important to be polite and professional in online networking? [3]

5. How can you make sure your references will be prepared to answer prospective employer's questions about you? [3]

6. What benefits can you gain by conducting career information surveys? [4]

7. What is the most important information you would hope to obtain in a career information survey? [4]

8. What methods can you use to connect with hard-to-reach employers? [4]

Want access to career resources, study tools, activities, and job information links? Get started at www.cengage.com/career/yourcareer.

TRIAL RUN

Working with a partner, take turns acting as interviewer and interviewee in a career information survey meeting. (Remember, in an informational interview, you—the job seeker—are the *interviewer* asking the questions; your networking contact is the *interviewee* answering the questions.) If possible, pair up with a classmate who has similar job interests or experience. Establish a time limit and use the sample questions from this chapter as well as the additional survey questions you have written. Be sure to practice:

- Introducing yourself.

- Asking prepared questions in a professional and courteous manner.

- Demonstrating that you have done your research.

- Sticking to your time limit and closing the interview.

- Thanking the interviewee for her or his time.

To make this activity as realistic as possible, dress professionally and follow up with a written thank-you note. At the end of each interview, give your partner constructive feedback and suggestions using the evaluation form below.

Evaluate the interviewer on the following elements:

Rating Scale: 1 to 4 (1 = minimal; 2 = adequate; 3 = strong; 4 = outstanding)

Element	Rating (1–4)
Interviewer introduced himself or herself politely, stood, and shook hands	_____
Interviewer asked prepared questions in a professional and courteous manner	_____
Interviewer demonstrated knowledge of the career/job	_____
Interviewer ended the interview on time and closed the interview skillfully	_____
Interviewer thanked the interviewee for his or her time	_____

Interviewer's Strengths:

Suggestions for Improvement:

CAREER ACTION   4-1   **Personal Support System Network** ②

People who boost your morale and encourage you to reach your goals should be tops on your list. Review the three areas to consider when selecting support system members. Then list below the names of the members of your personal support system. These people will become part of your larger job search network. File this list in your Career Management Files Tracker.

CAREER ACTION   4-2   **Job Search Network List** ②

Duplicate this form or use Career Action Worksheet 4-2 on the product website. List the names of everyone you can think of for your job search network. Be sure to include the members of your personal support system that you listed in Career Action 4-1. Keep your network organizer in your Career Management Files Tracker.

Networking Organizer

Name _____ Title and Organization _____

Mailing Address _____

Telephone Number(s) _____ Email Address _____

How I know this person _____

Date I received permission to use this reference _____

Date of reference letter on file _____ Date of last personal contact _____

Name _____ Title and Organization _____

Mailing Address _____

Telephone Number(s) _____ Email Address _____

How I know this person _____

Date I received permission to use this reference _____

Date of reference letter on file _____ Date of last personal contact _____

Name _____ Title and Organization _____

Mailing Address _____

Telephone Number(s) _____ Email Address _____

How I know this person _____

Date I received permission to use this reference _____

Date of reference letter on file _____ Date of last personal contact _____

CAREER ACTION

4-3 Internet Research on Networking Tips and Etiquette ③

Search the Internet for tips on effective job search networking. Select at least two articles that interest you and write a summary of each. File your research in your Career Management Files Tracker.

Here are some sites to get you started. (Links are provided on the product website.)

- *Career Transitions*
- About.com (Job Searching) (http://jobsearch.about.com)
- CareerBuilder
- The Career Key
- Monster
- Quintessential Careers
- The Riley Guide

CAREER ACTION   4-4   Career Information Survey Questions [4]

Develop a Career Information Survey form with two sets of questions:

1. Career information questions you will ask your contact during a survey meeting (questions about the job, career development, and hiring procedures)

2. Work environment questions you will answer yourself through observation

Start with the sample questions on page 73 and add questions that are relevant to your field. Jot your questions below or use the worksheet on the product website. For your meeting (Career Action 4-5 on the next page), you will need a copy of the questions with enough space below each question for your notes.

Projecting a professional image is important in all outside assignments, so put the questions in a professional-looking binder to use during the survey meetings. Take notes during the meetings, but don't try to write complete answers.

Questions about Job Scope and Career Development Opportunities

Questions about Applications, Interviews, and Hiring Procedures

CAREER ACTION   4-5   Career Information Survey Meeting [4]

In this activity, you will conduct at least one career information survey meeting. Schedule as many of these meetings as possible; the benefits of getting current information and possible job leads in your career field are great. Consider contacting people in your field who screen, interview, and hire job applicants to discuss the job hiring processes in particular. Contacting them could put you closer to a job interview if you perform impressively during your information-gathering meeting. Remember: Do not ask for a job or an interview during these meetings.

1. **Contact at least two people in your target industry who are recognized for their ability and accomplishments.** Ask your schools' career services staff, instructors, family, and friends to suggest people to contact.

2. **Call and ask whether your contacts can meet with you to discuss career development questions.** Schedule a time, date, and place to meet.

3. **Be well-dressed and on time.** Such meetings can lead to referrals or job offers.

4. **Project professionalism.** Keep your neatly prepared survey questions (from Career Action 4-4) in a professional binder.

6. **Be prepared to present your findings** in class or write a summary report about the event.

Follow-up and Evaluation

After the meeting:

1. **Follow up with a thank-you note.** In addition to thanking the person who met with you, consider sending a note to the people who were most helpful to you in getting the meeting.

2. **Summarize your findings and store them in your Career Management Files Tracker.** After each meeting, use a separate sheet of paper to write the answers to the questions you prepared in Career Action 4-4.

3. **Take the time to evaluate the entire process,** from greeting the first contact to saying good-bye at the end of the actual meeting. Think about what went well and what you need to improve for your job interviews.

For Your Career Management Files Tracker

File your completed Career Action worksheets in your Career Management Files Tracker.

CA 4-1   Personal support system network list

CA 4-2   Job search network list and organizer

CA 4-3   Internet research findings about networking tips and etiquette

CA 4-4   Career information survey questions

CA 4-5   Summary and evaluation of career information survey meetings

Research Careers and Find Job Leads

Outcomes

1. Explain the benefits of researching career fields, employers, and specific jobs.

2. Research career fields and organizations.

3. Find job leads using the Internet and traditional resources.

OVERVIEW Chapter 5 is a springboard for you to take charge of your investigation into the world of work. You will learn why it is important to know about your prospective employers and trends in your field and how to find current information, from the Internet to more traditional research methods. This chapter also provides strategies for using your research to improve your career-related vocabulary.

© Photographer/Image Source

JUMP START
Your Research Skills

How much do you know about researching a topic that interests you? Think about research projects you completed for a school assignment. How did you begin?

You may have already chosen a prospective career—a decision you made after researching the field and completing self-assessment profiles. In this way, you used multiple routes to gain the knowledge you needed. Your career research and search for job leads will be similar because you use many sources of information—the Internet, people, and organizations.

Pick a topic that interests you—graffiti, airplanes, the Rock and Roll Hall of Fame—and find as many sources of information as you can. Go online, visit the library, ask your friends, read a book, and see for yourself how many options you have to be informed.

Outcome 1 Get an Edge through Research

To find a job, the more you know and the better you are at finding information, the more likely you are to succeed. Researching your career field and prospective employers can affect the success of your job search in many ways, as follows:

- **Competitive edge.** Employers view job applicants who don't have solid knowledge of their businesses or industry as weak choices. If you are prepared to discuss products and industry facts, you will show that you have made a sincere effort to learn about the organization and the marketplace. Many applicants don't invest their time and energy in researching employers. If you do, you will have the competitive edge.

- **Better career decisions.** Having current knowledge about employers, industries, and job targets allows you to make informed career decisions and to assess your interest in and qualifications for specific jobs.

- **Improved ability to market your skills and get hired.** Researching employers improves your ability to discuss specifically how your

qualifications match the employers' goals and needs. Employers are most willing to invest training resources in applicants who demonstrate initiative and commitment through their research of the employer and the industry.

- **Compensation for lack of experience.** Industry knowledge helps you compensate for lack of actual or extensive job experience.

- **Increased confidence.** Being well informed helps you feel more confident, communicate more clearly, and project greater competence.

Learn What You Should Know

Strengthen your employability by improving your knowledge in these areas:

1. **Information about the career field.** Learn about current and predicted trends, general educational requirements, job descriptions, growth outlook, and salary ranges in the industry.

2. **Information about prospective employers.** Learn as much as possible about the companies you hope to work for. Learn about each company's products and services, markets and customers, reputation, performance, key

competitors, history and goals, corporate culture, divisions and subsidiaries, locations (U.S. and global), trends and growth indicators, number of employees and diversity, predicted job openings, and salary ranges and benefit plans.

3. **Information about specific jobs.** Get job descriptions; identify the required education and experience; and learn about working conditions, career paths, salary ranges, and benefit plans.

The information you collect through research will help you stand out when you apply for jobs and go on interviews. You will also turn up job leads in your field.

Learn about Industry Trends

Chapter 2 presents government data about growth occupations and careers in the United States. The number of expected job openings in each career field is an example of an *industry trend*. There are many industry trends, such as:

- Changes in products or services (for example, the voluntary switch from the original CD and DVD format to Blu-ray format)

- Changes in technology (for example, the business community's quick adoption of tablet computers)

- Changes in the business model (for example, the increase in white-collar jobs outsourced to developing countries)

- Financial statistics (for example, overall industry growth and salary data)

- Changes in competition (for example, new competitors, better-than-expected competitor successes, mergers, and bankruptcies)

Every career field also is affected by wider changes, such as:

- Economic changes (for example, the economic collapse that began in late 2008)

- Social changes (for example, baby boomers postponing retirement because of loss of savings and financial uncertainty)

- Increased workforce diversity. Did you know that by 2042, the United States will not have a majority race? The percentage of white Americans will drop to 46%, down from 65% in 2008. Already, nearly one in six residents is Hispanic and nearly 47% of children aged 5 and under are from minority families.

Take the time to learn about current trends in your career field. Search on your career field and the word *trends* (for example, *catering trends*). When you research specific companies, look for information about their response to these trends.

Expand Your Career-Related Vocabulary

What do *vacuum extraction*, *remediation system*, and *capture zone* mean? (Hint: If you know the answers, you might be an RET.) Every industry has its own vocabulary. Recognizing and understanding this vocabulary will help you understand your career research, write a resume and cover letter that stand out, and be informed during interviews.

Look up every unfamiliar word, acronym, and term you come across in your research. Employment directories, the Internet, and library resources have the information you need. In a search engine, enter "define *word*" (for example, *define blog*).

A strong career-related vocabulary projects competence, but don't overdo it. You don't want to sound like a know-it-all or a phony when you talk with people who already work in the career fields you are interested in.

> COMPLETE **CAREER ACTION 5-1**
>
> Build Your Career Vocabulary, p. 95

Use Many Sources of Information

The exciting reality of the research process is that there are many ways to approach it, and once you get started, you'll find many people and types of online resources to help you along the way. From your campus career center to

MAKE IT A HABIT

Remember Who You Are

At many websites, you must register as a user to have access to all of the resources available. Registration is usually free. When you visit the site, you sign in with your user name and password.

To keep things simple, consider using the same user name and password at all of the free information sites you use. Keep a record of your user names and passwords in your Career Management Files Tracker.

Mario7/Shutterstock.com

the Internet to trade journals, these resources are rich sources of information that can help you make smart decisions about career paths and jobs that match your values, interests, and qualifications.

The Indispensable Internet

The Internet affects every aspect of the job search process. It is filled with career advice, information about specific industries and employers, and job leads. Every "traditional" source of career information covered in this chapter also has an Internet presence, from the local chamber of commerce to the international professional association for your career field.

The social networking sites and job clubs in Chapter 4 are two tools for connecting with other job seekers and people in your field. You can also search on the name of your career field and the term *blog* or *discussion forum* (*oceanography discussion forum*, for example).

At all search engines and most large information sites, you can sign up for news alerts about the issues you are interested in. After registering at a site and selecting the topics you want to follow, you receive emails with links to newly posted articles on these topics. You can also get job alerts through email and text messaging.

Don't become overwhelmed by the vast amount of information on the Internet. Use the resources in this chapter and the links at the product website (www.cengage.com/career/yourcareer) to find reliable sites. Take good notes and bookmark the sites you think are best.

People in the Workplace

Regardless of how up-to-date and informative a company website is, current and former employees are the best resources for getting a feel for what it would be like to work there. To get the most complete picture, talk with people who have different types of information about the organization:

- **Employees of your target employer.** Current and former employees know about hiring procedures; employee satisfaction levels; job descriptions and responsibilities; skills, education, and experience required for jobs; company objectives; salaries; and advancement opportunities. Don't rely only on opinion, however, particularly when it's extremely negative or overly positive.

- **Your target employer.** When possible, visit your target employer to get a personal perspective. Be sure to dress appropriately. Ask for literature about the organization, such as a brochure, mission statement, or stockholder's report. If realistic and affordable, try the company's products or services.

- **Customers, clients, or patients.** Ask customers, clients, or patients for their opinions of the employer's service, reliability, products, and general reputation.

- **Competitors.** Research the competitors of your target employer to learn about the industry. Compare job openings, pay rates, and benefits as well as the education, skills, and experience required.

- **Instructors, professors, and counselors.** These people often know about local employers and industries. Because they may serve as job references for you, be professional, punctual, and reliable when dealing with them.

- **Recognized people in the field.** Successful people in your field are excellent resources for learning about the industry and prospective employers. See "Career Information Survey" in Chapter 4.

 ## Research Career Fields and Companies

You will not succeed in finding a job unless you are informed about the industry you want to work in and the companies you want to work for. Being smart about the career you are pursuing gives you credibility and helps you emphasize your related strengths and suitability for a job. "Insider information" is essential if you don't have real-world experience in the field.

Libraries

Your local library—public, college, and university—has extensive resources for job seekers. Reference librarians and staff can help you locate items such as those listed on the next page.

Tame the Internet Tiger

Angela Waye/Shutterstock.com

The Internet can be overwhelming. Take the time and effort needed to develop good research habits.

- If your search skills aren't the best, take a tutorial on Internet research. You can choose from dozens of free guides and lessons.

- Know what you are looking for. Learn how to use keywords effectively so that you don't get too many or too few "hits."

- Schedule research appointments in your calendar and set goals for each session. On Tuesdays and Fridays, for example, check for new job postings at the large job information sites. On Mondays and Thursdays, visit reference sites and other resources related to your field. Once a week, go to the websites of your target employers to check for new job postings.

- Bookmark the sites you think are best and keep a record of your user names and passwords.

- If it suits your learning style, keep a word processing file open while you work. Copy website content into it. Be sure to copy the addresses too.

- Follow the rules. The information on these sites may be free, but it is still copyrighted (that is, someone owns the rights to publish it). Assume that all of the sites you visit, except U.S. government sites, contain copyrighted information and respect the copyrights.

- Know when to stop searching and to start *using* the great information you find. ☺

- Company pamphlets, brochures, and annual reports
- Dun & Bradstreet's Million Dollar Database
- *Encyclopedia of Careers and Vocational Guidance*
- Thomas Register of American Manufacturers
- Standard and Poor's publications, such as Industry Surveys, Stock Reports, and Register of Corporations
- Value Line Investment Survey
- Moody's Manuals
- Business Periodicals Index
- Readers' Guide to Periodical Literature
- *Occupational Outlook Handbook*, published by the U.S. Department of Labor, Bureau of Labor Statistics
- Area telephone directories
- Encyclopedia of Associations
- Newspaper and journal articles
- *The Wall Street Journal* and business magazines such as *Fortune* and *Businessweek*

Ask librarians to help you locate international business information if you want to work outside the United States or if your target employer has international holdings or is based in another country. The main branch of a public library will have more extensive holdings than will neighborhood branches.

College Career Centers

These valuable organizations go by different names at different colleges and universities, such as Career Services and the Career Resources Center. Whatever its name at your institution, the center is a gold mine of career information with comprehensive resources for learning about industries, companies, specific jobs, local employers, and more.

The center may have many of the preceding library resources in addition to other resources directed to students, such as *Job Choices*, an excellent magazine published by the National Association of Colleges and Employers.

Find Job Leads with Twitter

Unlike many other social networking sites, Twitter users commonly chat and connect with complete strangers. This is great news for job seekers who are willing to be outgoing to meet others in their industry. A simple search can yield hundreds of people and businesses that hold the same interests and are willing to talk with you.

- Create a free Twitter profile, if you haven't already, and complete your profile indicating interest in your industry and career fields.
- Search for people and businesses that are interested and active in your field and "follow" them.
- Read tweets sent out by select companies to learn what's new with them and whether they're hiring. More and more companies tweet out current job openings.
- Follow experts who are active in your industry, read the articles and information they are tweeting, and ask them for advice.
- Send out tweets about your job-seeking interests.

Twitter users share information and links in real time, so you can often find the most up-to-date information on the Web. Search engines have to play catch-up because they need more time to find and index articles.

The staff can help with every area of a search: taking personal assessments and exploring suitable careers, writing resumes and cover letters, preparing for interviews, and possibly networking with alumni in your field.

If you have already graduated, find out what services are available to alumni. Some career centers also allow members of the community to use certain resources.

Job Information Sites

Also called career development sites, these comprehensive "one-stop-shopping" websites have job banks (lists of job openings) and information on every topic related to careers and job searches. They also provide interactive tools such as appointment calendars, follow-up reminders, updates about industry trends, and networking contact lists.

Company Websites

The vast majority of employers have websites where you can read about the organization and learn what jobs are available and how to apply for them.

Check the sites of several organizations in your career field to get a sense of the types of jobs and job titles and to view complete job descriptions and requirements. Try searching on each job title and the word *jobs* to find more job listings.

If your job search is more general, such as a plan to be an administrative assistant, and a prospective employer's industry is less important to you, use the general job information sites that list openings from a broad range of industries.

Professional Associations and Industry Trade Groups

In Chapter 4, you learned about networking through professional associations and industry trade groups. The websites of these groups are reliable sources of up-to-date information on every topic of interest in an industry. They publish online magazines and newsletters that

you can read at the site or that you receive in emails.

Most groups require membership to be able to access all of the resources, and many groups have reduced membership rates for students. To find an association, search on the name of the industry and the word *association* (for example, *occupational therapist association*). Many job information sites also have lists of associations and trade groups.

> **COMPLETE** **CAREER ACTION 5-2**
>
> Explore Company Websites, p. 95

Job/Career Fairs

Job fairs (also called career fairs) are a structured way to meet many prospective employers in one day. Use fairs to get company literature, talk to company recruiters, pick up industry vocabulary, and perhaps even schedule an interview. Get a list of companies before the event and research the ones that look promising.

Outcome 3 Find Job Leads

All of the resources you have learned about to this point are also sources of job leads.

- **Company websites** list available jobs and have instructions for submitting applications and resumes.

- **Job information sites.** These sites started out to connect employers and job applicants, and extensive job banks are still central to their mission. You can post your resume, search for jobs, and apply online.

- **College career centers.** Most college career centers host on-campus recruiting events. Recruiters from a range of companies come to campus to interview—and maybe hire—new graduates. The center may offer mock interviews before the real thing. Some centers digitally record the interviews, review them with you, and offer suggestions.

- **Professional associations and industry trade groups.** Most of these organizations maintain job banks, and they often announce job openings during meetings and in their publications. The membership directories are great resources for finding prospective employers. Check current and back issues of printed resources or Internet archives for help wanted ads and look for information about employment and job market trends. Companies are impressed with applicants who know about their industry associations and publications.

- **Job fairs.** Employers go to community, industry, and school-sponsored career or job fairs to find new talent, so you should go as well. You have to be there to be discovered.

> **COMPLETE** **CAREER ACTION 5-3**
>
> Search the Internet for Job Listings and Information, p. 95

Other Sources of Job Leads

The more resources you use, the more job choices you will have and the more quickly you will get results. Don't overlook these sources.

Want Ads

You can find want ads for jobs (also called help wanted ads) in print newspapers and other print media and on the Internet.

- **Newspapers.** Look in the help wanted section, the business section, and virtually all other sections of newspapers from locations that interest you. You can learn a great deal about the hiring, expansion, downsizing, or start-up of organizations in an area. Most newspapers also post their want ads on the Internet.

- **The Internet.** Check job listings and want ads on the Internet. Search the large job information sites and smaller niche sites that focus only on your career field or specialty.

- **Journals and other publications.** Check the classified sections of printed and online professional journals in your field and other publications that target job seekers.

Human Resources Departments in Private Companies

Contact the human resources department of private companies to learn about current job openings. If no openings are available, ask if you can leave your application and resume for future openings; then check back in a few months to ensure that your application is still active. Some organizations have telephone recordings about current job openings.

State Employment Services

Through the U.S. Department of Labor, each state has an employment agency that includes a job services or employment services office. These offices provide career counseling, job search techniques, referrals to opportunities to upgrade one's training or education, and information on area job openings.

Chambers of Commerce

Chambers of commerce have complete, current lists of local employers and often have names and telephone numbers of company executives. They also have information on new organizations coming to the area.

> **Statistics show that** job seekers who use many resources for findng job leads find jobs faster than people who use one or two resources. **"**

Local and Small Firms

According to the U.S. Small Business Administration, small businesses represent 99.7 percent of all employers and employ just over half of the private workforce. These data are clear reasons to research small businesses as sources of employment. Information on openings with small businesses is available through chambers of commerce, employer directories, the want ads, and your library or campus career center.

Government Agencies

Most city, county, state, and federal agencies have a civil service system that requires application and pre-employment testing through a central human resources department. Federal jobs are listed at a central website, USAJOBS. Every state has its own employment agency and job site. To limit your search to government jobs in a specific city or county, search on *city of [city state] job openings* or *county of [county state] job openings* (*city of wichita ks job openings* or *county of sedgwick ks job openings,* for example).

Educational Institutions

To find job openings for teachers, search on "teaching jobs [city state]." Many boards of education post openings on their websites and on the major job boards. To strengthen your qualifications, consider taking a contingency job as a substitute teacher or teacher's assistant. Search on "substitute teaching certificate" to get advice and to learn about state requirements. This can be a good way to prove your abilities, earn income, and possibly work your way into a regular teaching position.

Private Employment Agencies

Private contactors and employment or staffing agencies can be useful resources for finding prospective employers, particularly an agency that specializes in your field. The operations of these organizations vary. Some focus on connecting applicants with part-time jobs, while others focus on full-time jobs. Some employment firms connect employers and job seekers to facilitate a full-time hire by the employer.

Follow Current Events

During a job search—and throughout your career—it will be a challenge to stay on top of all of the news and information in your field on a regular basis.

Integrating personal education habits into your daily routine is key to maintaining an edge. Follow stories that affect the economy, your city, and your career field.

- Download a news app for your smartphone or put a news widget on your desktop.
- Listen to news programs such as NPR's *Morning Edition* during your morning routine or while you're commuting.
- Watch the nightly news and read newspapers to "make yourself smart" on national and international topics.
- When you read online articles, look at the reader comments to see what others think about the topic.

You'll find that having this knowledge and being able to discuss current events when talking to coworkers and when networking will benefit you in ways you would not have anticipated.

fotosipak/iStockphoto.com

Other employment firms serve as a permanent link between employer and employee, and the employment firm handles all human resource functions. This relieves the employer of activities such as hiring, compensation, and career development.

Some firms focus on hiring applicants to perform contract work on a temporary or project basis. Being a temp is one of the most accessible means of reentering the job market and is a stepping stone from unemployment to employment. This arrangement has two major benefits:

- It gives the employer and the employee an opportunity to check for a good fit without either party having to make a permanent commitment up front.

- The employment firm takes care of the administrative details. Many people find full-time jobs through this source by gaining experience in the temporary jobs.

You can find employment agencies in the Yellow Pages of the telephone directory and by searching the Internet for employment agencies, employment contractors, employment staffing agencies, or temporary help agencies.

A specific job may not fit your career target perfectly, but it can provide some outstanding benefits, including these:

- Entry or reentry into the job market
- Experience you may lack
- References for work done well
- Additions to your list of solid job leads
- A possible full-time job

WATCH OUT!

Do Your Research before Signing Up with a Private Employment Agency

- **Does the firm have a good reputation?** Ask the staff at your school's career services center, employers who hire the agencies to obtain employees, other job seekers, and the Better Business Bureau. Don't rely on one person's word. Also visit the agency you are considering.

- **How long has the firm been in business?** Does it have long-term relationships with employers?

- **Does the agency have expertise in placing people in your field?** What employment firms are associated with the ads for the jobs you are targeting?

- If you would accept employment outside your local area, **does the employment firm belong to a nationwide or regional system?** Is it familiar with job opportunities, hiring trends, and salaries throughout the areas you would consider?

- **What services will the employment firm provide?** Get a written agreement that spells out every service you will receive, including how long counseling will take and how long you are entitled to the agency's services.

- **Who pays the fees for securing a permanent job?** Policies vary regarding whether the applicant or the employer pays the fees for a permanent job. Always try to negotiate in your favor.

- **Do you understand the contract?** Read every word of it and make certain you are willing to accept all of the conditions. Ask the agency to clarify how it handles client dissatisfaction with job placement. Firms that guarantee a full refund are usually the most reputable.

EduLeite/iStockphoto.com

- On-the-job training and practical hands-on skill development
- Immediate income

CAREER ACTION 5-4

Job Leads Source List, p. 96

"Try Before You Buy"

Consider "practicing" in your career field to gain experience working side by side with people you can learn from. Cooperative education, internships, and volunteer positions are excellent opportunities for networking and may even lead to full-time employment.

Job seekers with experience have an advantage in the hiring process because of their familiarity with the field and because they have references who can verify their qualifications. Employers see these applicants as being able to contribute faster and needing less on-the-job training.

Cooperative Education

Cooperative education programs place you in a paying job in your field while you are still studying. Students alternate between school and work. Some co-op programs place students with the same employer more than once so that the students can gain new experiences and take on more responsibility after completing more advanced classes.

Internships

An internship is a period of supervised training in a workplace. Most internships are scheduled during breaks in the academic calendar. Some internships are unpaid, and some provide a living stipend.

Volunteer Work

Volunteering is perhaps easiest in nonprofit organizations that have limited resources to keep up with their goals and deadlines.

By volunteering and showing your commitment and ability to learn on the job, you will gain valuable information about the work and could be first in line for the next available opening. To get the most from any of these positions:

- **Demonstrate initiative.** Use your position to demonstrate initiative and achieve personal and professional development goals.
- **Be flexible and enthusiastic.** Offer to take on any tasks that need to be done. If you find yourself with some free time, ask for another assignment.
- **Act like you want to be taken seriously.** Dress professionally, be punctual, don't leave early, don't use office supplies or technology (including telephones and computers) for personal business, and don't date or flirt with coworkers.

Should You Try Self-Employment?

Don't overlook someone who might be your dream employer: you. Read these high-level tips to see if self-employment might be for you.

Learn under Another Employer First

To succeed in your own business, you must have adequate education, training, and knowledge. In addition, you can significantly improve your chances of successful self-employment by working for someone who has succeeded in the field. Learn the plusses and minuses of a business as an employee, not as a new business owner. Gaining experience and achieving solid accomplishments in the field provide the credibility you need to land work contracts on your own. Self-employment is worth considering if you have related work experience and can get endorsements from people who are satisfied with your performance.

Research to Succeed

If you are seriously interested in self-employment, plan every aspect of your business venture carefully.

MAKE IT A HABIT

Be Willing to Listen to Advice

It takes a large ego to start a company and go into business for yourself. Believing that you can succeed—and being willing to work very hard to make this happen—is a necessary personal quality for going out on your own.

It takes a *smart* ego to recognize that you can't know everything about building a successful company. According to a study by the Small Business Administration, one-third of small businesses fail within the first two years and fewer than half are still in business after four years.

No matter how much experience you have, be open to listening to advice from experts and friends. Don't insist on doing everything your own way.

ARENA Creative/Shutterstock.com

- Interview people in your field who are successfully self-employed to learn how they did it.

- Think through every aspect of your plans for your own business. You may not need to develop a formal written business plan if you are not looking for investors, but at least put your high-level plans on paper. *Do not skip this activity or skimp on the effort you put into it.* If planning sounds boring or sounds like too much work, you are probably better off working for someone else.

- Research the start-up costs and other expenses you can expect. Create a spreadsheet with realistic financial projections so that you know how much you need to earn and what your expenses will be. Keep in mind that you will need to earn enough money to pay for your health insurance and other benefits that an employer may have provided.

- Read about self-employment from published and Internet sources. The product website has links to resources for new entrepreneurs.

Networking Is Essential

To succeed in your business, you must network regularly with people in your field, potential clients, and customers. Market yourself by being active in professional or trade associations and clubs related to your career field.

Start Small and Build

A smart way to begin self-employment is to work for yourself part-time to develop a client base and essential references. Volunteer with groups to prove your skills. Start small, keep expenses at an absolute minimum, and expand only when the demand for your product or service requires it.

Chapter Checklist

Underline each action you are already taking and circle the actions you need to work on.

- Develop and regularly expand my career-related vocabulary to demonstrate competence and knowledge. [1]

- Know how to use many sources of career and job information, including libraries, college career centers, websites, professional associations, and job fairs. [2]

- Know where to look for job leads: the sources above in addition to want ads, human resources departments, state employment services, chambers of commerce, local and small companies, government agencies, educational institutions, and private employment agencies. [3]

- Know how to get experience in the career fields I'm interested in through cooperative education, internships, and volunteer work. [3]

- Know when to consider working for myself and know some success strategies for getting started the right way. [3]

Critical-Thinking Questions

1. What are the advantages of researching career fields that interest you? [1]

2. Describe two websites you have visited that provide useful information about your field. Give three examples of the types of information you found at each site. [2]

3. How can internships, temporary jobs, and volunteer work help the job seeker? [3]

4. Which information sources do you think will be most useful to you in your job search? Explain your answer. [3]

Want access to career resources, study tools, activities, and job information links? Get started at www.cengage.com/career/yourcareer.

TRIAL RUN

A key element in your research success is your ability to stay organized. Make a weekly research appointment calendar that includes your research topic, goals, and sources. If your goal the first week is to uncover the greatest amount of information on your career field, outline how you will do this and where you plan to go for the information. If you want to learn how to research, spend the first week mastering search engines, taking tutorials, and reading about careers and job searching.

Complete this planner to organize your research schedule.

Week	Topic	Source 1	Source 2	Time
Goal 1: Research the skills needed, projected openings, changes in policy	Medical insurance claim industry	Internet	Library for *Occupational Outlook Handbook*	Monday 6 hours
2				
3				
4				
5				
6				
7				

CAREER ACTION   5-1   **Build Your Career Vocabulary** [1]

Follow these steps to create a vocabulary list. Use these terms to make your resumes, cover letters, interviews, and follow-up communications stand out.

1. **Obtain two general job descriptions for the type of job you are seeking.** Get these directly from employers or from job postings on the Internet. You can also find more general job descriptions for your job target in *Career Transitions* or the *Occupational Outlook Handbook.*

2. **Obtain at least two job postings for positions that are similar to your job target.**

3. **Carefully read through the job target material.** Underline all action verbs (for example, *compile, analyze, operate,* and *supervise*) and all keywords and nouns used to describe required or related skills, education, and experience, including the specific names of software and computer-related knowledge. Underline vocabulary, abbreviations, special terminology, and buzzwords that are used in the career field.

4. **Make a list of these terms, spelling each word correctly, and include their definitions.** If you don't know the definition of a term, find it. Categorize the terms as follows: (a) action verb, (b) keyword noun, (c) specialized terminology, (d) abbreviation, and (e) industry buzzword.

5. **File this vocabulary list in your Career Management Files Tracker.**

CAREER ACTION   5-2   **Explore Company Websites** [2]

Use printed, people, and *Career Transitions* resources to research at least two companies that interest you. Learn about the company's products or services, objectives, locations, salaries, and trends and research any further details that interest you. Prepare a written summary of your findings.

CAREER ACTION   5-3   **Search the Internet for Job Listings and Information** [3]

Visit at least four of the sites listed on the next page. File your report in your Career Management Files Tracker.

1. Describe the sites that have the most relevant information to your job target and field.

2. Summarize or print job listings for your field and indicate the sources of the listings.

3. Summarize job trends and other useful information.

You should also visit at least one specialty site in your field. Links to the sites on the next page are found on the product website.

- America's Job Bank
- The Black Collegian Online
- CareerBuilder.com
- EmploymentGuide.com
- Indeed.com

- JobCentral.com
- Monster
- NationJob Network
- Net-Temps
- Saludos.com

CAREER ACTION   5-4   Job Leads Source List ③

Review each source of job information and leads in the chapter, including the websites you used in Career Action 5-2. List the sources you think would be effective in your job search. Make additional copies of this worksheet or use the worksheet on the product website.

Name of Source _____

Address of Source _____

Internet Address (URL) _____

Telephone Number(s) _____

Email Address _____ Twitter Account _____

Facebook Account _____ LinkedIn URL _____

Action Plan for Using This Source:

Name of Source _____

Address of Source _____

Internet Address (URL) _____

Telephone Number(s) _____

Email Address _____ Twitter Account _____

Facebook Account _____ LinkedIn URL _____

Action Plan for Using This Source:

Name of Source _____

Address of Source _____

Internet Address (URL) _____

Telephone Number(s) _____

Email Address _____   Twitter Account _____

Facebook Account _____   LinkedIn URL _____

Action Plan for Using This Source:

Name of Source _____

Address of Source _____

Internet Address (URL) _____

Telephone Number(s) _____

Email Address _____   Twitter Account _____

Facebook Account _____   LinkedIn URL _____

Action Plan for Using This Source:

Name of Source _____

Address of Source _____

Internet Address (URL) _____

Telephone Number(s) _____

Email Address _____   Twitter Account _____

Facebook Account _____   LinkedIn URL _____

Action Plan for Using This Source:

For Your Career Management Files Tracker

File your completed Career Action worksheets in your Career Management Files Tracker.

CA 5-1   Career vocabulary list

CA 5-2   Information from company websites

CA 5-3   Internet research about job listings and career information

CA 5-4   List of job leads

3

Essential Job Search Communications

PART 3 shows you how to create resumes and cover letters that will convince employers to give you a job interview.

© Jim Calloway Photography

ADVICE FROM THE EXPERT

Regina Russo
Director of Marketing and Communications Cincinnati Art Museum

The Cincinnati Art Museum, where Regina Russo is Director of Marketing and Communications, advertises job openings through CareerBuilder and arts organizations job banks and in the local newspaper. After HR looks through the 200 or so applications for each position to select the candidates with the best credentials and potential, Regina typically looks more closely at the top 40 or 50 candidates.

While job seekers are routinely told that a reader will skim a resume for about 30 seconds, Regina spends several minutes reading a cover letter and resume. She is impressed by "a cover letter that is written in an authentic voice. I want to feel like the person is in the room talking to me."

A good cover letter can "absolutely make up for a so-so resume. A good cover letter tells a compelling story about who the person is, and it tells me that they can write and that they are passionate about what they do."

For every position she fills, Regina is keenly aware of the importance of excellent communication skills. A "good" resume, she believes, is "organized and it has a 'voice'—I can get a sense of who the person is and not just what he or she does."

If a resume has a LinkedIn URL, Regina looks at the profile when assessing an applicant's fit. She believes that "We are in a new age. Most of us have an online life through social media, and we need to make sure our employees have good judgment. We don't hire positions—we hire people."

Regina advises job applicants to make the most of the brief time they have to get an employer's attention.

© Cengage Learning

Robin McCraw
Web-Based Training Developer

About a year ago, Robin McCraw's manager invited her to a meeting to discuss their department's new organizational plan. Fifteen minutes later Robin learned that she was among 8,000 "displaced" employees.

Robin's took two weeks to "catch up on all the sleep" she'd missed by working 50 hours a week in her dream job as Senior Global E-Learning Manager for a Fortune 25 company. "Writing my resume reminded me how accomplished I was, and I was ready to go. I set productivity goals and made myself keep them," says Robin. "I had decided to move, so I looked for jobs online. In the beginning, I spent about six hours a day, five days a week online. I posted my resume on more than a dozen job sites and signed up for search alerts to find jobs that matched my qualifications. I knew employers wanted strong evidence of my technical skills and creativity, so I created a knockout eight-page resume and an online portfolio."

Robin learned that "a job search has a lot of moving parts. Job sites are an easy way to find leads and apply for jobs, but each application takes a long time. I have different versions of my resume and customize the cover letter for every job. I have a folder for each job: resume, letter, application, emails, and my notes before and after phone interviews."

Her search has taken more time than Robin expected. "For some reason, the longer it's gone on, the less panicked I am. I'm more selective about the openings I apply for. I want a job I love with people who are thrilled to work with me."

After months of what she calls "the big silence," Robin has five weeks to pack up her house and move across the country. "I knew the right job was out there," she says.

→ Ready, Set, **PLAN**

Read the outcomes on the first page of Chapters 6 and 7 and mark the ones that are most important to you. What do you want to accomplish by reading these chapters and doing the assignments?

How much time is in the syllabus for Chapters 6 and 7?

List the dates for reading assignments and the dates for turning in homework and projects for this class.

What are your other major commitments in the coming weeks (for other classes, work, home)? For each task, include the estimated time and when you will do it.

If you are doing any group projects, list information that will help the project go smoothly: project goal and due date, each person's assignments and phone number, dates for completing each part of the project, meeting dates, and anything else.

Resumes

Outcomes

1. Identify the purpose and role of a resume.
2. Describe the main sections of a winning resume.
3. Write clear and concise resume content.
4. Select the best organization for your resume.
5. Create an effective print resume and plain text resume.
6. Customize your resume to target specific jobs and employers.
7. Use the Internet to research resume tips and trends.

OVERVIEW Chapter 6 shows you how to write and deliver resumes that get you interviews. A good resume is your key to getting an interview. Most employers consider candidates based on a quick visual screening or computerized search of the many resumes they receive. Employers then look for a match between their needs and the applicants' qualifications and select a few people to interview. Your resume must be organized, written, and formatted so that it passes both an initial screening and a more detailed analysis. This chapter explains how to create resumes that will pass these tests. Through the activities in this chapter you will prepare and evaluate a resume draft, revise it, and format your print and plain text resumes.

CHAPTER 6

CAREER ACTIONS

6-1: Objective Statement and Profile

6-2: Resume Outline

6-3: Resume Action Verbs and Keywords

6-4: Resume Draft

6-5: Final Print Resume

6-6: Plain Text Resume

JUMP START Your Resume

Self-reflection, research, and planning are necessary to prepare a resume that achieves its purpose: to get interviews. Before you start writing and assembling your resume, review or complete these key activities in Chapters 2, 3, and 5:

- Identify your most important qualifications. Look at Chapter 2 and complete Career Action 2-2, Workplace Skills and Competencies Profile, and Career Action 2-3, Career Competencies Inventory.
- Document your qualifications. Look at Chapter 3 and complete Career Action 3-1, Education, Training, and Activities Inventory, and Career Action 3-2, Experience and Skills Inventory.
- Set a career target. Complete Career Action 3-6, Career Targets, and Career Action 3-7, Job Qualifications Profile.
- Read about the career field you are interested in. Look at Chapter 5 and complete Career Action 5-1, Build Your Career Vocabulary; Career Action 5-3, Search the Internet for Job Listings and Information; and Career Action 5-4, Job Leads Source List.

akva/Shutterstock.com

Outcome 1 — What Is a Resume?

A **resume** is a brief document, typically one or two pages, that details your qualifications for a particular job or job target. It is a record of your relevant work experience and education, and it is a tool for marketing yourself to prospective employers and getting job interviews. Your resume is an evolving document that you must revise and rewrite as your experience and career goals change over time.

A winning resume gets you a job interview. Your resume needs to compel the reader to want to learn more about you and contact you for an interview.

Consider the following steps that a typical large employer uses to process resumes and determine which candidates to interview:

1. The organization receives resumes in response to a job listing—via email, a website, or mail. Resume scanning software scans the resumes and stores the contents in a database for analysis, distribution, and retrieval. The software searches each resume for words and phrases that indicate a match with the job requirements and flags the resumes that appear to be a good fit.

2. Human resources staff members review the resumes selected by the software. Resumes of the most qualified candidates are forwarded to departmental hiring managers for interview consideration. The other resumes are stored for future consideration or discarded.

3. The hiring managers review the resumes and choose candidates to interview based on the candidates' qualifications and whether they appear to be a good fit with the department's needs.

From these steps, you can conclude that a winning resume achieves multiple objectives. A winning resume:

- Quickly shows that the candidate has the qualifications for the job and can meet the employer's needs.

❝The top third of page 1 is the most valuable real estate in your resume. Put your most impressive and important information here.❞

- Is accessible to resume scanning software and human reviewers.
- Offers a professional image and an example of good written communication skills.
- Previews the type of employee the candidate will be (professional, results-oriented, attentive to details, etc.).
- Convinces prospective employers that the candidate deserves an interview.

If you haven't done so, review the self-assessment and research activities in the Jump-Start feature on page 101. Have access to your completed Career Action worksheets listed in the Jump-Start feature.

Plan Your Resume Content

Outcome 2

Writing a great resume that gets you an interview typically does not happen on the first try. You begin by planning and developing a master resume that you can customize for different job listings. (Your **master resume** is the generic version of the resume you use for networking and distribute at job fairs.)

The rest of this chapter walks you through all of the stages of preparing, writing, formatting, and submitting a winning resume:

1. Identify the most appropriate resume sections (beginning on this page).
2. Write and edit each section to showcase your marketable assets (pages 107–110).
3. Choose the most appropriate resume organization: chronological, skills-based, or combination (pages 110–111).
4. Format your resume for different distribution channels: print, electronic, and/or Web (pages 111–116).
5. Customize your master resume for specific job listings (pages 116–117).

Your goal is to use organization, writing, and formatting to create a professional-looking document that can be skimmed quickly for key information and read critically to reveal impressive details.

Don't rush the process. If you skip any of the steps or try to rush through them, you will diminish your chance of achieving the purpose of your resume: getting the interview and, ultimately, the job.

In most situations, your resume is part of an application "package" that includes a cover letter and maybe even a business card. Chapter 7, Job Applications and Cover Letters, has instructions for submitting your resume and cover letter in print and electronic form.

Your Resume Sections

Resumes use headings to organize the content into major sections that are easy to skim for the key facts. Review these guidelines to get a sense of how to focus the content of your resume and include the sections that are most appropriate for your experience in the order that best fits your target employer's needs and best highlights your experience. Place the most important and impressive sections near the top of the resume.

Look at the sample resumes in this chapter to see a variety of ways to present the sections of a resume. The following sections will fulfill the resume needs of most job seekers. Modify the section headings to best fit your experience and qualifications.

Contact Information

At the top of your resume, list your name, mailing address, telephone number, email address, and LinkedIn URL. Follow these tips:

- Your contact information is your resume's letterhead. Format it the same way on your print resume, print cover letter, and business cards. You can read about cover letters and business cards in Chapter 7.

- Use the name you are best known by, such as Michael Hardesty, not Michael J. Hardesty III.

- Provide one reliable phone number. Put the area code in parentheses to indicate that it is optional depending on where the user is calling from. (While it's on your mind, listen to your voice mail greeting. Do you state your name as you use it in your job search? Does your greeting sound professional?)

- Omit a fax number. Fax machines have been largely replaced by email. If a prospective employer wants to fax a document later in the interview or hiring process, you can provide a number then.

- Avoid crowding your contact information, but also avoid making it so prominent that the rest of the resume looks compressed.

- If your resume is two pages, put your name and page number at the top of the second page. Include your email address and LinkedIn URL if space permits, but do not repeat all of your contact information.

- Do not use the heading *Resume* or *Contact Information*. The contact information is the only section of a resume that does not have a heading.

- Use an email address that won't get tossed out by an employer's spam filter. An address such as john.waters@email.com is professional and appropriate. Sk8trBoy@email.com is not. Also follow this advice for your social media user names.

Objective

The **Objective** is a concise statement of your immediate employment goal (not your long-term career goal). It is the first section of the resume, immediately below the contact information on the first page. The objective:

- Can be stated as a job title or the type of work desired (Medical Laboratory Technician at ABC Healthcare Systems; Office manager for a travel agency)

- Can reflect the needs the employer stated in the job listing (Health Information Technician position requiring the ability to perform detailed clerical tasks, to change priorities quickly, and to communicate well)

- Can include one or more of your most important job-specific skills and areas of specialization (Information Systems Analyst I position in a financial environment requiring system design, programming, investigation, reporting skills)

- Can be customized for the job listing (Server position in an exclusive restaurant where knowledge of international cuisine is an added value; Server position in a four-star French restaurant where knowledge of the French language and cuisine is an added value)

- Should not focus on what you want (Expand my programming skills in the software development field)

An objective statement is especially important on resumes intended for entry-level jobs, for candidates with a diverse work history, and for candidates who do not have extensive work experience in the career field.

In large organizations, human resources professionals and the organization's resume scanning software will use your objective to know which job opening you are applying for. Use a customized job objective for every unique position you apply for. (It is not unusual to have two or three resumes that are identical except for the job objective.) Omit the objective statement in your master resume that you use for networking and distribute at career fairs.

Profile

The **Profile** section is a brief statement that describes you by stating your most relevant experience and qualifications. Think of it as the best you have to offer the current target employer and change the emphasis as needed for each job listing.

Use a Profile instead of an Objective on your master resume. If you can describe your qualifications with a job title (based on your overall experience, not just your current job), use the title as the heading for this section. Career Focus is a good title for the Profile section if you don't have a job title.

Some resume consultants recommend a profile for job seekers who have a great deal of experience and a job objective for those with limited experience who are seeking an entry-level position. Every job seeker, however, should be able to write a profile statement that describes her or his qualifications, skills, and personal traits.

Profile Personable and professional Server with four years restaurant experience, in-depth knowledge of international cuisine, and excellent customer communication skills.

If you have many years of relevant experience and it is difficult to describe your experience in one statement or if a statement is long, use a bulleted list of skills or a bulleted list of several profile statements.

 **CAREER ACTION 6-1**

Objective Statement and Profile, p. 139

Qualifications

The **Qualifications** section is a bulleted list of skills that highlights why you are the ideal candidate for the job. Because this section is a focal point for employers, use it to emphasize specific and relevant skills, capabilities, and related accomplishments such as the following:

- Software skills. If you can list several applications and have different levels of expertise with them, consider grouping the applications into categories labeled Master, Intermediate, and Basic. (Better yet, set aside time during your job search to take free online tutorials to increase your skills. But don't exaggerate your skills; newly hired employees are often given tasks using their hard skills while they learn their other responsibilities, and you aren't a master user if you can't use advanced features confidently starting on day one.)

- Years of experience in a specialized field and/or specialized skills

- Relevant credentials and degrees

- Relevant accomplishments in work or volunteer experiences, community involvement, and other activities

Other titles for the Qualifications section are Qualifications Summary, Skills Summary, and Career-Related Skills or, for business and technical careers, Core Competencies. Regardless of the name, spend time crafting this list to be a concise statement of your skills that quickly tells the employer that you are capable of doing the job.

Review your completed Career Actions 2-2, 2-3, 3-1, and 3-2 for your qualifications, skills, key personal traits, and other attributes you can list to best match the job list. List them in order of importance as they relate to your job objective. For example, if you are applying for a position with a doctor's office, start with your courses and volunteer work in the medical or emergency response fields.

Format the Qualifications section as a bulleted list to draw attention to each item; for example:

- Graphic and multimedia design, including streaming audio/video, analysis graphs, and custom web graphics

- General ledger, inventory control, and accounts receivable and accounts payable experience
- Proven team-player skills demonstrated in three successful internship projects

In the appropriate section of your resume (Work Experience, Education, or Related Activities), provide proof of the qualifications you have listed in the Qualifications section. If you do not have strong work experience related to your job objective, use the Qualifications summary to emphasize your accomplishments and skills in areas other than paid work experience.

Work Experience

In the **Work Experience** section of a resume, list the jobs you have held, starting with the most recent one. Start each entry with the most important information: your job title and dates of employment. On the next line, list the name of the organization and the city and state. Continuing on this line or starting on the third line, write a brief results-oriented description of your responsibilities. Use the present tense to describe your current job duties (*conduct, organize, reduce,* etc.).

Organize your descriptions so that they begin with the results and benefits of your work. Give specific, measurable examples of your accomplishments, such as increased sales, decreased costs, and reduced errors. Quantify where possible (with a percentage, a specific dollar figure, the number of items sold, etc.); for example, "Increased sales by 45% through skillful negotiation with automotive clients."

If you have held increasingly more responsible jobs with one employer, show this to demonstrate your reliability and your ability to learn and achieve on the job. List only new responsibilities and accomplishments for each promotion. (The reader will assume continuing job duties.) See Figure 6-13 on pages 134–136 for an example.

If you have little work experience, list your part-time and summer work, internships, school projects, volunteer work, and community involvement. Invent a job title if necessary and

MAKE IT A HABIT

Keep Your Skills Inventory Up to Date

During your job search and throughout your career, you will need to update your inventory of skills. Get into the habit of reassessing your skills and accomplishments twice a year. As you develop new skills and gain more experience, training, and education, your goals will change or expand.

Repeating the self-analysis activities in this chapter at turning points in your career will also help you identify your skills and see where you fall short compared with other candidates and employees. You can then seek the training and experience you need to help ensure that you will continue to be an asset to employers and will grow in your career.

iofoto/Shutterstock.com

emphasize the accomplishments and skills you developed—even if they do not relate directly to your job target. For example, if you recently graduated, one accomplishment might read as follows:

> Earned 85% of school expenses working part-time during school years and full-time during summers

This example demonstrates work experience, initiative, and the ability to make the most of a challenging situation. Employers consider these qualities real pluses, particularly for entry-level applicants.

Related Experience

Use this section to highlight other experience that relates to your job objective. Include activities such as memberships, awards, and leadership positions earned in professional or trade associations; honorary groups; and social, service, and school organizations. All of these activities show achievement and ability to work with others.

Instead of the heading *Related Experience*, consider a heading that may be more appropriate for your achievements and experiences, such as *Awards and Honors*, *Volunteer Work*, *Community Service*, *Certificates*, *Activities*, or *Professional Associations*.

Education

List your education in reverse chronological order (most recent first). List the technical schools, colleges, and universities you have attended, the years of attendance, and the degree(s) or certificate(s) you earned. Include relevant certifications, specialized training, and seminars.

If you are (or will be) a recent graduate with limited work experience, list Education before Work Experience. Highlight school activities and achievements in the Education section.

Support your job objective by listing related major(s), minor(s), and courses.

If your overall GPA or your GPA in your concentration area is high and you graduated with honors, include this information on your resume.

If you have several years of work experience related to your job objective, emphasize your work experience by listing it before your education and condense the education section.

Optional Resume Sections

Add the following sections if they are appropriate for your situation.

Military Service

Include any military experience that is relevant to your job objective, emphasizing relevant training, responsibilities, and accomplishments. Highlight any rapid progressions, significant promotion(s), and special commendations.

Consider listing your military record in its own section if it is significant; you can also list it in the work experience section. Translate the military jargon into terminology that your readers will understand—and that showcases your relevant qualifications.

ImageryMajestic/Shutterstock.com

WATCH OUT!

Never Lie or Stretch the Truth on Your Resume

If you can't prove it, it doesn't belong on your resume.

It is *never* acceptable to lie or stretch the truth about your work experience. Employers can and will verify all of the facts on your resume (including degrees, job titles, and dates of employment) and will contact your references. If you are caught in a lie, you will gain a bad reputation and will have no chance of being hired.

Even if you get away with a lie and are hired anyway, the truth has a way of coming out. When your employer discovers the truth, you may be fired immediately.

Personal Information

In most cases, resumes should not include personal information such as your age and marital status. Fair employment laws prohibit employers from requesting such information. Do not include your photograph: to avoid discrimination, many employers will not consider a resume with an enclosed photo. The only exception to this rule is a position that requires a certain appearance, such as modeling.

If your job target is in the field of nutrition, physical fitness, or sports and you want to provide relevant information about your own health consciousness, fitness level, or suitability for an active job, do so in a Related Experience section with the name Activities and Awards or something similar. In that section, you can list hobbies and/or accomplishments such as these:

- Completed two marathons in 2011
- Finalist in Eat Your Veggies Recipe Competition, Charleston WV, 2011
- Cofounded running team at Northside Montessori, 2010

References

If you are selected for a job interview, your prospective employer will more than likely check with your **references**, people who can attest to your work abilities and personal qualities, before offering you the job. (You can read about selecting references in "Your Connections" beginning on page 41 in Chapter 3.)

Although the References section is listed here as being optional for your resume, the standard advice is to omit references from your resume in most situations. It is unnecessary to state "References available upon request." Use this space for more valuable information, such as your accomplishments or experience.

Prepare a separate reference sheet with your references' names, titles, and phone numbers and take it to interviews. To protect your references' privacy, do not include email addresses and do not put your references' names and contact information on any resume that you submit electronically. A model reference sheet is available at www.cengage.com/career/yourcareer.

COMPLETE **CAREER ACTION 6-2**

Resume Outline, p. 139

Outcome 3 Write and Edit Your Resume

Once you have determined the appropriate sections for your resume, the next step is to write each section using professional and straightforward language and tone and excellent word choice. Your goals are to impress readers with your accomplishments through evidence and details *and* to use terminology that scanning software will identify.

Be Clear and Concise

Even in organizations that use resume scanning software to select the most promising resumes, deciding which applicants to interview is time-consuming. Employers want to find important information quickly. Make every word count as you emphasize how you meet the employer's needs. Use phrases, not complete sentences, and omit I, *me*, and *my*. The reader knows the resume is about you.

A resume for a recent graduate should be one full page. If you have extensive work experience, two or more pages are acceptable. In this case, use logical page breaks and repeat the current heading at the top of the next page so that the reader can follow the flow.

Use Specific Examples

Your resume will be clearer and more powerful if you use specific terms and examples to describe your accomplishments. Notice the more forceful impact of the following specific examples:

General/Vague	Specific
Reduced costs significantly	Reduced costs by 20%
The leading producer	Top producer of 30 employees

The most persuasive resumes describe the applicants' accomplishments with numbers, percentages, and dollar amounts to emphasize how the accomplishments can meet the prospective employers' needs. Use numbers whenever possible to enhance the credibility of your achievements.

Notice how the numbers in the second example below strengthen the accomplishment:

- Processed more orders than any other member of the work team

- Processed 40% more orders than any other member of the work team

Use Action Verbs

To satisfy resume-search software, you need to include terminology (usually nouns) that reflects the employer's requirements (see "Use Keywords Strategically"). Ultimately, however, you want a person to view your resume; so you also need to include concrete statements that use action verbs and are persuasive to human readers. These action verbs and phrases are the resume **action verbs** (also called *power verbs* and *power words*).

Use action verbs to show that you take initiative and actively participate in problem-solving and decision-making processes. Notice how the action verbs and sentence fragment in the second example convey a stronger image.

- My duties included reviewing marketing trends, analyzing statistical data, and preparing annual sales reports

- **Conducted** extensive market research; **analyzed, diagrammed,** and **reported** results of sales data; **wrote** annual sales reports

Figure 6-1 has a list of common action verbs. Select verbs that convey your qualifications most *powerfully* and use the past tense for jobs you held in the past. Compare the first two examples below and notice the use of more specific action verbs in the second example. *Designed* and *implemented* clearly describe the applicant's scope of responsibility and convey a greater sense of accomplishment.

- **Started** inventory tracking system

- **Designed** and **implemented** inventory tracking system

- **Organized** and **trained** volunteers who solicited contributions and **raised $55,000** for citywide elder-help campaign

- **Coordinated** school's student body elections and **reduced** final ballot processing time by **25%**

Use Keywords Strategically

Resume scanning applications look for **keywords**—terms that represent the qualifications the company has programmed the software to search for. The software searches for applicants with the required skills, knowledge, and capabilities for a position.

Employers will also search for these keywords when they read resumes. Think of keywords as the magnets that draw attention to your resume and strive to include as many appropriate keywords in your Qualifications section as possible.

Keywords name attributes that qualified candidates must have. Appropriate keywords for your job target include industry terminology and specific words or short phrases in job descriptions and ads.

Review the websites and publications of specific companies and professional associations in your career field to identify relevant keywords. These words describe employer-valued qualifications. Use this list of sources to help identify appropriate keywords to include in your resume.

- Job titles

- Skills and specialties

- Work and volunteer experience
- Education, certifications, licenses, and course work
- Community and other clubs/activities
- Relevant personal qualities
- Computer/software/hardware skills and specialized tools
- Industry buzzwords, jargon, and acronyms
- Accomplishments
- Industry/professional organizations
- Awards

Include keywords throughout your resume, and repeat critical keywords. The more keywords the resume-search software identifies, the more likely it is that your resume will be selected and you will be considered for an interview.

Employers may use different terms in their search criteria, so use synonyms for keywords (for example, *budget* as a synonym for *forecast* and *supervisor* for *manager*). Include the abbreviation and the full name of your degree, as in *B.A.* and *Bachelor of Arts*.

Resume-search programs typically seek nouns. In searching for AutoCAD drafters, for example, the software may look for nouns (and noun synonyms) such as *CAD, engineer, AA degree, certified drafter, Computer-Aided Drafting, AutoCAD, wiring diagrams,* and *physics*.

Use the career-related vocabulary you developed in Chapter 5 to enhance the number of keywords you use. Figure 6-2 has examples of typical keywords used to select resumes to fill two positions.

COMPLETE **CAREER ACTION 6-3**

Resume Action Verbs and Keywords, p. 142

accomplish	conduct	evaluate	manage	prove	select
adapt	consolidate	examine	monitor	provide	sell
administer	control	execute	motivate	publish	serve
advise	coordinate	expand	negotiate	purchase	setup
analyze	create	expedite	obtain	raise	solve
approve	customize	forecast	operate	rate	specialize
arrange	delegate	formulate	order	recommend	start
assemble	deliver	generate	organize	reconcile	streamline
assess	demonstrate	guide	originate	record	strengthen
audit	design	handle	overhaul	redesign	structure
budget	detect	identify	oversee	reduce	study
build	develop	implement	participate	reorganize	summarize
catalog	diagnose	improve	perform	repair	supervise
change	diagram	increase	plan	report	support
clarify	direct	inspect	prepare	represent	teach
coach	discover	install	present	research	test
collaborate	distribute	instruct	process	resolve	track
collect	draft	integrate	produce	respond	train
communicate	earn	introduce	program	review	update
compile	edit	investigate	promote	revise	upgrade
complete	eliminate	lead	propose	schedule	validate
compute	establish	maintain	protect	screen	write

Figure 6-1 Examples of Resume Action Verbs

Position Title	Sample Keywords	Position Title	Sample Keywords
Accountant	CPA, audit, accounting, accounts receivable/payable, statistics, spreadsheet, finance, systems training, computer, database, team player, B.B.A. Accounting, accurate, project leader, customer relations, accounting database, tax code, ethics, Sarbanes-Oxley compliance, data integrity	Web-based training developer	e-learning, WBT, instructional design, distance learning, synchronous, asynchronous, ADDIE, training, project management, Lectora, Flash, Sharepoint, Dreamweaver, CourseBuilder, Centra, SCORM, Section 508, DeBabelizer, Director, Captivate, Acrobat, LMS, SABA, SumTotal, Illustrator, Photoshop, PageMaker, Persuasion, Fireworks, Premiere, Sound Forge, Movie Maker, Javascript, SQL, Lingo

Figure 6-2 Sample Keyword Search Terms

Organize Your Resume

The way you organize your resume sections and details helps an employer quickly identify your most important skills, qualifications, and experience. The most common resume organizations are chronological, skills-based (also called functional), and combination.

Chronological Resume

The **chronological** organization is the most traditional resume structure. Use a chronological resume to showcase work experience, skills, and a career progression that are directly related to the job target. At the top of the resume (after the contact information), place the resume section that best supports your job objective or career focus.

In this organization, you will have a large Work Experience section. (You may or may not need a Qualifications section.) List each position you have held, starting with the most recent and going in reverse chronological order. Include the start and end dates and stress the major accomplishments and responsibilities of each position. Avoid repeating details that are common to several positions.

Follow this same reverse chronological order in the Education and other sections. Choose this layout when you want to emphasize steady, related work experience without major employment gaps or numerous job changes.

Most of the resumes at the end of the chapter are organized chronologically.

Skills-Based Resume

Another resume organization is the **skills-based** resume (also called a *functional resume*). Use the skills-based organization if you have relevant work skills that are related to your job target but you lack formal work experience that is directly related to the job target.

A skills-based organization is also appropriate if you have gaps in employment. Instead of showing that you have held similar jobs or have always been employed, the skills-based resume uses bullet items to emphasize your skill categories.

The Qualifications section is the most prominent section of a skills-based resume. Starting with the most important skill for the job, list your skills that relate to the job objective and back them up with measurable details and accomplishments. Instead of emphasizing job titles, dates, and length of employment, focus on your qualifications and transferable skills. Then in a brief Work Experience section, list your employer names and dates of employment. Figure 6-7 on page 123 is an example of a skills-based resume.

Combination Resume

The **combination** resume organization uses the best features of the chronological and skills-based organizations to emphasize the match between your skills and a position's requirements. Consider the combination organization if you want to emphasize your skills or if you have limited experience.

In the combination organization, both the Work Experience and Qualifications sections are emphasized. List your Qualifications section just below your objective or profile. Then incorporate your accomplishments in a reverse chronological list of Work Experience. Add credibility by linking your achievements with specific employers and time periods.

Place your education summary where it best supports your objective. If your education is more closely related to the skills required for your target job, place your educational information before your work experience information. Figure 6-8 on page 124 is an example of a combination resume.

COMPLETE | **CAREER ACTION 6-4**

Resume Draft, p. 143

Format Your Resume

The appearance of your resume may well be an employer's first impression of you. Even if the content is well written, an employer may not take the time to read your resume if it is sloppy or looks hard to read or process.

You need at least two resume formats: (1) a print resume (typically a .doc or .pdf file) that can be sent through the mail and attached to an email message or an online application and (2) a plain text resume (a .txt file) that can be pasted into an online application or the body of an email message. In some career fields, having a web resume is an asset.

Print Resume

Every job applicant needs a **print resume**, a printed, word-processed resume designed to be:

- Visually appealing.
- Delivered by regular mail, delivered in person, or attached to an email message or an online application.
- Scanned accurately into a resume database.

Formatting Do's for Print Resumes

- Use a clean format that is visually attractive.
- Use the whole page effectively. Space sections to fill the entire first page with an attractive layout framed by one-inch margins on all sides. Use areas of white space to draw attention to important items.
- Create a visual hierarchy in each section. Draw attention to headings by using capital letters and/or bold and indent text to emphasize items. (Don't overdo this, however.)
- Use a standard font. Keep the font size between 11 points for body text and 14 points for headings.
- Place the most important information at the top left of the page or section—where readers naturally begin reading.
- Single-space body text, double-space between items (such as jobs), and triple-space between sections. (Adjust the guidelines to fit on one page or to have logical page breaks.)

- Use bulleted lists instead of paragraphs.
- Be simple and consistent. Format the same elements the same way.
- Use one space after periods and add a space before and after slashes (for example, HTML / XML).
- Use only standard format elements: bold, italics (sparingly), centering commands, solid bullets, and tabs.
- Use color sensibly. For example, try dark blue for the contact information and section headings. Experiment with color before you send your resume and don't make color a "feature."
- Print your resume on a laser printer on one side of white or cream-colored paper. If the paper has a watermark, print with the watermark facing up and toward the reader.

Use your master resume for the first version of your print resume. Save the document with full formatting (.doc) or as a Rich Text Format (.rtf) file. (RTF files are less vulnerable to viruses but may not retain full formatting.) Both .doc and .rtf files can be converted to a PDF file (.pdf). A Portable Document Format file retains all formatting, is invulnerable to viruses, and is compatible across all platforms. Most users have the free software for reading PDF files, but the resume scanning software may have more difficulty searching PDF files for keywords.

A PDF file is your best choice if your word processing skills aren't top-notch. The person who receives a .doc or .rtf file as an email attachment can view the format coding to see how skilled you are with the program. A PDF file shows the finished product—and nothing more.

However, you may not have a choice about the file type. Many sites require a .doc file that their scanning software can read and that can be edited if necessary. Most employment agencies, for example, have their own "look" for the resumes they send to employers. They reformat everyone's resume in their own style and replace the contact information with an identifier, such as a date and time stamp, so that employers can't contact job seekers directly. (If you have free time while you are looking for a job, invest some of it in perfecting your word processing skills so that your .doc files will pass inspection if someone looks at the formatting symbols. You will be more efficient and more valuable on the job.)

Use the "do's" on the previous page and the "don'ts" below to format your print resume so that it will scan clearly, present a professional and attractive image, and keep you in the running for an interview.

Final Evaluation and Revisions

After you have drafted and formatted your print resume, review it, paying careful attention to every detail and marking areas for improvement.

- Rewrite sections to strengthen your qualifications.

Formatting Don'ts for Print Resumes

- Don't use the headings *Resume* or *Contact Information* at the top of a resume.
- Don't use excessive decorative fonts and formatting. These elements look unprofessional and do not scan well.
- Don't put the section headings in a narrow left column if this format crowds the page. There are better uses for the trapped white space under each heading.
- Don't crowd the text to fit everything on one page. Check your writing again and see where you can be more concise. If the text still doesn't fit, end the first page at a logical stopping point near the bottom of the page. If a section carries over, repeat the heading on page 2 (for example, Education, continued).
- Don't use a newsletter layout or multiple columns. Scanning software assumes that the text reads from left to right across the page in one column.

- Don't adjust the spacing between characters. Use the standard left-margin alignment for body text. (Headings can be centered.)
- Don't use formatting that can blur or corrupt the scanned image. Avoid the following:
  - Light-colored text
  - Shadow effect
  - White text on a black background
  - Boxed text
  - Vertical lines (You can use a single horizontal line as a separator between sections if you leave enough space above and below the line so that it doesn't touch any letters.)
- Don't fold or staple the resume. (Creases and staple marks can cause scanning errors.)
- Don't print page 2 on the back of page 1; use two sheets of paper attached with a paper clip.

- Eliminate unnecessary words; substitute stronger, clearer terms for weak one and add more action verbs and keywords if needed.

- Edit the text and make formatting changes to fit the resume attractively and neatly on the page.

- Check your resume against the Resume Checklist on page 115 and edit as needed.

After you revise your resume, recruit help from one or two objective members of your support network who have good writing skills. Give them a copy of the checklist on page 115 and ask them to critique your resume and give you honest feedback.

COMPLETE **CAREER ACTION 6-5**

Final Print Resume, p. 144

Plain Text Resume

You also need to have a **plain text resume**, a text file (.txt file) that has no formatting (no bold, no tables, no bullets, etc.). The main purpose of this text file is to serve as the source file for online applications.

- At some sites, you paste the entire plain text resume into one text field.

- Other sites use the headings in your resume to fill in fields automatically; you check each field and correct any errors (for example, if the program puts your job duties in the skills field).

- At other sites, you paste sections of the resume into labeled text fields. Less frequently, you may paste your plain text resume into the body of an email message.

Follow these steps to create a plain text resume. Start with the final version of the print resume you are using to apply for a job.

1. Save the print resume as a.doc file with a different name. Format the file so that it will convert to a clean .txt file. Replace bold text with all caps and bullets with hyphens; remove the tabs and start every line at the left margin.

   If your resume has two pages, delete the page break and the header at the top of the second page.

WATCH OUT

Save It for the Interview

Be careful not to put yourself out of the running for an interview by placing something unnecessary on your resume. It is not necessary to volunteer negative information about yourself. For instance, if you were fired from a job, do not indicate this fact on your resume. If necessary, discuss it during an interview, where you will have an opportunity to explain the situation.

Likewise, reserve any discussion of salary until you have had adequate opportunity to discuss your qualifications in an interview. Placing a salary requirement on a resume could eliminate you from a job or seriously weaken your negotiating position. If employers require your salary expectation, use broad numbers (the mid-thirty thousands, for example) and indicate that your salary is negotiable.

YURALAITS ALBERT/Shutterstock.com

2. Save the "stripped down" Word file as a .doc file and a .txt file. Close both files.

3. Open the folder with the .txt file and double-click the filename to open it. Windows opens the .txt file in the text editor program Notepad. *Do not open the .txt file in Word.*

4. Always finalize the *format* of a plain text resume (and cover letter) in Notepad, not in Word. To keep both versions of the current resume in sync, make *text changes* in the formatted print resume and re-create the unformatted.doc file and .txt file.

5. Check the format of the .txt file to make sure you didn't miss anything when you formatted the .doc file in Step 1. If necessary, add blank lines to make the resume more readable. Notepad ignores automatic line breaks in the .doc file and displays paragraphs, such as a description of job duties, as one continuous line of text that runs off the screen. Divide these long lines into lines of 65 characters, including spaces, by inserting a hard return at the end of each new line.

Look at the sample plain text resume in Figure 6-5 on page 120.

◄ COMPLETE **CAREER ACTION 6-6**

Plain Text Resume, p. 145

Web Resume

A **web resume** is formatted in HTML so that it can be posted on the Internet as a web document. It is designed to showcase the applicant's HTML skills and may also link to a web portfolio of artistic, specialized computer, and other abilities (for example, graphic art, charts, CAD drawings, and video or musical performance clips).

A web resume is created in HTML and published on the Internet. This resume format is more flexible than the others because it supports more sophisticated elements, such as animated graphics, sound clips, and video clips.

Keep Track of Your Resumes

Unless you get very lucky and are offered the first job you apply for, you will develop several versions of your resume during your job search. For example, you may need to change the job objective, emphasize different skills and capability in the qualifications section, or add specialized keywords. See "Customize Your Resume" on pages 116–117 for details.

Your goal is the same every time you apply for a job: to get an interview and have a shot at getting hired. For every interview, you need an attractive, carefully crafted print resume to take to the interview or to mail to the interviewer, with your thank-you note after a phone interview.

The information in each customized print resume and corresponding plain text resume must match. You need a system that keeps both versions in sync so that you can respond quickly and accurately to job listings.

Always edit your formatted print resume (not the stripped down, unformatted .doc file you saved in Step 2 above) when you customize your resume for a specific job. Use the edited file to create a new unformatted .doc file and new .txt file. In other words, create a new .txt file every time you change the text in your formatted print resume. *Do not try to make the same changes in both files.*

Develop a naming convention for each pair of resume files. To be organized and able to respond to job listings quickly, for each job you apply for, create a folder on your computer (and/or on a flash drive reserved for your job search and career management files). Keep a copy of the job listing, both versions of the resume, both versions of the cover letter (Chapter 7), copies of all emails related to your application, and—if you get an interview—your interview notes and the text of your thank-you letter.

Resume Checklist

Objective and/or Profile

✓ Does the Objective or Profile include the job title or required abilities specified by the employer?

Qualifications

✓ Do your Qualifications contain keywords that reinforce requirements for the job?

✓ Are the Qualifications relevant to your stated job objective? Have you included all of your major strengths?

Education

✓ If your education supports your job objective better than your work experience does, have you placed the Education section first (or vice versa)?

✓ Have you emphasized courses, internships, degrees, certificates, etc., that best support your objective?

✓ If your GPA is impressive, have you included it (overall or major/minor related to your job objective)?

Work Experience

✓ Does each job listing contain the employer's name and address (city and state), your job title, and dates of employment?

✓ Does each job listing describe your responsibilities and specific accomplishments?

✓ In your job descriptions, have you used power words and keyword nouns to support your job objective?

✓ If your work experience is limited, have you included relevant paid and nonpaid internships and volunteer or other pertinent activities?

Related Activities

✓ Have you included your involvement in professional and other organizations that support your job objective?

✓ Have you included relevant awards, achievements, and offices held?

Overall Content and Appearance

✓ Have you included all relevant information and targeted the content to the specific job objective?

✓ Is the length of the resume appropriate for your level of experience?

✓ Is the content logically organized and presented in order of importance to your job objective?

✓ Is the resume content truthful and correct (free from all grammar, spelling, and punctuation errors)?

✓ Do you use sentence fragments and omit the articles *the, a,* and *an* and the words *I, me,* and *my*?

✓ Is the overall design visually appealing and easy to read?

✓ Print resume only. Have you used appropriate fonts; white space; and acceptable enhancements such as bold, bullets, and tabs for indenting? Have you used italics sparingly?

✓ Did you follow the steps on page 113–114 to create your plain text resume and to keep the print and plain text versions in sync?

✓ Have you created a folder system and naming conventions for your print and plain text resumes? (Store your customized cover letters with the corresponding resumes.)

It is a good tool for displaying your expertise in computer technology (HTML, website and graphic design, and more). Web resumes can also be creative sales tools for people who want or need to display their artistic abilities, such as photographers, artists, singers, models, architects, and graphics and computer specialists.

Web resumes are most commonly used in high-tech industries, but they are also used in other fields. Research to determine whether a web resume is appropriate in your career field. Also note that a web resume should be used in addition to—not as a substitute for—your print and plain text resumes. Figure 6-12 on page 132 is the first page of a web resume.

Customize Your Resume

Outcome 6

Do not send the same resume to every prospective employer. A resume that you have taken the time to customize is more effective than your master resume is at showing how you meet the requirements stated in the job listing, and it will increase your chances of getting an interview. Customize your resume for specific job titles, job listings, and employers.

- Use the name of the company or industry in your objective.
- Use keywords in your job objective or profile and throughout your resume that match the terms in the job listing.
- Use appropriate industry terminology.

Figure 6-3 shows excerpts from a resume for a service manager position along with changes made to customize the resume for a position as an automotive insurance adjuster.

When the jobs you are applying for are quite similar, the adjustments may be minimal. If you are applying for different types of jobs in a similar industry or if you are trying to change career fields, you will need to revise your resume to fit each new career objective.

- Open a copy of your master resume in a window on the left side of the screen. On the other half of the screen, use your browser to read about the new career field and read

"Before"	"After"
Objective: Service manager in multiline dealership	**Objective:** Insurance adjuster in automotive collision repair industry
Auto Repair Customer Service	**Modified to Focus on Claims Management**
Scheduled appointments, performed pre-inspections, achieved upgrade sales on 95% of accounts, quoted estimates, wrote work orders, performed post-repair inspections, explained statements to customers, and increased referrals from customers by 40%	Scheduled client appointments, determined mechanical and auto body damages within 45 minutes, negotiated repairs with clients and insurance companies, prepared job documentation (pictures, work orders, billing), performed post-repair inspections, and explained statements
Parts Management	**Modified to Focus on Cost Containment**
Managed ordering and stocking of mechanical and auto-body parts inventories, selected suppliers and negotiated vendor discounts that averaged 25% to 30% below wholesale, reconciled shipping invoices to billing statements, and approved payments	Obtained clients' permission to use appropriate after-market and/or rebuilt parts on 95% of jobs; located replacement parts; negotiated price, delivery, and discounts, averaging 25% to 30% below wholesale; returned unused parts for credit; reconciled billing discrepancies; approved payments

Figure 6-3 Excepts from "Before" and "After" Resume

several job listings, including listings for jobs you are not considering. Compare your resume against the industry terminology for the new field. Highlight text in your resume that you can modify and paste the new terminology in your resume where appropriate. Look for ways to increase the number of keywords that match the career or job. For example, you might list different courses you have taken if a course title includes a keyword that you cannot use when describing your work experience. A teacher who is applying for jobs as a corporate trainer would use the terms *trainer, instructor, presenter,* and/or *facilitator* instead of *teacher.*

- Create new skill and experience headings by grouping related items from your updated skills list into categories. Use a heading that describes each category.

- Now that you have appropriate content, begin drafting and refining your new career resume. In other words, once you have completed this exercise of identifying appropriate content for a new job objective, you can revise and edit your master resume to match your new job objective.

 Internet Resources

Outcome 7

Just as no two resumes are the same, resume guidelines vary widely and are constantly changing. The Internet is a rich resource for staying on top of resume trends and locating additional resume writing and formatting suggestions. As you continue to revise and fine-tune your resumes, use your favorite search engine to:

- Research resume strategies.
- Find answers to specific resume questions.
- Search for writing and formatting guidelines.
- Find examples of power words and industry keywords.
- Access sample resumes, content ideas, and templates from different careers.
- Locate resume consulting services.
- Find resume-posting sites and services.
- Investigate quality sites that offer useful resume development advice. See the links at the product website.

Create Your LinkedIn Resume

LinkedIn was launched in 2003 with the idea of fostering business networking opportunities among professionals. Today it is the job seeker's most useful social networking tool. LinkedIn helps you create a full online resume that anyone can view and offers many features to help you build your network. With LinkedIn, you can do the following:

- View a full array of resumes and summaries of qualifications from people in many different fields and use them as examples for your own resume.
- Build a personal network of "connections" with people you know or have worked with and see the people in their networks.
- Create a "Recommendations" area where you can show off references from friends and past coworkers.
- Join industry-specific groups and discuss trends and issues; network with others who are interested in similar topics.
- Search a jobs database, which that you can easily filter by keyword.

Sample Resumes

The following sample resumes are on pages 119–136:

Print Resume and Plain Text Resume

- Figure 6-4: Print Resume (Registered Environmental Technician)
- Figure 6-5: Plain Text Resume (Registered Environmental Technician)

Chronological, Skills-Based, and Combination Print Resumes

- Figure 6-6: Chronological Resume (Administrative Assistant)
- Figure 6-7: Skills-Based Resume (Administrative Assistant)
- Figure 6-8: Combination Resume (Administrative Assistant)

Print Resumes

- Figure 6-9: Print Resume (Private Security Guard)
- Figure 6-10: Print Resume (Medical Assistant)
- Figure 6-11: Print Resume (Health Information Technician)

Web Resume

- Figure 6-12: Web Resume (Instructional Designer)

Two-Page Print Resume

- Figure 6-13: Two-Page Print Resume (Mid-career Job Seeker)

ERIKA ALLEN

10173 Jeffrey Street • Hoboken, NJ 07030
(551) 555-0129 • eallen@email.com • linkedin.com/in/erikaallen

REGISTERED ENVIRONMENTAL TECHNICIAN

PROFILE

Award-winning RET with A.S. in Environmental Sciences, OSHA Certification, knowledge of federal and state regulations, and strong technical writing abilities

CORE COMPETENCIES

- Soil and groundwater sampling and soil vapor extraction
- Environmental site mapping and assessment
- Technical writing and reporting
- Mapping and data entry
- Microsoft Office 2010 (expert user, Word and Excel), GIS, AutoCAD

CERTIFICATIONS AND TRAINING

- **RET – Registered Environmental Technician**
  Certification from National Environmental Health Association 2007

- **Emergency First Response**
  Primary and Secondary Care 2006

- **OSHA Health & Safety Training**
  40-hour course 2008; 8-hour refresher course 2011

AWARDS

Three-time recipient of Envirocorp Safety Recognition Award – 2010, 2011, 2012

RELEVANT WORK EXPERIENCE

Environmental Technician
Envirocorp, Burlington, NJ   January 2010–Present
- Survey sites and conduct field analyses and environmental site assessments
- Conduct soil and groundwater sampling
- Operate and maintain remediation systems
- Oversee drilling and excavation and monitor well installation
- Collect data and develop technical reports and maps using Word, Excel, GIS, AutoCAD

Soil and Water Extraction Technician
Environmental Consultants, Inc., Oakwood, NJ   April 2007–December 2009
- Completed laboratory tests on water samples in accordance with schedules set by supervisor
- Collected and preserved soil and groundwater samples
- Used Microsoft Word and Excel to record historical research and perform data entry

EDUCATION

A.S. in Environmental Science
Ocean County College, Toms River, NJ   May 2007
GPA 3.8

Figure 6-4 Print Resume (Registered Environmental Technician)

ERIKA ALLEN
10173 Jeffrey Street
Hoboken, NJ 07030
(551) 555-0129
eallen@email.com

PROFILE

Award-winning RET with A.S. in Environmental Sciences, OSHA
Certification, knowledge of federal and state regulations, and
strong technical writing abilities

CORE COMPETENCIES

- Soil and groundwater sampling and soil vapor extraction
- Environmental site mapping and assessment
- Technical writing and reporting
- Mapping and data entry
- Microsoft Office 2010 (expert user, Word and Excel), GIS,
AutoCAD

CERTIFICATIONS AND TRAINING

- RET, Registered Environmental Technician. Certification from
National Environmental Health Association 2007
- Emergency First Response. Primary and Secondary Care 2006
- OSHA Health & Safety Training. 40-hour course 2008; 8-hour
refresher course 2011

AWARDS

Three-time recipient of Envirocorp Safety Recognition Award - 2010,
2011, 2012

RELEVANT WORK EXPERIENCE

Environmental Technician
Envirocorp, Burlington, NJ
January 2010-Present
- Survey sites and conduct field analysis and environmental site
assessments
- Conduct soil and groundwater sampling
- Operate and maintain remediation systems
- Oversee drilling and excavation and monitor well installation
- Collect data and develop technical reports and maps using Word,
Excel, GIS, AutoCAD

Soil and Water Extraction Technician
Environmental Consultants, Inc., Oakwood, NJ
April 2007-December 2009
- Completed laboratory tests on water samples in accordance with
schedules set by supervisor
- Collected and preserved soil and groundwater samples
- Used Microsoft Word and Excel to record historical research
and perform data entry

EDUCATION

A.S. in Environmental Science, May 2007
Ocean County College, Toms River, NJ
GPA 3.8

Figure 6-5 Plain Text Resume (Registered Environmental Technician)

Analysis of Figures 6-4 and 6-5
Print and Plain Text Resumes (Registered Environmental Technician)

Design	Erika uses the Calibri typeface for her letterhead and for the resume headings and uses Times New Roman for the content. She places her recognizable job title immediately below her contact information. She uses horizontal lines to separate the major sections of her resume.
Profile	Erika uses a profile statement for her master resume; she does not list a specific job objective. She will upload her print resume as a PDF file when she applies for jobs through online job sites. Figure 6-5 shows the plain text resume that Erika will use to complete online applications.
Core Competencies	Erika uses the strong heading Core Competencies to list her most important qualifications, including skills that are often required in Environmental Technician positions. She uses industry keywords that she found in job descriptions.
Certifications and Training	Because Erika has important technical, regulatory, and safety certification and training that will impress employers, she lists these near the top of her resume in a separate section. She includes dates to show that her training and certifications are recent and up-to-date.
Awards	Erika is well aware that safety is prized in the environmental industry. Because her awards are measurable proof of her commitment to safety and excellence on the job, she creates a separate section to highlight these awards.
Relevant Work Experience	Because of her strong work experience, Erika uses the heading Relevant Work Experience and omits other jobs she has held. Her work experience shows advancement and increased responsibility, so she emphasizes her experience over her education. She uses industry keywords and abbreviations that resume scanning software and employers will recognize, and she uses action verbs to describe her job responsibilities.
Education	Since Erika has relevant work experience that is more important than her education, she lists her education last. Because of her strong skills and qualifications (and to keep her resume on one page), Erika omits a list of courses she has taken. She includes her high GPA.

Kimi Okasaki

148 Barrister Street • Tucson, AZ 85726

(520) 555-0136 • kimi.okasaki@email.com • linkedin/in/kimi.okasaki

OBJECTIVE

Administrative Assistant for MegaMall Property Management Inc.

EDUCATION

Associate of Applied Science, A.A.S., 2012, Westfield Community College, Tucson, AZ
Major: **Administrative Office Technology,** GPA 3.6

Related Courses and Skills

- Advanced Word Processing (Office 2010 for Windows, Office 2011 for Mac)
- Keyboarding at 75 words per minute
- Spreadsheet (Excel 2010, Apple Numbers) and Database Management (Access and Oracle)
- Records Management
- Bookkeeping I and Computerized Bookkeeping (QuickBooks Pro)
- Ten-key at 250 strokes per minute
- Office Management

EXPERIENCE

Community Volunteer, Tucson, AZ   December 2009 to December 2011

- **National Diabetes Foundation.** Developed and customized Excel spreadsheet report to track three fund-raising activities, reducing reporting time by 50%.

- **Secretary-Treasurer, Valley Elementary School Parent-Teacher Organization**
  Published electronic newsletters and maintained correspondence. Tracked budget in QuickBooks Pro; satisfied yearly CPA audits.

- **Meals on Wheels.** Developed and maintained Access database for survey responses from 1,200 participants.

Katz Department Store, Tucson, AZ   March 2009 to December 2010

- **Department Supervisor, Part-Time.** Supervised four salesclerks; trained new salesclerks. Computed daily cash receipts, balanced two registers, attained highest part-time sales volume, had fewest sales returned. Coordinated weekly deliveries and returns; managed annual inventory.

Value Variety, Tucson, AZ   Summers 2008, 2009

- **Salesclerk, Floater.** Provided complete customer service in sales and returns.

Figure 6-6 Chronological Resume (Administrative Assistant)

Kimi Okasaki

148 Barrister Street   •   Tucson, AZ 85726
(520) 555-0136   •   kimi.okasaki@email.com   •   linkedin/in/kimi.okasaki

OBJECTIVE

Administrative Assistant for MegaMall Property Management Inc.

EDUCATION

Associate of Applied Science, A.A.S., 2012, Westfield Community College, Tucson, AZ
Major: **Administrative Office Technology,** GPA 3.6

PROFESSIONAL SKILLS

Document Preparation. Expert in Office 2010 for Windows, Office 2011 for Mac. Enter text at 75 words per minute. Integrate tabular data and graphics into documents using Access and Excel. Write, format, and proofread printed and electronic business correspondence, slide shows, and newsletters.
- Published electronic newsletters and maintained correspondence for Valley Elementary School Parent-Teacher Organization (VES-PTO) for two years.

Spreadsheet Management. Develop and maintain Excel and Apple Numbers spreadsheets.
- Developed spreadsheet to track three fund-raising activities for the National Diabetes Foundation that reduced reporting time by 50%.

Database Management. Configure, maintain, and generate reports with Access and Oracle.
- Developed and maintained Access database for survey responses from 1,200 participants.

Bookkeeping. Perform manual (ten-key at 250 strokes per minute) or computerized (QuickBooks Pro) bookkeeping functions from journal entry to end-of-period reports.
- Maintained books for VES-PTO for two years and satisfied yearly CPA audits.
- Computed daily cash receipts and balanced two registers as part-time department supervisor of a department store.

Human Relations. Successfully cooperate with store managers, representatives of delivery companies and community organizations, and the general public.
- Held positions of responsibility in three community organizations over the last three years.
- Worked in two department stores: promoted to department supervisor, trained new salesclerks, coordinated weekly deliveries, provided customer service in sales and returns, attained highest part-time sales volume, and had fewest sales returned. Coordinated weekly deliveries and returns; managed annual inventory.

EXPERIENCE

Community Volunteer, Tucson, AZ	December 2009 to December 2011
Katz Department Store, Tucson, AZ	March 2009 to December 2010
Value Variety, Tucson, AZ	Summers 2008, 2009

Figure 6-7 Skills-Based Resume (Administrative Assistant)

Kimi Okasaki

148 Barrister Street • Tucson, AZ 85726
(520) 555-0136 • kimi.okasaki@email.com • linkedin/in/kimi.okasaki

OBJECTIVE

Administrative Assistant for MegaMall Property Management Inc.

QUALIFICATIONS

- Advanced word processing (Word 2010 for Windows, Word 2011 for Mac)
- Spreadsheet generation with Excel and Apple Numbers
- Database design and maintenance using Access and Oracle
- Experienced in use of PDF files and FTP
- Keyboarding at 75 words per minute
- Write and proofread printed and electronic business correspondence, reports, newsletters
- Presentation preparation using PowerPoint and Presentation software
- Internet research and email correspondence using Netscape and Explorer
- Bookkeeping using QuickBooks Pro and ten-key at 250 strokes per minute
- Proven ability to work successfully with store managers, delivery companies, community organizations, and the general public

EDUCATION

Associate of Applied Science, A.S.A., 2012, Westfield Community College, Tucson, AZ
Major: **Administrative Office Technology,** GPA 3.6

EXPERIENCE

Community Volunteer, Tucson, AZ   December 2009 to December 2011

- **National Diabetes Foundation.** Developed and customized Excel spreadsheet report to track three fund-raising activities, reducing reporting time by 50%.

- **Secretary-Treasurer, Valley Elementary School Parent-Teacher Organization** Published electronic newsletters and maintained correspondence. Tracked budget in QuickBooks Pro; satisfied yearly CPA audits.

- **Meals on Wheels.** Developed and maintained Access database for survey responses from 1,200 participants.

Katz Department Store, Tucson, AZ   March 2009 to December 2010

- **Department Supervisor, Part-Time.** Supervised four salesclerks; trained new salesclerks. Computed daily cash receipts, balanced two registers, attained highest part-time sales volume, had fewest sales returned. Coordinated weekly deliveries and returns; managed annual inventory.

Value Variety, Tucson, AZ   Summers 2008, 2009

- **Salesclerk, Floater.** Provided complete customer service in sales and returns.

Figure 6-8 Combination Resume (Administrative Assistant)

Analysis of Figures 6-6, 6-7, and 6-8
(Chronological, Skills-Based, Combination Resumes)

Resume Organization	Figures 6-8, 6-9, and 6-10 show the same content organized as a chrono-logical, skills-based, and combination resume, respectively.
Objective	Because Kimi is applying for a specific entry-level job, she uses the title of the position in the job listing as her objective.
Education	In each resume, Kimi emphasizes her degree and major by placing the Education section near the top of the page. She has a high GPA, so she includes this as well.
	In Figure 6-6, her chronological resume, Kimi uses the subheading Related Courses and Skills to emphasize her computer skills and show the relevant classes she has taken.
Kimi's Qualifications	Figure 6-6: Kimi's chronological resume does not have a separate list of qualifications. Instead, she combines her course work and skills into one list in the prominent Education section at the top of the resume.
	Figure 6-7: As you would expect, the centerpiece of Kimi's skills-based resume is the prominent Professional Skills section at the top of the resume. She groups her skills into five categories that are essential for administrative assistants and lists relevant job duties to show how she used each type of skill at work.
	Figure 6-8: Kimi's combination resume starts with a Qualifications section that is an expanded version of the list of courses and skills in her chrono-logical resume.
Experience	Because her community volunteer work is related to her job objective, Kimi lists it with her paid positions and uses the title "Experience" instead of "Work Experience." She describes her activities using results-oriented, measurable language.
	Figure 6-6: Kimi's chronological resume lists her experience in reverse chronological order.
	Figure 6-7. For her skills-based resume, Kimi reworks the Experience section of her chronological resume. She rewrites and reorganizes the job descriptions and puts them in the Professional Skills section to show how she has used each set of skills in her work. The Experience section at the end of the resume simply lists the name of each organization and the dates she worked there.
	Figure 6-8: Kimi's combination resume emphasizes her qualifications *and* her work experience. The Qualifications section at the top of the resume is an expanded version of the list of courses and skills in her chronological resume. The Experience section is identical to the one in her chronological resume.

THOMAS STANLEY

tom.stanley1066@email.com   linkedin.com/in/tomstanley1066

(607) 555-0157   123 Forest Drive, Springfield, NY 13333

OBJECTIVE

Private Security Guard position requiring ability to perform safety, security, and surveillance procedures; current licensing; excellent communication and interpersonal skills

CERTIFICATIONS AND TRAINING

- New York State Security Guard License, 2011
- Carrying Concealed Weapons (CCW) License, 2010
- First Aid and CPR Certification, 2007
- Physical Fitness Specialist, 2008
- Fire Prevention and Safety Training, 2009
- Burglary Prevention Training, 2009
- Practical experience in closed-circuit video surveillance and switchboard operations
- Proficient in Windows 7 and Microsoft Office 2010

EDUCATION

Crown Community College, Buffalo, NY
Associate of Applied Science, 2011
Major: Criminal Justice   GPA: 3.75

RELEVANT WORK EXPERIENCE

Buffalo Juvenile Justice Center, Buffalo, NY   September 2011–November 2011
Juvenile Corrections Intern
Under the direction of the Juvenile Corrections Officer, monitored and ensured the safety and security of juvenile detainees. Enforced facility safety and security rules. Escorted juvenile offenders to classes, counseling sessions, and work-release programs. Conducted security checks, searches, and pat downs.

Erie County Sheriff's Department, Hamburg, NY   Summer 2009, 2010
Assistant Supervisor, County Fairgrounds Grounds and Maintenance
Supervised groundskeeping and maintenance crew of eight work-released juveniles for the County Sheriff's Department. Quickly resolved worker disagreements and scheduling issues using training in conflict resolution techniques. Evaluated work crew weekly; submitted thorough and timely paperwork to the Sheriff's Department.

Baker Sporting Goods, Buffalo, NY   April 2008–May 2009
Security Guard, Part-Time
Monitored customers and employees to maintan internal and external loss-theft control. Conducted closed-circuit video surveillance of store and building exterior. Responded swiftly to all employee and customer security and safety requests. Handled switchboard operator duties. Wrote and submitted daily loss prevention reports.

Figure 6-9 Print Resume (Private Security Guard)

Analysis of Figure 6-9
Print Resume (Private Security Guard)

Design

Thomas uses the same font, Calibri, for the letterhead and section headings. The resume text is in Georgia, which has very strong bold letters. He saves bold for the most important information: his college and degree, his employers, and his job titles. A reader who skims the resume will focus on these qualifications.

Objective

Thomas states a clear, targeted job objective using a job title that is clearly understood in the field. To capture the attention of employers and emphasize his qualifications, he includes job-related competencies that match those listed in employers' job postings.

Certifications and Training

Because security guard positions can have several certification requirements, Thomas lists his training, certificates, and licenses with dates to show that they are current. He uses industry keywords and stresses experience and training that show his emphasis on safety, fitness, and security. He also lists his practical experience in video surveillance, switchboard operations, and computers because security guards often perform a variety of surveillance and communication tasks.

Education

Thomas reinforces his qualifications by placing his degree near the top of his resume. He uses bold to highlight his Criminal Justice major and includes his respectable grade point average.

Related Work Experience

Thomas uses the heading Related Work Experience to call attention to his three positions in the criminal justice field. The descriptions of his work experience show that he can be productive immediately in a job in the security field. His internship at the local Juvenile Justice Center gave him broad criminal justice experience. He highlights safety and security procedures by listing them as the first job duty, and he starts each job duty with a strong action verb for his field *(monitored, enforced, escorted, conducted)*.

In the description of his summer job at the county fairgrounds, Thomas emphasizes his use of conflict resolution and interpersonal skills, both of which are important qualifications for security guards. He also describes his ability to complete and submit essential paperwork.

Although Thomas's job at Baker Sporting Goods was a part-time position, it gave him practical experience in a variety of common security guard tasks. He uses action verbs and keywords and emphasizes his ability to manage multiple surveillance and communication tasks.

SHEREE LONG

5077 Pine Run • Bonifay, FL 32425 • (850) 555-0181 • s.long@email.com • linkedin.com/in/sheree.aama

CERTIFIED MEDICAL ASSISTANT, AAMA

Current AAMA certification. Front office and back office procedures.
Associate of Science, A.S. Fluent in Spanish.

QUALIFICATIONS

- Certified Medical Assistant, 2012
- Associate of Science, A.S., 2011
- Four-month Medical Assisting internship with front office administrative and back office clinical experience
- Medical records management experience in ICD-10 coding, alpha and color-coded filing systems
- Medical terminology courses
- Fluent in Spanish

EDUCATION

Associate of Science, A.S., 2011, College of Applied Careers, Orlando, FL   **Major: Medical Assisting**

Related Courses and Skills

- Human Anatomy and Physiology
- Clinical and Diagnostic Procedures
- Medical Office Practices
- Patient Relations
- Phlebotomy
- Medical Law and Ethics

- Pharmacology and Medication Administration
- Laboratory Techniques
- EKG and Basic X-ray
- Medical Terminology
- Business Communications
- Office Technology

CERTIFICATIONS

- Certified Medical Assistant, 2012
- CPR / BLS Certificate, 2010
- IV Therapy and Blood Withdrawal Certificate, 2011
- Basic X-ray Machine Operator License, 2011

EXPERIENCE

Dr. Jean Esteban, Sanford, FL   April 2012 to Present
Assistant Office Manager, Part-Time. Greet and register patients. Prepare patient charts. Conduct patient interviews and record patient history summaries. Maintain online records for all patients, including active and inactive files. Maintain supplies and instruments and prepare examination rooms. Assist physicians with vital signs and diagnostic testing, minor laboratory testing, and EKGs. Answer telephones and schedule appointments. Submit insurance claims. Received Standards & Procedures Award for maintaining safe and healthy work environment.

Seminole Medical Center, Sanford, FL   September 2011 to December 2011
Medical Assisting Intern. Greeted and registered patients. Answered telephone and scheduled appointments. Submitted insurance claims. Prepared examination rooms.

ASSOCIATION

American Association of Medical Assistants, AAMA

COMMUNITY SERVICE

Blood pressure screening, Holmes County Senior Center, April and October 2012

Figure 6-10 Print Resume (Medical Assistant)

Analysis of Figure 6-10
Print Resume (Medical Assistant)

Design
Because medical assistants are not required to be certified, Sheree places her job title at the top of the resume so that readers will know this about her while they skim the rest of the resume. Because this is Sheree's master resume and because her job title indicates the position she is seeking, she lists her major qualifications immediately under her job title and omits a job objective. She repeats the qualifications in other parts of the resume.

Sheree usees the Arial font for her name and the resume headings. In the body of the resume, she uses bold to highlight the most important text. She uses the regular font for the year she graduated and the city, state, and dates of employments.

Qualifications
Sheree uses keywords that readers and resume scanning programs will search for when seeking a medical assistant. She lists her qualifications in a clear bulleted list and emphasizes her Certified Medical Assistant certification by listing it first. She includes her practical experience in medical records management and medical terminology and highlights her ability to speak a second language, which is an increasingly important patient communication skill. She lists her degree in the Qualifications section because resume scanning programs are likely to use this keyword. She uses
the name and the abbreviation of her degree.

Education
Sheree reinforces her qualifications by placing her degree near the top of her resume. She repeats the title of her degree to highlight her Medical Assisting major. She lists the classes that are especially pertinent to employers because the course titles allow her to include keywords that she might not be able to use other-wise, such as *clinical, diagnostic, phlebotomy*, and *pharmacology*.

Certification
Because Medical Assistant positions can have several certification requirements, Sheree is careful to include all of the relevant certificates and licenses she has, along with dates to show that they are current. She places her national certification near the top of the resume to emphasize her qualifications and to show that she takes her profession seriously.

Experience
Sheree uses industry keywords to emphasize her contact with patients and her medical records experience. She places her Standards & Procedures Award at the end of the description so that a reader who skims the section is likely to notice it. She explains the purpose of the award ("for maintaining safe and healthy work environment") to show that her job performance is above average and to highlight her attention to a safe and healthy environment, which is a primary job requirement.

Sheree's internship allowed her to work and learn at a local medical center. The internship lasted four months, provided hands-on experience, and is directly applicable to Sheree's job objective; so she places the intern-ship in the Experience section of her resume and repeats industry keywords in the description.

Association
The association noted on Sheree's resume reinforces her strong interest in the medical field and shows that she takes her profession seriously.

Community Service
Space is tight on the page, so Sheree limits her list of activities to one in her career field. She knows that this section is not important enough to warrant a second page.

SONYA REID

2332 Clovis Boulevard • Savannah, GA 31401 • (912) 555-0109

sonya_reid@email.com • linkedin/in/sonya_reid

OBJECTIVE

Health Information Technician position requiring the ability to perform detailed tasks, change priorities quickly, and communicate well

QUALIFICATIONS

- RHIT, Registered Health Information Technician, 2012
- Family practice receptionist, 1.5 years
- Awarded Superior Service Certificate twice
- Five-month internship as assistant to Health Information Technician, Community Hospital
- Associate of Science, A.S., 2012

EDUCATION

Associate of Science, A.S., 2012, Savannah College of Georgia, Savannah, GA

Major: **Health Information Technology**, GPA 3.6

Related Courses and Skills

Medical Terminology • Clinical Classification Systems • Health Information Management
Health Delivery Systems • Health Data • Introduction to Health Law and Ethics
Human Disease Mechanisms • Health Care Reimbursement • Alternative Health Care Settings
Business Communications • Word • Excel • Access • PowerPoint

CERTIFICATION

Registered Health Information Technician, 2012

EXPERIENCE

- **Community Hospital**, Savannah, GA   January 2012–May 2012
  Clinical Internship. Under the direction of the Health Information Director, assisted Health Information Technician in reviewing and assigning diagnosis codes and DRGs. Abstracted appropriate information and retrieved medical records. Assisted with Medicare/Medicaid coding for three months. Checked charts into and out of records department.

- **Family Practice Partnership**, Savannah, GA   July 2010–December 2011
  Evening Receptionist. Answered telephone, scheduled appointments, and kept waiting room neat. Checked in patients, obtained insurance and billing information, and pulled charts for nurses. Copied requested records for transport to other medical offices. Provided cheerful, efficient service to patients; awarded Superior Service Certificate in 2010 and 2011.

ASSOCIATIONS

- Community Hospital Volunteer   2010–Present
- American Health Information Management Association   2010–Present

Figure 6-11 Print Resume (Health Information Technician)

Analysis of Figure 6-11
Print Resume (Health Information Technician)

Objective	Sonya is looking for her first job after graduation, so she lists her job objective instead of using a Profile section. She uses an industry-standard job title to state her job objective concisely. To catch the attention of employers and to advertise her work-related characteristics, she includes job-related competencies that her target employers use in job postings.
Qualifications	Sonya uses terms that resume scanning software and human readers typically search for when filling a health information technician position. She emphasizes her Registered Health Information Technician certification by placing it first because it is a primary requirement for the job she is seeking. She highlights her relevant work experience and her hospital internship assisting a Health Information Technician. She spells out the title of her degree and uses the abbreviation so that the resume scanning software will pick it up regardless of which form it has been programmed to search for.
	Notice that all five bulleted qualifications are repeated elsewhere in Sonya's resume. Sonya uses the Qualifications section to highlight her most important qualifications and to catch a human reader's attention.
Education	Sonya lists her courses as a way to include industry keywords. She reserves bold for the two most important pieces of information: her degree and her major.
Certification	Because Sonya just graduated and has limited work experience, she places her certification in its own section of the resume to emphasize her qualifications and to show that she takes her profession seriously.
Experience	Sonya's internship through her college allowed her to work and learn at a local hospital. Because her internship lasted five months, gave her hands-on experience, and is relevant to her job objective, she places it in the Experience section of the resume, not in the Education section. Notice how Sonya uses action verbs and keywords to describe her job duties.
	Although Sonya's job at the family practice clinic was at a medical facility, she did not have any responsibilities that directly relate to her current job objective. She puts her award for superior service at the end of the job description.
Associations	The associations reinforce Sonya's professionalism and commitment to the medical field. She includes her volunteer work because she knows that target employers value community service.

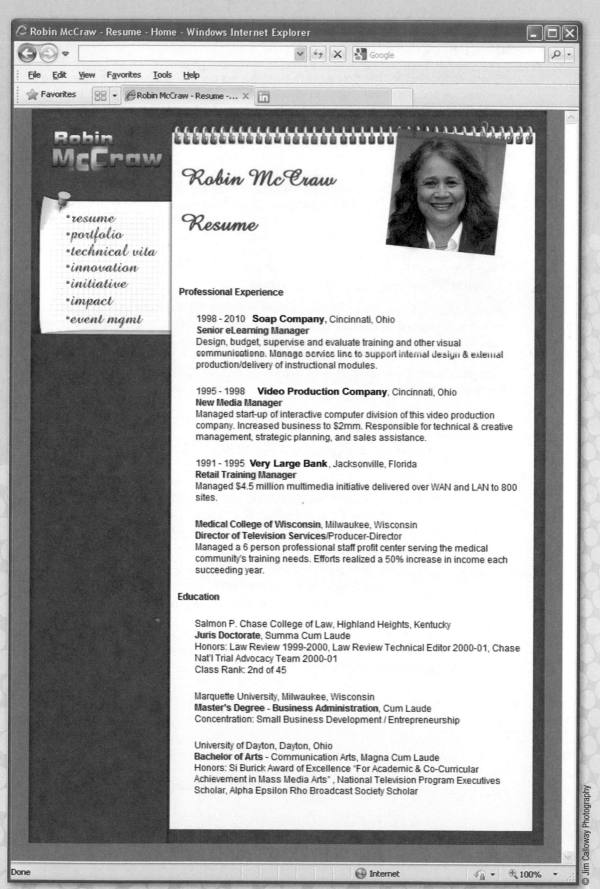

Figure 6-12 Web Resume (Instructional Designer)

Analysis of Figure 6-12
Web Resume (Instructional Designer)

Design

Note: Robin's resume has been modified for this textbook.

Robin displays her Web expertise by creating a sophisticated multipage website. To save time and money, she modified a $50 template she found online. Because many employers will not take the time to look at this resume, she is confident that posting her photo will not put her out of the running.

Professional Experience

Robin is a mid-career job seeker. She includes her position as director of television services for a large medical college, but she omits the dates because this position was much earlier in her career.

Education

Although she is not looking for a job as an attorney, Robin lists her J.D. degree to show that she enjoys intellectual challenges and is a critical thinker. She does not list the dates of her MBA and BA degrees.

Portfolio (listed in menu; page not shown)

Robin puts several samples of work on this page and links to her larger portfolio at behance.net. Because of confidentiality issues, she was limited in the samples she could use. She showed generic projects and removed identifying information from other work.

Technical Vita (listed in menu; page not shown)

Because Robin has an impressive list of technical skills (see the list for the Web-based training developer in Figure 6-2 on page 110), she creates a vita (another word for *resume*) to describe some of the work she has done to confirm her level of expertise with the tools she can use.

Innovation Initiative Impact (listed in menu; pages not shown)

Because Robin is a mid-career job seeker, she has a long list of accomplishments. For maximum effect, she uses three "*I*'s" that will appeal to employers looking for a senior instructional designer or department manager.

Robin worked at the company when the intranet was in its initial stages. On the Innovation page, she shows how she helped develop the company's intranet standard and online "look and feel." Because she kept good records of her work, she also can describe innovation in more recent projects.

Robin uses the Initiative page to describe projects where she was proactive in helping her internal clients (other departments in the company) see how they could use the company's intranet most effectively. She took the initiative to show them features they had not thought of.

Robin uses the Impact page to show that she is effective at developing solutions that will have a positive effect on the company's bottom line. For example, she writes, "Flash applications are very difficult to modify and expensive to edit, but using Flash as an animation tool is a great way to make a training program more appealing."

Event Management (listed in menu; page not shown)

Although she is not applying for jobs in event management, Robin has strong experience in this field. A prospective employer looking at this page will see her customers' assessment of her event management skills, providing strong evidence of her transferable competencies, such as her ability to troubleshoot and overcome problems, develop strategic partnerships with suppliers, manage multiple priorities, and work under pressure.

S. CAMILLE BRADLEY

1537 Donaldson Place | Marlinton, WV 24954
(304) 335-0120 | scbradley822@email.com
Camillecooks.com | Linkedin.com/in/scbradley822

CORE STRENGTHS

✓ Highly organized and self-directed
✓ Comfortable working in a fast-paced environment
✓ Strong customer service orientation
✓ Leadership experience and traits
✓ Strong team player with collaborative mind-set
✓ Can visualize and implement efficient solutions to meet needs of various groups (departments, managers, coworkers, clients)

✓ Excellent oral written communication skills
✓ Excellent creative and critical-thinking skills
✓ Impeccable work ethic
✓ Proactive, eager learner; wide variety of interests
✓ Outgoing personality
✓ Experience developing and maintaining document workflow processes for transition from paper to online environment

TECHNICAL SKILLS

Master skills Windows 7, Office 2010, Acrobat X Pro, Xerxes library portal system
Intermediate skills Microsoft Access, SharePoint, OneNote

EMPLOYMENT HISTORY

YMCA OF ELK COUNTY (Marlinton, WV)   January to June 2012
AppalKids After School
- Lead instructor for kindergarten and Grades 1 and 2
  - Created new learning activities to expand on standard curriculum
- Conducted field trips for all grade levels
- Tutored international students in English and math

PUBLIC LIBRARY OF MARLINTON AND ELK COUNTY (Marlinton, WV)   2001 to 2011
Senior Librarian Services Assistant 2006 to 2011
Librarian Services Assistant 2001 to 2006
- Information Desk: Helped patrons with reference queries (in person, online, on telephone)
- Circulation Services: Maintained patron records and holds. Developed streamlined process for organizing and tracking materials to be distributed back into library collection (system continues to be used)
- Represented Circulation Services on major project to implement new, enterprise-wide library software adopted by state library consortium (OCLC). Trained staff; converted and maintained patron records
- Commended for excellent service by coworkers four times

PERSONAL CHEF and CATERER (Marlinton, WV)   1995 to present
- Cook for families; cater art gallery openings
- Plan themed catered events such as Taste of the World New Years at Main City Grill
- Created and led Eat for Art series at Comet Restaurant, 2011

STARBUCKS COFFEE COMPANY (Marlinton, WV)   2004 to 2008
- Opened store every morning (selected for role because of dependability; reported to work at 5 a.m.)
- Oversaw shift changes to ensure smooth shift transfers

Figure 6-13 Two-Page Print Resume, page 1 (Mid-career Job Seeker)

S. CAMILLE BRADLEY

ELK COUNTY BOARD OF EDUCATION (Marlinton, WV) 2001 to 2002
- Assistant to Director of Marlinton Charter School Board
- Paralegal duties: Researched educational and real estate laws for charter schools

MENTIS INTERNATIONAL SCHOOL (Marlinton, WV) 2000 to 2001
- Managed school attendance at inner city charter school
- Mediated truancy hearings among school, students, and families
- Filed truancy paperwork, represented school at truancy court hearings
- Instituted lunchtime etiquette program

ELK COUNTY PROBATE COURT (Marlinton, WV) 1998 to 2000
Deputy Clerk
- Set court dates for hearings
- Organized and distributed files
- Processed marriage licenses
- Organized and prepared printed records for transition from paper to electronic record keeping. Maintained electronic records for court filings

LIFEGUARD (Marlinton,WV) 1994 to 1998
Elk Recreation Commission, Jerry West YMCA, Greenbrier YMCA, University of Charleston
- Responsible for opening and closing pools and pool upkeep
- Coached inner city Hartwell Swim Team for 3 years; won second place in citywide recreational swim meets 3 years in a row
- Taught basic swimming skills to all age groups
- Performed life-saving maneuvers on two occasions; helped organization avoid lawsuit through quick and effective response
- Received highest job performance ratings at every organization

CAMELOT MUSIC STORES (Marlinton, WV) 1997 to 1998
Assistant Manager
- Opened and closed store
- Oversaw customer service; trained new employees; made daily bank deposits
- Managed promotional events

BEST BUY (Marlinton, WV)
Supervisor of appliance department 1996 to 1997
Retail sales associate 1992 to 1995

EDUCATION

University of Charleston, Marlinton, WV, 1996 to 1999

Winston-Salem State University, Winston-Salem, NC, 1995 to 1996

Greenbrier High School, Marlinton, WV, Graduated 1995

Figure 6-13 Two-Page Print Resume, page 2 (Mid-career Job Seeker)

Analysis of Figure 6-13
Two-Page Print Resume (Mid-career Job Seeker)

Background	Camille, 34, has worked since she was a sophomore in high school. Her greatest regret is postponing her senior year of college after her brother was seriously injured in a car accident the last week of her junior year. She "never dreamed" that a dozen years later she still would not have a college degree.
	Since losing her full-time job in the public library in late 2011 because of budget cuts, Camille has been able to find only part-time work. In the summer of 2012, she worked on the Cirque du Soleil local crew for five weeks, and she is currently a chef for a wine bar three nights a week. But because she needs a full-time job with benefits and because she wants a "desk job," Camille decides not to list those jobs on her resume. If her job search continues, she will list her position as a chef to avoid showing gaps in her work history.
Format	Camille needs a two-page resume to show employers that she is versatile and was given increasing responsibilities in the jobs she has held.
Core Strengths	Camille knows that her skills, although strong, are generic: she is not a nurse or an IT network manager and has the best chance of getting a job where soft skills are important (front desk clerk, for example). She puts this list of strengths at the top of her resume to showcase her strong soft skills and transferable competencies (skills and attitudes that can be applied in different work situations)—and to be selected for a job interview.
Technical Skills	Camille lists her skills before her work history so that they appear first on the page.
Employment History	Camille uses bulleted lists for her job duties. For each job, she highlights an accomplishment that makes her stand out, such as creating new learning activities for students, being commended for excellent work by her coworkers, being trusted to open the coffee shop, even helping her employer avoid two lawsuits when she worked as a lifeguard.
Education	Because she is not a college graduate, Camille lists her high school and her date of graduation.

Chapter Checklist

Underline each action you are already taking and circle the actions you need to work on.

- Know how organizations select which resumes to consider for a job listing. [1]

- Know the requirements for a winning resume. [1]

- Write a clear, appropriate objective and/or profile to focus my entire resume. [2]

- Choose the resume sections and organization that best support my job objective and qualifications. [2]

- Use measurable details and accomplishment statements to market myself. [3]

- Use appropriate action verbs and keywords to demonstrate that I have the required skills and knowledge. [3]

- Select the most effective organizational structure: chronological, skills-based, or combination. [4]

- Format my print and plain text resumes correctly. [5]

- Customize my resume to meet the needs of the employer and match my resume to the job description by using specific terms and industry terminology. [6]

- Use the Internet to review resume tips and trends tips. [7]

Critical-Thinking Questions

1. When should an applicant use different objectives or different resumes? [2]

2. In what order should you present your resume data to best support your objective? [2]

3. Why is it effective to include a Qualifications section immediately below the Objective on a resume? [2]

4. Why is it essential to use power words and keywords in a resume? [3]

5. Why is a chronological resume the preferred organization for job seekers who have a significant amount of work experience? [4]

6. Why do you need a plain text resume? What are the requirements for this resume, and how do you create it? [5]

7. How can you tailor your resume to target a specific job or employer? Give at least three examples from your own resume. [6]

Want access to career resources, study tools, activities, and job information links? Get started at www.cengage.com/career/yourcareer.

TRIAL RUN

A good way to get started on creating a resume is to review sample resumes online. However, these samples are only guidelines and are not intended to be used as shown. They are intended to be evaluated, revised, reorganized, and reformatted to fit a job seeker's skills and career objective.

Search the Internet for free sample resumes in your career area. Choose one that is relevant to your job target and evaluate it using the Resume Checklist in the chapter. List the changes needed to make the resume better fit your qualifications and experience and to fit the formatting guidelines in this chapter.

Copy and paste the text of the sample resume into a word processing file and make the necessary revisions. Format the resume as a print resume (.doc) or plain text resume (.txt).

Print out the revised resume and edit it carefully for mistakes and typos. Pair up with a classmate and exchange resumes for peer editing.

Evaluate resumes on the following elements:

Rating Scale: 1 to 4 (1 = not really; 2 = sometimes/somewhat; 3 = usually; 4 = definitely)

_____ 1. The Objective or Profile includes the job title or required abilities specified by the employer.

_____ 2. Qualifications contain keywords that match requirements for the job.

_____ 3. Qualifications are relevant to the stated job objective. Major strengths are included.

_____ 4. If education supports the job objective better than the work experience, it is placed first (or vice versa).

_____ 5. The candidate emphasizes courses, internships, degrees, certificates, etc., that best support the objective.

_____ 6. The overall GPA and/or GPA in the concentration area is included (if impressive).

_____ 7. Each job listing contains the employer's name and address (city and state) and job title.

_____ 8. Each job listing describes responsibilities and specific, measurable accomplishments.

_____ 9. Job descriptions use power words and keyword nouns that support the objective.

_____ 10. If work experience is limited, relevant paid and nonpaid internships and volunteer or other pertinent activities are included.

_____ 11. The candidate emphasizes involvement in professional and other organizations that support the job objective.

_____ 12. Relevant awards, achievements, and offices held are included.

_____ 13. The overall design is appealing.

_____ 14. The content is correct (grammar, spelling, and punctuation).

_____ 15. The content is logically organized and presented in order of importance to the objective.

_____ 16. Resume meets all print or plain text resume formatting requirements.

CAREER ACTION   6-1   Objective Statement and Profile ☐2

Using one of the job descriptions you collected earlier, write two Objective statements for your target job. Follow the guidelines on pages 103 and 104. Add one of these statements to the Objective tab under Write a Resume on *Career Transitions*.

Now suppose you need a master resume to hand out to multiple employers at a job fair. Write a Profile statement that you can use in place of an Objective on that resume.

CAREER ACTION   6-2   Resume Outline ☐3

Create an outline for your resume using this worksheet (here or on the product website) or a word processing document. Use your completed Career Actions in Chapter 3 for help with this activity.

Once you have completed the worksheet, number the sections of the outline, ranking them in order of importance and relevance to your job objective. Continue building your online resume by adding this information to *Career Transitions*. Later you will present the material in your final resume in this order. For example, if your education is more relevant to your job objective than your work experience is, place the education information before the work experience information. Likewise, you will need to group items from your Related Experience, Activities, and Awards section in the way that best presents your accomplishments. File your completed worksheet in your Career Management Files Tracker.

Name _____

Mailing Address _____

_____

Email Address_____   LinkedIn URL _____

Telephone Number_____   Website URL _____

OBJECTIVE and/or PROFILE

QUALIFICATIONS (*Use terms and keywords that are related to your target job to describe your capabilities and accomplishments.*)

WORK EXPERIENCE (*State your accomplishments in measurable terms if possible. Start with the most recent job and list each job in reverse chronological order, ending with your earliest work experience. If you have little actual work experience, list internships in this section.*)

Company Name _____

City and State _____

Dates of Employment _____

Job Title and Description _____

Tasks and Accomplishments:

Company Name _____

City and State _____

Dates of Employment _____

Job Title and Description _____

Tasks and Accomplishments:

Company Name _____

City and State _____

Dates of Employment _____

Job Title and Description _____

Tasks and Accomplishments:

Company Name _____

City and State _____

Dates of Employment _____

Job Title and Description _____

Tasks and Accomplishments:

EDUCATION *(If you have attended more than one school, list the schools in reverse chronological order—the most recent one first. Do not list high school if you have higher-level schooling unless the high school is considered very prestigious.)*

Name of School	**City, State**	**Degree(s)/Certificate(s)**	**Years Attended**

(Job seekers with little or no work experience should expand the education section and list it before the Work Experience.)

Major(s) _____

Minor(s) _____

Overall GPA _____ GPA in concentration area _____

Relevant Courses of Study:

Certifications and Licenses:

RELATED ACTIVITIES/EXPERIENCE *(Include internships, volunteer work, service clubs, etc. List the name of the program or organization and the dates you were involved. Briefly summarize your experience, accomplishments, and activities.)*

SCHOOL-RELATED ACTIVITIES *(Include organizations, clubs, tutoring, class projects, honor groups, internships, leadership positions, etc.)*

INTERESTS *(List interests that are related to your job target and that demonstrate well-rounded qualities, including interaction with people, intellectual pursuits, artistic ability, physical fitness, continuing education, and personal/professional development.)*

MILITARY SERVICE *(List branch of service, highest rank, training, areas of specialization, major duties, skills and knowledge developed, honors, location of service, and discharge status.)*

AWARDS and HONORS *(List all awards, honors, and commendations you have received. Note that they do not have to be workplace awards, but they should be relevant to workplace skills.)*

ASSOCIATIONS and MEMBERSHIPS *(Include membership and leadership positions in professional or trade associations, community organizations, social organizations, and volunteer groups.)*

CAREER ACTION   6-3   Resume Action Verbs and Keywords ③

Use this worksheet or a separate sheet of paper to complete this activity.

1. Prepare a comprehensive list of appropriate action verbs and keywords (industry term; acronyms; terms describing your job positions, experience, education, skills, etc.).

2. Use the list on page 109 and the Internet as a primary resource in your research.

3. Print a report with (a) your lists of action verbs and keywords and (b) the resources you used to identify them.

4. File your summary report in your Career Management Files Tracker for future reference.

Resources for Identifying Action Verbs and Keywords for Your Resume

- *Your Career: How to Make It Happen* website at www.cengage.com/career/yourcareer
- Job advertisements and descriptions for positions you are considering (print or online)
- Websites of employers you are considering
- Government publications such as the *Occupational Outlook Handbook* (print or online)
- Professional associations in your field (check their websites, publications, and meetings)
- Internet searches on *resume keywords*, *resume action verbs*, *resume power verbs*, and *resume power words*
- Online encyclopedias and dictionaries

CAREER ACTION   6-4   Resume Draft [5]

Review the sample resumes on pages 119–136. Mark the organizational schemes and sections of the models that are useful to you. Resumes typically should contain all of the standard sections below. Include the optional sections when they support your main job objective or when an employer requests them. Note how the sample resumes include differences in the section headings. Mark the headings that best suit your experiences and preferences.

Standard Resume Sections

- Name and Contact Information (no heading)
- Objective or Profile
- Work Experience
- Qualifications
- Education
- Related Experience (or Activities)

Other Resume Sections to Consider

- Military Service
- Awards and Honors
- Associations and Memberships

Determine which organization is best for you. (If you have extensive work experience, the chronological organization might be best. If you have limited work experience but plenty of relevant skills, the skills-based or combination organization will highlight your skills.)

Prepare a written or word-processed rough draft of the content of your resume using the resume outline in Career Action 6-2 as a reference and starting point. You can also print your resume from *Career Transitions* if you built in the information from the previous Career Actions. Be selective about the quality and quantity of information you include. Make every word count. Emphasize your qualifications and measurable accomplishments and include appropriate power words and keywords from Career Action 6-3. File your draft in your Career Management Files Tracker.

CAREER ACTION   6-5   Final Print Resume [5]

Use a word processor to prepare your final print resume or print from *Career Transitions*. (If you hire an expert to prepare your resume, be sure to request the file so that you have it for revisions and updates.)

Use the checklist on page 115 as a guide for evaluating and revising your resume. For each category that contains a question to which you answered no, revise your resume content according to the guidelines in the chapter. Proofread and edit the content until your resume is as close to perfect as you can get it. Make sure your print resume is scannable and avoid formatting that does not scan clearly. File your resume in your Career Management Files Tracker and in your Career Portfolio.

If you want more ideas for your resume, browse the links on the product website. Also check with your school's career services center, which is typically an excellent resource for developing a resume.

	Yes	No
Objective and/or Profile My Objective and/or Profile statement includes the job title and/or the required abilities specified by the employer.		
Qualifications My Qualifications contain keywords that reinforce requirements for the job.		
My Qualifications are relevant to my stated job objective.		
I have listed all of my major strengths.		
Education If my education supports my job objective better than my work experience does, I have placed the Education section first (or vice versa).		
I have emphasized courses, internships, degrees, certificates, etc., that best support my objective.		
I have included my overall or major/minor GPA if it is impressive; otherwise, I have left it out.		
Work Experience For each job listing, I have included the employer's name and address (city and state), my job title, and dates of employment.		
In each job listing, I have described my responsibilities and stated specific accomplishments.		
In my job descriptions, I have used power words and keyword nouns to support my job objective.		
I have included relevant paid and nonpaid internships and volunteer or other pertinent activities.		
Related Activities I have included my involvement in professional and other organizations that support my job objective.		
I have included relevant awards, achievements, and offices held.		

	Yes	No
Overall Content and Appearance		
I have included all relevant information and targeted the resume content to the specific job objective.		
I have made sure the length of the resume is appropriate for my level of experience.		
I have organized the content logically and presented it in order of importance to my job objective.		
My resume content is truthful and correct (free from all grammar, spelling, and punctuation errors).		
My resume is visually appealing and easy to read.		
I have used appropriate fonts, white space, and acceptable enhancements (boldface, bullets, indents).		
I have avoided graphic enhancements, columns, and decorative fonts.		

CAREER ACTION   6-6 Plain Text Resume ⑤

Part 1. Convert the print resume you created in Career Action 6-5 to a plain text resume. Follow the steps below and review the sample plain text resume, Figure 6-5 on page 120. (The product website has the .doc files used to create the .txt file in Figure 6-5.)

1. Save the print resume you created in Career Action 6-6 as a .doc file with a similar name (for example, *MasterResume_plain text source file.doc*).

2. Format the new .doc file so that it will convert to a .txt file that needs less manual formatting. Newer versions of Word create cleaner .txt files, so experiment with the formatting you need to change.

   - Start every line of contact information at the left margin.

   - Replace bold headings with all caps.

   - Add blank lines to emphasize sections as needed. For example, insert two blank lines before the section headings.

   - Replace bullets with hyphens or asterisks. (Newer versions of Word convert bullets to asterisks automatically.)

   - Format tables as lists.

   - For each company in the employment section, put the dates of employment under the company.

   - If your resume has two pages, delete the page break and the header at the top of the second page.

3. Save the "stripped down" Word file as a .doc file. Use Save As to save it as a .txt file. Close both files.

4. Open the folder with the .txt file and double-click the filename to open it. Windows opens the .txt file in the text editor program Notepad. *Do not open the .txt file in Word.*

   Always finalize the *format* of a plain text resume (and cover letter) in Notepad, not in Word. To keep both versions of the current resume in sync, make *text changes* in the formatted print resume and create a new unformatted.doc file and .txt file.

5. Check the format of the .txt file to make sure you didn't miss anything when you formatted the .doc file in Step 2. If necessary, add blank lines to make different sections of the resume stand out more. Because Notepad does not wrap text automatically, look for long lines of text that run off the screen. Insert hard returns to divide these long lines into lines of 65 characters, including spaces.

6. Save the .txt file. Repeat these steps—create a new plain text resume—every time you modify your print resume. For this exercise, leave the .txt file open.

Part 2. Email your plain text resume to yourself.

1. Open your email program and create a new message addressed to yourself. To ensure clean transmission, set your format to Plain Text format (not Rich Text or HTML).

2. Select (highlight) all of the resume text and copy and paste it into the email message window.

3. In the email subject line, enter a reference number from a job listing you have found.

4. Key the words *cover letter* above the first line of your resume (your name). (If you have a plain text cover letter, paste the entire letter above the resume.)

5. Key a line of asterisks or equal signs under the words *cover letter* (or under the last line of the cover letter) to mark the end of your cover letter and the beginning of your resume.

6. Clean up any odd spacing or other formatting problems.

7. Send the message to yourself and check the format of your resume. Repeat this process until your plain text resume comes through as a clean, attractive, and readable document.

8. Save printed copies of the plain text resume and the email message containing the resume in your Career Management Files Tracker.

For Your Career Management Files Tracker

File your completed Career Action worksheets in your Career Management Files Tracker.

CA 6-1   Job Objective and Profile statements

CA 6-2   Resume outline and notes

CA 6-3   List of resume action verbs and keywords

CA 6-4   Resume first draft

CA 6-5   Final print resume and electronic file (file your resume in your Career Portfolio too)

CA 6-6   Printout of plain text resume and .txt file

Job Applications and Cover Letters

Outcomes

1. List the items needed to apply for jobs.

2. Complete employment applications.

3. Apply for jobs using a paper employment application.

4. Write cover letters that get employers' attention.

5. Apply for jobs online.

6. Assemble and use print documents in your job search.

© Photographer/Image Source

OVERVIEW You will be screened into or out of an interview (and a job) based on the quality and effectiveness of your job search package: resume, cover letter, and employment application. If you carefully completed the activities in Chapter 6, your resume should be top-notch. This chapter presents tips and activities for preparing winning employment applications and cover letters. Remember: The qualified job applicant who does only an average job of preparing these documents is screened out; applicants who prepare these documents well remain in the running for the job. Chapter 7 explains how you can market yourself by writing a results-oriented cover letter and by completing print and online applications correctly.

CHAPTER 7

CAREER ACTIONS

7-1: Create an Application Data Sheet

7-2: Complete a Paper Employment Application

7-3: Internet Research on Cover Letter Strategies

7-4: Draft of Master Cover Letter

7-5: Print Version of Master Cover Letter

JUMP START

Your Employment Application

Download two or three job applications in your career area or request printed applications from local businesses. Work with a partner to review them carefully and make a checklist of the common information that is requested on all of the forms or websites (for example, name, address, and available hours).

Make a second checklist of information that is requested on only one or some of the forms.

Make a third list of application questions, terminology, and abbreviations that you do not understand and research them online to find more information.

With your partner or as a class, discuss why you think certain information is required on all forms and other information appears on some applications but not others.

akva/Shutterstock.com

Outcome 1 Applying for Jobs

In Chapter 6, you learned how to create a winning resume—a resume that will be selected by the resume scanning software and forwarded to the hiring manager, who will read about your qualifications and experience and decide to interview you for the job.

In Chapter 7, you learn about two other items that hiring managers use to decide which applicants to interview: an employment application form and a strong cover letter that convinces the hiring manager to read the applicant's resume. Chapter 7 covers the following topics:

- Completing employment application forms (most of the information is in your resume)

- Applying for a job with a specific employer

- Writing effective cover letters

- Applying online for jobs posted at career websites and company sites

- Using your print "job search package" in your job search (cover letter, resume, and optional items such as your business card and work samples from your Career Portfolio)

- Following up with an employer after applying for a job

Outcome 2 The Employment Application

An **employment application** (or **job application**) is a form with a set of questions used to collect information about a job applicant's skills, qualifications, and experience.

Many job seekers think of the application as something to get through quickly so that they can get on with the interview. Wrong! Employers carefully consider employment application forms, cover letters, and resumes. They use these documents to select interviewees and to weed out people who do not look to be qualified on paper.

In this section, you will learn how to complete an employment application correctly and professionally. This will help ensure that your application passes the screening process.

Application Forms

Employers design application forms to get the information they consider most important to making hiring decisions. They use the forms to collect the following:

- Consistent information from every applicant so that they can compare applicants accurately and objectively

- Information needed to evaluate an applicant's qualifications and match with the job, such as the starting and ending salary for previous jobs
- Information needed to judge the type of employee the applicant would be, such as the reason for leaving each job
- Background and legal information needed to make a job offer, such as Social Security number and proof of citizenship or proof of legal right to work in the United States

Employers use a variety of application formats. The length and complexity of forms vary greatly—from preprinted paper forms to sophisticated online forms. Some applications have questions that require detailed answers. Some organizations ask questions that test applicants' knowledge of the job or career field. Treat every question seriously and answer it completely. Applicants who submit incomplete applications with mistakes are the first to be eliminated.

Many employers require online applications. Others scan paper applications and file the information electronically. Applications are searched for information (education, work experience, etc.). If you omit important information, your application may be passed over.

Preparation and Practice

Search the employer's website for an application you can print and use as a practice version. If you can't get an application ahead of time, get one from a competitor or a related organization.

If you pick up an application in person and plan to fill it in by hand, take the form home with you: do not fill it in on the spot. Ask for two copies or photocopy the application and fill in a practice form so that you can do your best work. Filling in applications by hand includes deciding how to summarize the information in your resume to fit in the space provided. Employers judge neatness, completeness, and the quality of answers. It usually takes more than one try to achieve the wording and effect you want.

Following directions is important to employers. Be sure to demonstrate this ability when you apply for a job. Read the instructions carefully and *follow them exactly*. Before you pick up your pen (black or blue ink; fine tip if possible), *read the entire application* to see how sections are related and which sections require more or less detailed answers. This will help you avoid duplicating information, ensure that you enter information in the right places, and learn what other information you may need. By the way, you can fill in a preprinted paper application with a typewriter—if you can find one.

Completing an Employment Application Form

This section has guidelines for completing the major parts of a typical preprinted paper application form (and the online version of the preprinted form). Refer to the completed sample application in Figure 7-1 on pages 152–153. Do not leave any section of a form blank. Enter "NA" or "N/A" (not applicable) if a question does not apply to you.

As you read this section, note that you will be asked to provide information that is not in your resume. So that you have all of the information with you when you complete an application, create a plain text application "data sheet" with all of the information you will need. The sole purpose of the data sheet is for your own use when filling in job applications. Because the data sheet is a plain text file, you can paste text from it into an online application form. Use Career Action 7-1 to record additional information you may need.

Personal Information

In this section, you provide your name, address, contact information, Social Security number, and information about any history with the organization. If the application asks for a current address and a permanent address, repeat your current address in the permanent address section rather than leave it blank. If the form asks for a second phone number, list a phone number where messages can be left. Provide a working email address that you check regularly. It is acceptable to write "Upon Hiring" in the field for your Social Security number.

Position Information

List a definite position objective, title, or number. If you submit your application online, the scanning software will use this information to match your application to the job you are applying for. Moreover, employers are not impressed with applicants who list "anything" as the position desired. This hints of desperation, a lack of confidence, or a lack of focus or direction.

If you can start work right away, enter "Immediately" for Date Available. If you are currently employed, think about the amount of notice you will give (typically two weeks). You may be asked about your available days, hours, or shifts and your willingness to relocate.

Because salary is such an influential factor in employment, use "negotiable" as the salary desired. Don't risk eliminating yourself before you have a chance to present your qualifications in an interview. Save any discussion of salary until the employer has expressed a definite interest in you. If the position is advertised at a set, nonnegotiable salary, list that figure.

Education

List all schools/colleges attended, your major, your degree/diploma, and your graduation dates. Figure 7-1 lists one high school and one community college.

- If you attended more than one high school, list the most recent one you attended and indicate the year you received your diploma. List your GPA only if it is requested or if it is high.

- If you have attended more than one post-secondary educational institution, list the most recent one first and work back to the first one you attended.

- If necessary, attach a separate keyed list of additional schools you attended.

If the form has a space to list additional information, include items such as subjects of study, research, special skills (such as a foreign language), or other activities; also give examples of your capabilities and activities that relate to your job objective. Summarize the information and use abbreviations if space is tight.

Employment History

List your most recent job first. Most forms ask for the month and year you started and stopped each job. If the application does not have a separate section for your military service, list it in your employment history.

Before you fill in the application, decide which information to put in the education section and which to put in the employment section.

References

List three professional or personal references. Whenever possible, tie your references directly to your work experience. Most prospective employers value good references from former reputable employers because former employers know firsthand how you performed at work. In Figure 7-1, notice how the first two references are the applicant's coworkers at previous jobs.

Some applications specify that references be people other than former employers or supervisors. Consider teachers, members of volunteer organizations, and members of your network who know your skills and capabilities. This is just one reason it is important to read every word of an application carefully.

Remember that you must talk to your references in advance and get their permission to list them on an application. See the feature "Respect Your References" for important information about safeguarding your references' telephone numbers.

Additional Information

This section, which is sometimes at the beginning of an application, collects information the employer needs to have on file before offering you a job, such as alternative names you used in the past and information about any felony and misdemeanor convictions.

If an application asks permission to contact your current employer, answer yes only if your employer is aware of your job search and approves. Otherwise, protect your current job by answering no.

You will be asked for information that protects the employer if you are hired. You must indicate that you are a U.S. citizen or have the legal right to work in the United States, and you must indicate whether you are willing to take a drug test. If you have been convicted of a felony or misdemeanor, you will be asked about the nature of the crime, when and where you were convicted, and the disposition of the case. (Note that you can only be asked about convictions; employers are not permitted to ask if you have been arrested.) Answer these questions truthfully and indicate "will discuss at interview." Your best option is to explain any negative history in person, where you must be prepared to take responsibility for your actions and explain what you learned.

The application will probably inform you that the employer may procure an investigative consumer report on you as part of considering your application. If so, the investigative report could include information about your criminal record, education, credit history, and driving record. Any misrepresentation on your part would be identified, and you would be eliminated from consideration for the job.

Sign the Application

Because an employment application is a legal document, when you sign the form, you literally take an oath that the information you provided is true and accurate (or in an online form, when you check the box indicating that the information is correct). On a more practical

MAKE IT A HABIT

Respect Your References

When you apply for a job online, you must supply a great deal of personal information. This is the price applicants "pay" for the convenience and ease of applying for jobs online.

A person cannot be a reference for you without providing a phone number for prospective employers' use. Whether or not you discuss privacy issues with your references, they expect you to guard this information.

On a printed application that you fill in by hand, it is acceptable to include your references' phone numbers.

When you complete an online application form or email a copy of your resume, do not include your references' phone number or attach a reference list with their phone numbers. Instead, enter "Upon request" in the field or on the list. A prospective employer will not call your references before meeting you, and you can provide the phone numbers during the interview.

Never include your references' email addresses in an online application. When a site will not accept an application without references' email addresses, one job applicant enters "uponrequest@uponrequest.com" in these fields. She has been selected for phone interviews by organizations when she has done this. During the interview, she gives the phone numbers verbally so that the interviewer can include them in the interview notes.

Comstock/JupiterImages

APPLICATION FOR EMPLOYMENT

ABC Company

This application is used in the selection process and both pages <u>must</u> be completed. Attach extra sheets if necessary (references to resumes are <u>NOT</u> acceptable).

A P P L I C A N T   I N F O R M A T I O N

Last Name **Martinelli**	First **Elizabeth**	M. I. **S.**	Social Security Number **999-00-0088**	Home Phone **208-555-0106**	Alternative Phone **208-555-0170**

Permanent Address – No. & Street **6518 Willow Way**	City **Boise**	State **ID**	Zip **83706**	Date **01/15/--**

Have you previously	☐ applied to OR ☐ been employed by ABC Company?	Where and when? **N/A**	E-mail Address **emartinelli@provider.net**

Do you have relatives working for the ABC Company? ☐ Yes ☒ No If yes, give names and departments where they work.

P O S I T I O N

Position Desired **Sales Supervisor**	Salary Desired (per month) **Negotiable**

Willing to relocate? ☒ Yes ☐ No	Do you want ☒ Full-time ☐ Part-time	Date Available for Work **Immediately**

E D U C A T I O N

Highest Educational Level Completed:

Name of School	Location	From	To	Degree or Diploma	Major	Minor
High School **Idaho Falls High School**	**Idaho Falls, ID**			**Diploma**		
Community College **Central Community College**	**Boise, ID**	**9/08**	**1/10**	**A.A.**	**Marketing**	
College or University						
Graduate School						
Special Training						

Languages Other Than English (if required in employment announcement):	Speak **Spanish**	Read **Spanish**	Write **Spanish**

EMPLOYMENT HISTORY & RELATED EXPERIENCE   List present or most recent experience first. Include armed services experience and volunteer work.

Employer Name **Kevington's Emporium (Part-time)**	Employer Address **3315 Front Street Boise, ID 83705**	Dates (Mo./Yr.) From **12/08** To **Present**
Position Title **Assistant Sales Supervisor**	Supervisor **Charlie Wu**	Phone **208-555-0131** Ext. **125**
Reason for Leaving **Still employed**	Salary: Start **9.00/hr** End **11.58/hr**	No. Hours Per Week: **20**

Duties:

Training, supervising, and scheduling staff of six

Promoted to Assistant Sales Supervisor after only six months

Employer Name **Crown Sportswear (Part-time)**	Employer Address **1800 Orchard Street Boise, ID 83704**	Dates (Mo./Yr.) From **5/08** To **11/08**
Position Title **Sales Clerk**	Supervisor **Connie Pratt**	Phone **208-555-0114** Ext. **418**
Reason for Leaving **Took new job**	Salary: Start **8.50/hr** End **8.50/hr**	No. Hours Per Week: **10-15**

Duties:

Sales, customer service, and design and setup of all merchandise displays

Performed managerial and closing duties for store three nights a week

Figure 7-1 Sample Employment Application Form

APPLICATION FOR EMPLOYMENT

Employer Name **Value Market Variety (Part-time)**	Employer Address **460 Park Way** **Idaho Falls, ID 83402**		Dates (Mo./Yr.) From **12/05** To **3/08**
Position Title **Salesclerk**	Supervisor **Tevia Levitt**		Phone **208-555-0199** Ext. **420**
Reason for Leaving **Moved to college location**	Salary: Start **7.00/hr** End **8.25/hr**		No. Hours Per Week: **15**

Duties:

Sales, customer service, and inventory stocking tasks

Selected "Customer Service Employee of the Month" twice in one year

Employer Name	Employer Address		Dates (Mo./Yr.) From To
Position Title	Supervisor		Phone Ext.
Reason for Leaving	Salary: Start End		No. Hours Per Week:

Duties:

REFERENCES

Name	Address	Telephone	Occupation	Years Known
Charlie Wu **(Kevington's Emporium)**	**3315 Front Street** **Boise, ID 83705**	**208-555-0131** **Ext. 125**	**Sales Manager**	**2 years**
Tevia Levitt **(Value Market Variety)**	**460 Park Way** **Idaho Falls, ID 83402**	**208-555-0199** **Ext. 420**	**Supervisor**	**3 years**
Dr. Robert Cornwell	**Business Department** **Central Community College** **8500 College Way** **Boise, ID 83704**	**208-555-0143**	**Professor, Marketing** **and Sales**	**2 years**

ADDITIONAL INFORMATION

Φ Are you currently employed? ☒Yes ☐No   May we contact your employer? ☒Yes ☐No   May we contact your former employers? ☒Yes ☐No

Can you (if accepted for employment) provide proof of your legal right to remain and work in the U.S.? ☒Yes ☐No

A separate affidavit on felony and misdemeanor convictions is REQUIRED to be completed on the attached form.

I hereby certify that all statements on this application are true and complete to the best of my knowledge and belief. If employed, I understand that any untrue statements on the above record may be considered grounds for termination.

Date *01/15/--*   Signature *Elizabeth S. Martinelli*

Figure 7-1 (Continued)

note, unsigned applications cannot be processed. You may lose valuable time—and face—if the organization has to take the extra step of asking you to sign your application.

COMPLETE **CAREER ACTION 7-1**

Create an Application Data Sheet, p. 173

Outcome 3

Apply for a Job with a Preprinted Application

Not every job application requires a cover letter and resume. A preprinted application form by itself may be all you need to apply to an organization where many people have the same job (a discount retailer or a national restaurant chain, for example). You may be able to fill in a preprinted application, or you may need to apply online through the company website or at an application kiosk. (See "Apply for Jobs Online" on pages 163–164.)

If you apply in person at a small business, you will probably be given a blank application to fill in by hand. Fill in the application at home and return the completed form with a customized version of your print resume and, optionally, a cover letter.

Follow these tips to make the best impression when you apply for a job in person with a preprinted paper job application.

- **Look the part and be ready to interview.** Never visit an employer's place of business without dressing conservatively and looking professional (business casual is fine). You could be invited to meet the manager and even interview on the spot. Be sure you get the manager's full name. Prepare by studying the interview chapters in this book, Chapters 8–11.

Explaining Gaps in Employment and Reasons for Leaving a Job

Use brief, positive phrases to explain reasons for leaving a job and periods of unemployment: "returned to school," "changed careers," "reorganization," "employment ended," "business closed," or "took a position with more responsibility." Avoid negative language ("couldn't find a job," "quit," "personal conflict," "fired for no reason") that may lead an employer to question your abilities and judgment.

If you were fired from a job, be as brief and positive as possible and leave longer explanations for the interview. Be prepared to describe what happened using unemotional and professional language. Take responsibility for your actions (don't blame others), explain what you learned from the situation, and explain how you could have handled the situation differently. It may help to write out an explanation, but your best chance at getting a job will come from explaining the situation in person. It also will be essential to have a reference who will give you a solid recommendation.

Nicholas Moore/Shutterstock.com

Be prepared to answer the question "Why do you want to work here?" This question may be tricky to answer if the job is not your ideal choice. A safe answer is "I looked at your website and was impressed by. . . ." (Be sure you have looked at the site, of course.)

- **Bring your driver's license or other proof of identification.**

- **Come alone and do not conduct any business during your visit.** Do not order food or come to the customer service desk carrying a bag of purchases.

- **Allow enough time for your visit.** You may be asked to take a survey or an employment test; so allow plenty of time for your visit. You do not want to miss out on an opportunity because you have to rush to another obligation.

- **Proofread the application carefully.** The application is your "ambassador"; make sure it represents you well. Check it for accuracy, neatness, completeness, and the quality of your answers.

- **Sign and date the application.** Your signature certifies that the information in your application is true and correct.

- **Keep a copy of the application.** Create a filing system for all of your applications. Include a sheet of paper with the manager's name and contact information and any notes about the application process.

- **Ask to meet the manager when you return the application.** Ask if you can give your application to the manager. Be gracious if the answer is no and ask for the manager's name and the name of the person who takes the application.

   If you are applying at a small business, return the application with a copy of your resume.

- **Check back in a week if you don't hear from anyone.** Call or visit if you haven't heard from the organization within a week. If you really want the job, go in person and leave a copy of your resume.

COMPLETE **CAREER ACTION 7-2**

Complete a Paper Employment Application, p. 174

Outcome 4 # Cover Letters

A **cover letter** is a letter of inquiry or introduction that introduces you to a prospective employer. *Every resume you submit should have a matching cover letter.* You state your interest in the advertised position or ask about openings in the organization. Most important of all, you answer the all-important questions in the mind of every person who reads a cover letter: "How will this person help us?" and "Should I take the time to look at the resume?"

Your cover letter must make an excellent first impression. It must be well written, be designed to get the reader's attention and interest, and provide information that convinces the reader to read your resume and offer you an interview. An effective cover letter highlights your most important qualifications and emphasizes how those qualifications can meet the employer's needs.

Even if a job listing does not mention a cover letter, employers expect you to include one. Your letter demonstrates the type of professionalism and initiative they want employees to have and shows that you take assignments seriously and do them well. The letter also indicates that you are serious about this particular job opening. Submitting your resume without a cover letter could cost you further consideration for employment.

Job seekers use three types of letters depending on their purpose and the type of job they seek.

- **Application cover letter.** The applicant responds to an advertised opening and states his or her interest in and qualifications for that job (Figure 7-5, page 167).

- **Prospecting cover letter.** The applicant writes to a prospective employer to ask about possible job openings when none have been advertised (Figure 7-6, page 168).
- **Networking letter.** A job seeker contacts a member of his or her network to request information or assistance with the job search.

Standard Cover Letter Content

Keep your cover letter brief—four or five paragraphs and no more than one page. Use the standard format for business letters and follow the structure below. Figures 7-6 and 7-7 (pages 168 and 169, respectively) are examples of proper cover letter formatting and content. You can also find many examples online.

Address, Date, and Salutation

Place your name, address, and contact information at the top of the letter followed by the date, inside address (employer's name, title, and address), and salutation ("Dear Ms. Och:").

The Opening

Introduce yourself and state your purpose. Mention the position you are applying for and explain how or where you heard about it. If you learned about it through an advertisement or announcement, include the date and where you found the notice. Explain why you are interested in the organization and state the type of job you are seeking (or use the title from the job listing).

Mention any earlier communications you have had with the person you are writing to. If you have a contact who knows the person, ask your contact if you can mention his or her name in the letter.

The following excerpt is from a networking letter by Kimi Okasaki, whose resumes for an administrative assistant position are on pages 122–124 in Chapter 6. Kimi mentions a person who is well known to the addressee.

> Carmine Garduno from the Health Services Bureau recommended that I talk with you about the possibility of your needing an administrative support person with experience in educational and community activities. I am confident that my experience as a volunteer in the Valley Elementary School Parent-Teacher Organization (VES-PTO) and the Diabetes Foundation would be useful in helping you achieve success with your new five-year education and community plan.

The Sales Pitch

This is the heart of your letter. Focus on what you have to offer—your most relevant qualifications for the job. Include two to four results-oriented descriptions of capabilities and accomplishments that show how you can benefit the employer and handle the job. Be truthful and remember that you must be able to verify these accomplishments during an interview. Do not duplicate information exactly from your resume. Express interest and enthusiasm for the job and focus on your strengths, experience, and achievements.

Somewhere in the letter, refer to the job description or something specific you know about the organization's activities or requirements. This demonstrates initiative and interest in the company.

Write one to three short paragraphs or use a bulleted list to highlight the qualifications you want to emphasize, as in this example:

> Through my volunteer work, I learned about the disease-prevention techniques your department teaches to day care workers. The potential to help families fight disease while doing work I enjoy is irresistible. I recently completed an Associate in Science degree, majoring in Information Management Technology, with an overall GPA of 3.5. As Secretary-Treasurer of the VES-PTO, I used Excel and Word to generate and track correspondence with more than 500 student families.

Figure 7-2 shows a reader-friendly way to highlight your qualifications for the job. The left column lists the key job requirements (quoted exactly from the job listing), and the right column describes your matching experience. Figure 7-2 shows the example on the previous page in a table. Use a table only in your print cover letters, not in plain text letters.

The Closing

Ask for a meeting or an interview—not a job—and indicate how and when you will follow up. State that your resume is enclosed and include a courteous sentence that expresses appreciation or thanks. Here's a good example:

> My resume is enclosed for your review. I would appreciate meeting with you to discuss the possibility of our working together. I will call you on Thursday to check on your availability, or you may reach me at 404-555-0136. I would welcome the opportunity to contribute to the exceptional community outreach efforts of the Department of Disease Prevention. Thank you for your consideration.

Tips for Writing Effective Cover Letters

Review "Write and Edit Your Resume" in Chapter 6 for guidelines about the writing style in resumes. The advice to write clearly and concisely also applies to your cover letters. In addition:

- **Don't duplicate the wording in your resume.** Also make sure your letter does not contradict anything in your resume.

- **Be positive.** Share your positive qualities. Project confidence and show interest in the job.

- **Write clearly and concisely.** Work on your master cover letter until you are sure that every word counts. You will be more motivated to customize the letter for other job listings when you start with an excellent letter.

- **Don't use overblown or empty words to describe your abilities.** Use specific, measurable terms; for example, "My program increased reported customer satisfaction by 35%."

Job Requirements	My Qualifications
GPA of 3.0 or higher	Word processing and data processing experience
	I completed an Associate of Science degree, majoring in Information Management Technology, with an overall GPA of 3.5.
Interest in health and disease prevention	Through my volunteer work, I learned about the disease prevention techniques your department teaches to day care workers. I am highly motivated by the desire to help families and fight disease.
Community involvement	I am actively involved in community volunteer work and serve as Secretary-Treasurer of the VES-PTO.
	I use Word and Excel to generate and track correspondence with more than 500 families.

Figure 7-2 Employer's Requirements and Applicant's Qualifications

MAKE IT A HABIT

Show Off Your Writing Skills

Use your cover letters to show employers that you have business writing skills. Work on your letter (and get help from your network) until it is concise, articulate, and convincing. An error-free, grammatically correct letter shows that you are conscientious and detail-oriented.

Never allow slang, informal language, or texting abbreviations to sneak into your job search correspondence. Use well-crafted sentences and businesslike language to demonstrate your professionalism and readiness to communicate in the workplace.

You can write more concisely if you avoid clichés, dated expressions, and "inflated" words. Here are some common examples and alternatives:

Clichéd/Dated	Concise
At this point in time	Now
Ballpark figure	Estimate
Explore every avenue	Explore the options
In a timely manner	On time; promptly
In the event that	If
In the near future	Soon
Last but not least	Finally
State-of-the-art	Latest

Complex/Wordy	Concise
Advantageous	Helpful
Attempt; endeavor	Try
Equitable	Fair
Initiated	Started
Possess	Have
Proficiency; proficient	Skill; skilled
Regarding	About
Remainder	Rest
Timely	Prompt
Transmit	Send
Utilized	Used

- **Be truthful.** Never misrepresent yourself or give false information. Be honest about your education, background, and experience.

- **Emphasize your skills as a team player.** Don't try to convince the employer that you are a one-person miracle worker.

- **Incorporate specialized terminology** from your industry and job target where appropriate.

- **Do your research.** Make sure you have researched the organization and/or the job enough to make informed comments. A statement suggesting that you are unfamiliar with the employer will eliminate you from consideration.

- **Read the letter aloud.** "Listening" to your cover letter will give you distance from your writing and help you judge the letter from the reader's perspective. Do you sound likable and sincerely interested in working for *this* company? Are *you* convinced to give your application a closer look?

Customize the Content

Cover letters require thought and effort and can be difficult to write. To avoid the stress of writing a letter from scratch for every job application, write a master cover letter and then take the time to tailor the content of the letter to emphasize your fit with the job you are applying for. Edit the text to match the job title, objectives, and requirements of each job.

- **Demonstrate your knowledge of the organization or industry.** Use your company research to personalize the letter. Mention your interest in a new or popular product or service; the expansion of the firm; recent organizational accomplishments; the company's reputation (for example, the quality of its products or services, excellent customer service, or community involvement); or a special achievement of the person you're writing to or the organization in general. Mention only one thing and keep your praise short.

- **Emphasize how you can meet the employer's needs.** Restating the duties and qualifications in the job listing or advertisement shows how you meet them. For example, consider an applicant who has the education and work experience to apply for customer support jobs and IT jobs in both the accounting and insurance industries. Each letter (and resume) should use concrete, specific terminology and examples that highlight the writer's qualifications, experience, and education and training in the field (customer support or IT) and the industry (accounting or insurance) of the job opening.

- **Edit the text carefully.** Check every part of the letter, including the date, inside address, salutation, name of the organization, and job title.

Even when you are starting with an excellent master cover letter, do not underestimate the time you will need to write a convincing letter that tells the reader that you have done your homework and are genuinely interested in the organization and the position. Because customizing your cover letter typically takes more time than customizing your resume, plan accordingly.

Address the Letter Appropriately

A job advertisement will indicate the address of the person or department that should receive the cover letter and resume. Use the person's full name and title in the inside address. Use "Ms." for a woman.

With a prospecting cover letter, you may not know the name of the person who should receive the letter. Some organizations do not accept unsolicited cover letters and resumes. Applicants who address communications to the human resources department may receive a form letter stating that no applications are currently being accepted.

To boost your chances of getting an interview, address a prospecting letter to the person who has hiring authority for the position. Never address your cover letter "To Whom It May Concern." This type of salutation may target your letter for the wastebasket.

How do you get the right person's name? If you do not yet know the person to address your cover letter to, consider one of these methods:

- Call your target employer and say that you are researching careers and want to write to the person who specializes in your area. Get the person's full name and title and verify the spelling and mailing address or email. When you call, introduce yourself and thank the person by name for his or her help. Always say that you are a student or that you are doing research. The person you speak to could help you later, and using names establishes a courteous, friendly tone.

- Search the organization's website for an organizational chart or contact information. If this is not available, contact the human resources office (if your target employer has one). Ask whether there is an organizational chart you could use for your career planning class or personal research. The chart should provide you with the name of the department head to whom you should address your cover letter.

If these methods are not effective, ask members of your job search network to help you devise a workable approach. As a last resort, address the prospecting letter to a Hiring Manager, Department Head, or Human Resources Department and use the address from the organization's website.

You also need to decide which department to send the resume and letter to. If you send your cover letter and resume only to the human resources department, the hiring manager in the department you are interested in may never see them. On the other hand, if you send your prospecting letter and resume directly to the person you would work for, your chances of getting an interview will be increased, but the

"**Your cover letter** tells the reader who you are. Look at examples online, but write about *you*."

human resources department may resent being circumvented.

How do you handle this situation? If the employer is accepting applications, send one letter and resume to the human resources department and one letter and resume to the department head. Indicate in your letters that you have sent similar communications to each party. At worst, both letters wind up in the human resources department. If the employer is not officially accepting applications, send your cover letter and resume to the department head only. You could still get an interview.

Revise and Edit the Letter

Carefully review and edit the draft of your cover letter before sending it. Be choosy—downright hypercritical—about every word. Every word counts! Use the spell checker, but also read your letter carefully for errors. Mistakes can be costly. Any error in spelling, punctuation, or grammar can lead the reader to believe that you are careless and prone to making mistakes.

Most people find it difficult to edit their own resumes and cover letters because they overlook important aspects (such as punctuation and omission of details) while concentrating on the wording. Ask a friend or a contact who has strong communication skills and knows your background to evaluate your letter. Your contact may think of additional items to include that you have overlooked. Choose a good writer who will give you honest criticism. Consider asking:

- A hiring expert you know who can tell you how your cover letter stacks up against the ones he or she reviews and can suggest how you can improve yours.

- A friend or an acquaintance who knows you and your work well enough to help you clar-

ify confusing statements or to spot where you have left out important information or qualifications.

- A professional who does not know you well who is willing to serve as a final test for your cover letter. Make it clear that the cover letter is not yet final and that you are seeking suggestions for improvement.

COMPLETE **CAREER ACTION 7-3**

Internet Research on Cover Letter Strategies, p. 174

Format the Cover Letter

As you do for the resume, you need two cover letter formats: (1) a print letter (.doc or .pdf) that can be sent through the mail and attached to an online application or an email message and (2) a plain text letter (.txt file) that can be pasted into the cover letter field of online application or into the body of an email message.

Print Cover Letter

Every job applicant needs to have a **print cover letter** that is formatted like a standard business letter. To develop your print cover letter, consider customizing a template or sample from a job search website or begin with one of the Microsoft Word templates or wizards.

Use a clean overall format to make your letter visually appealing. Follow these formatting guidelines and look at the letters on pages 167–169.

- Format the letterhead to match your resume. Include the same contact information, formatted the same way, as in your resume. If your resume letterhead is in color, use the same color in the letter. Do not use color for any other part of the letter.

- Print the letter on the same paper you use for your resume (white or cream-colored 8 1/2-inch by 11-inch paper). If the paper has a watermark, print the letter with the watermark facing up and toward the reader. Use a laser printer, not an ink-jet printer.

- Use the standard format for business letters.

- Use one-inch margins and center the letter on the page. Do not write more than one page.

- Use one simple, standard font such as Times Roman, Arial, or Calibri in size 11 or 12 point.

- Single-space the body text and double-space between paragraphs and sections.

- Use bulleted lists to break up lengthy paragraphs.

- Do not assume that the employer will print your letter or resume unless you are scheduled for an interview. Most print cover letters and resumes are read online to save time. Do not put the letterhead in the document header.

- Use one space after periods at the end of sentences. Use periods in your degree (B.A. instead of BA).

- Don't use excessive decorative fonts and formatting (such as underlining, shadows, backgrounds, or colored text). These elements will look unprofessional.

- Use the standard left-margin alignment.

- Avoid distracting or elaborate graphics.

- Hand-sign every print cover letter. Create a PDF file (recommended format) online;

Don't Forget Your Business Card

Take the time to create matching business cards when you design and format your cover letter. Cards are invaluable when you network and interview. (Exchanging business cards with the interviewer is more professional and more natural than simply taking the person's card.) A business card is also an impressive addition to a print job search package.

If you are employed and changing jobs or careers, do not use your card from your current job.

Use a smaller version of your letterhead formatted closely to match your cover letter and resume. If you want your card to be more eye-catching, consider using the same font for your name as in the letterhead. Your card should look as professional as possible. If some of the text is in color (a good idea), use color sparingly; do not make your card "shout" to be heard.

Now that you know how to write effective resumes and cover letters, consider bartering with a graphic artist for a professional card. If you design your card yourself, look at the design, spacing, and wording on other cards to get ideas. Most business cards use a smaller font to achieve generous white space.

In days past when printing was more expensive, business cards were printed on one side only. Consider using the back of the card for a bulleted list of your major qualifications or a short statement that tells the reader who you are. Keep this text short with generous margins.

You can print business cards:

- Using precut card stock and your laser printer.
- At your local copy shop.
- Through one of the many websites that sell low-cost (sometimes free) business cards.

do not scan the .doc file. Insert a graphic file with your signature into the Word file.

- Make the final letter perfect—no errors! Proofread and proofread again!

Plain Text Cover Letter

You also need a **plain text cover letter**, a text file (.txt) with no formatting (no bold, no tables, no bullets, etc.). You will use this version of your cover letter to complete online application forms that have a text field for inserting the text of a cover letter. Pasting in unformatted text is the only way to ensure that the job application database displays the text properly. Follow these guidelines to create and format the plain text version of your letter.

- To create the plain text file, save your print cover letter as a .doc file with a different filename, edit the text, and save the file as a .txt file. Check the formatting and look for long lines of text that run off the screen. Insert hard returns to divide these long lines into lines of 65 characters, including spaces.

- Keep your cover letter concise but clear. An email cover letter should be only two or three paragraphs long and under 150 words. It should reveal your interest and sell the target employer on one or two of your outstanding capabilities.

- Follow standard business letter guidelines. Even though email is less formal than a paper letter, you should not omit parts of the letter such as the salutation or closing.

- If you paste the letter in the body of an email message, use a brief, informative subject line that stimulates the reader to open the email and read the letter. Consider a subject line such as "Experienced CPA for Auditing Director" rather than "Re: Job No. 3872."

- Make the most of keywords. Focus on keywords that will increase the chances of your letter being retrieved in a database search. Because of the possibility of a database search, it is more important to use noun phrases than action verbs in an electronic cover letter.

- Provide sufficient contact information for the prospective employer. This includes your name, address, phone number, and email address.

Ask Your Network to Review Your Cover Letter

Employers base hiring decisions largely on trust and are more likely to consider letters that mention people they know. Members of your network are statistically the strongest source of job leads and can form the bridge to your perfect job. They can give you suggestions for improving your letters and resumes and can put you in touch with prospective employers in your field. Consider the following networking options:

- Make an appointment to meet in person with the most viable member(s) of your network. Briefly review your job objective and ask for recommendations. Give each person a copy of your cover letter to review. Do not expect the person to review the letter on the spot.

- Call the person. If you cannot arrange an appointment, make a telephone call. Briefly review your job objective and ask for recommendations. Ask if you can send a copy of your cover letter and resume to get your contact's feedback.

- Send a networking letter or email. If you cannot arrange a meeting or reach the person by telephone, send a networking letter or email. Professionally and politely identify your job target and job search goals and request specific assistance or feedback on your cover letter and/or resume. See Chapter 4, page 69, for an example.

COMPLETE | **CAREER ACTION 7-4**

Draft of Master Cover Letter, p. 175

COMPLETE **CAREER ACTION 7-5**

Print Version of Master Cover Letter, p. 177

Outcome 5 Apply for Jobs Online

If you have applied for a job in the 21st century, you probably have firsthand experience with submitting your resume and cover letter online. This section describes the basic process of applying for jobs online.

REMEMBER: If the job listing includes the name of the employer, apply through the company's website too. If the listing includes the name of the hiring manager for this position, also send a copy of your print resume package.

Register with a Career Site

You must register with a career site to apply for the jobs posted there. Registration for job seekers is free because the sites earn their revenue from the fees that employers pay and from advertisements. Some professional organizations charge nonmembers a fee to use their sites. If you have an informal email address, create a free account using the name on your resume and letter. If you register at several sites, create a highly secure password to use at all of them—and don't forget what it is.

You create a profile when you register, with your contact information, job objective(s), career field(s), and skills and qualifications. Your profile is posted at the site where employers can find it; so use as many keywords as you can.

Submit a Job Application

The product website has a PDF file with screen shots of a typical online application form (www.cengage.com/career/yourcareer; OnlineApplication.pdf).

Because you can see only part of the application at a time, the top of each page in the example application has a diagram of the steps in the application process that shows where

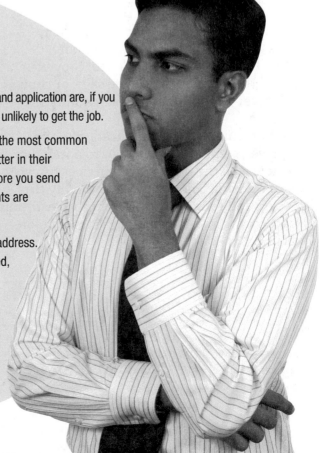

WATCH OUT!

Did You Forget Anything?

No matter how qualified you are and how well written your cover letter and application are, if you forget something important, you will be viewed as careless and will be unlikely to get the job.

According to a recent Career Builder survey about cover letters, one of the most common errors made by applicants is forgetting to enclose a resume or cover letter in their envelope or neglecting to attach a document to an email message. Before you send an envelope or email, take a moment to make sure all of your documents are enclosed or attached. Don't forget . . .

Contact information. Always include your phone number and email address. Because applications, cover letters, and resumes can become separated, it is essential that your contact information is on all documents.

The date, salutation, or closing on the cover letter. Use proper business letter format and include all sections of the letter.

Your signature. On a cover letter, the signature shows your personal attention. On an application, your signature is required to certify and validate your information.

you are in the process (Figure 7-3). Notice that at this job site, you attach your resume and cover letter before you start filling in the form. An excellent print resume and print cover letter are as essential in the new world as they were when employers and job seekers used the help wanted section in newspapers to find each other.

You can fill in most of the fields by pasting in text from the application data sheet you created in Career Action 7-1. Employers get a report with the data you enter into the form and the print copies of your resume and cover letter.

Figure 7-4 shows the first page of a job application at an employer's website. The applicant attaches the print resume file and pastes the contents of the plain text cover letter into a text field.

Apply via Email

Some employers ask applicants to apply by sending an email with the cover letter and resume attached. Put the title or number of the job listing and your name in the subject line. Attach PDF files of your print cover letter and print resume if the organization does not specify a file format.

Use the default email font. In the body of the email, you can write a brief note saying that the files are attached, copy your cover letter into the email message, or copy your cover letter and your resume into the message.

Before emailing your application to the employer, send it to yourself or to a friend to see how well the documents survive the cyberspace transfer. You may need to modify the spacing and formatting. Always proofread your attachments and the data in the form before you click "Send."

Do not attach files to the email application unless the employer requests them. Some organizations block emails that contain attachments. Because no one wants to receive an email with a lot of attachments, do not attach items from your Career Portfolio. Save them for the interview.

Outcome 6 Distribute Your Print Job Search Package

Because you will apply for most jobs through career sites and company websites, your typical "job search package" will consist of your completed online application and a print cover letter and print resume that you upload when you submit your online application. This section covers several ways to use your print job search package.

Mail Your Job Search Package or Deliver It in Person

If you mail your print job search package or deliver it in person, put the documents in a large white envelope so that you do not have to fold them. Documents that lie flat on the desk are easier to read and easier to scan into the computer.

Address the envelope to a real person. Print the recipient's address and your return address on labels or directly on the envelope. You can also write the address neatly in black ink. Place your cover letter on top with your business card clipped to it. If your resume is longer than one page, clip the pages together with a paper clip and place it under the cover letter. Place the reference list behind the resume. Then add a few impressive items from your Career Portfolio. Use only a few items; save some for the interview.

Home   Search openings   Search results   Job details   Submit resume   Resume profile information   Submit attachments   Questions   Additional information   Confirmation   ? Help

Figure 7-3 Typical Online Application Process

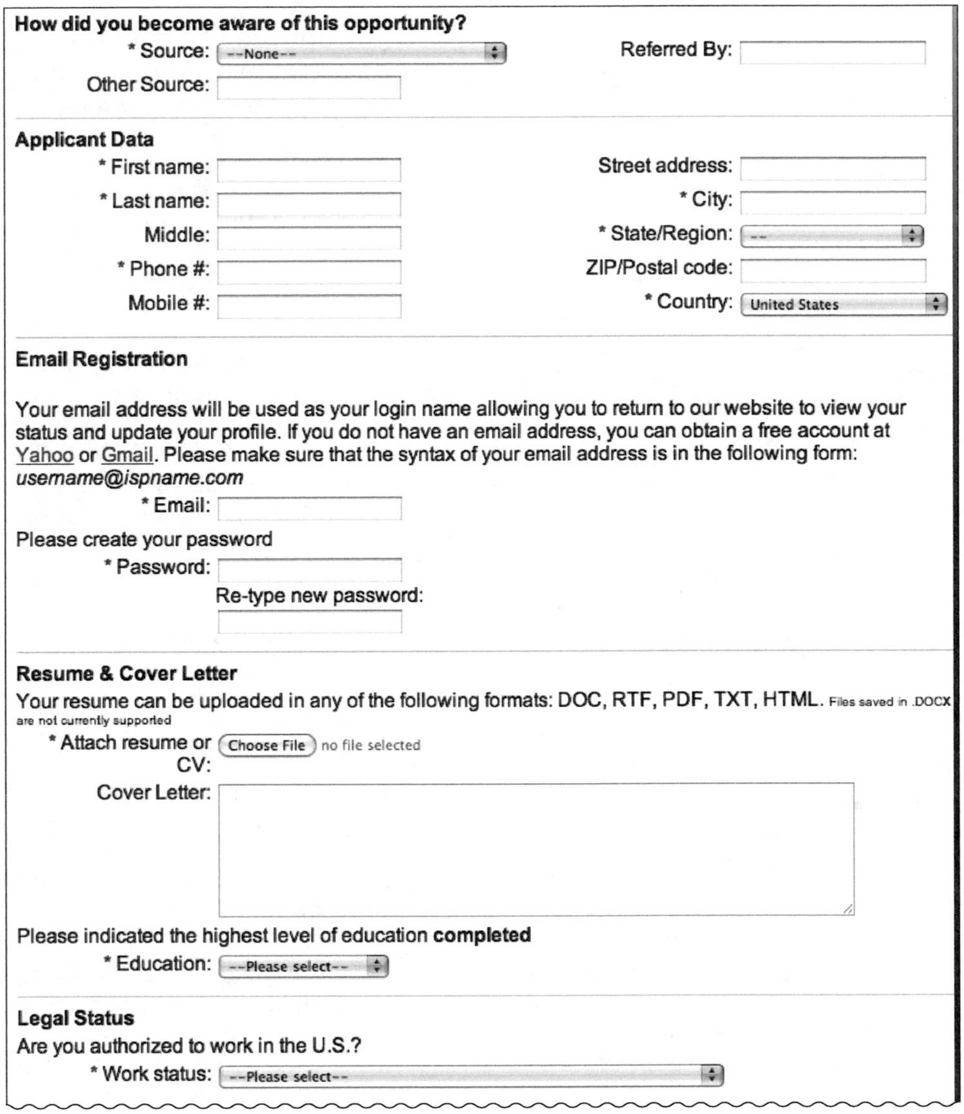

How did you become aware of this opportunity?

* Source: [--None-- ▼] Referred By: [   ]

Other Source: [   ]

Applicant Data

* First name: [   ] Street address: [   ]

* Last name: [   ] * City: [   ]

Middle: [   ] * State/Region: [-- ▼]

* Phone #: [   ] ZIP/Postal code: [   ]

Mobile #: [   ] * Country: [United States ▼]

Email Registration

Your email address will be used as your login name allowing you to return to our website to view your status and update your profile. If you do not have an email address, you can obtain a free account at Yahoo or Gmail. Please make sure that the syntax of your email address is in the following form: *username@ispname.com*

* Email: [   ]

Please create your password

* Password: [   ]

Re-type new password:

[   ]

Resume & Cover Letter

Your resume can be uploaded in any of the following formats: DOC, RTF, PDF, TXT, HTML. Files saved in .DOCX are not currently supported

* Attach resume or (Choose File) no file selected
CV:

Cover Letter: [   ]

Please indicated the highest level of education **completed**

* Education: [--Please select-- ▼]

Legal Status

Are you authorized to work in the U.S.?

* Work status: [--Please select-- ▼]

Figure 7-4 First Page of Application on Company Website

If the envelope contains items from your portfolio, have it weighed at the post office. Don't risk missing the deadline for applications because you didn't put enough stamps on the envelope.

Other Ways to Use Your Print Job Search Package

Your print job search package will be useful in many other situations, including:

- Unsolicited job applications and applications for unadvertised job openings.

- Job interviews. Take several copies of your print cover letter, resume, and Career Portfolio items to interviews.

- A physical "thank-you package" after a telephone interview. Clip the envelope with your handwritten thank-you note to your resume.

Follow Up with the Employer

Do not rely on just your cover letter and resume to get job interviews. It's a mistake to mail your print application package to several organizations and then wait for the telephone to ring. Applicants who contact the organization demonstrate initiative and increase their name recognition.

- If you applied by mail, contact the person you sent your application to.

- If you applied through the company's website, contact the human resources department and tell the receptionist which position you applied for (have the reference number when you call) and ask for the hiring manager's name, phone number, and email address.

- If you applied through a career site to a job listing that includes that hiring manager's name, contact the manager directly.

- If you applied for several jobs through a career site or if the job listing did not include the manager's name, decide whether getting the information is the best use of your time.

Keep the conversation or email brief. Here's an example of a phone call:

> Hello, _____. Thank you for taking my call. I'm Jennifer Ortiz calling from Raleigh. I applied for the system support programming job and wanted to make sure you received it.

Sample Cover Letters

The following sample cover letters are on pages 167–170:

- Figure 7-5: Sample Application Cover Letter (Printed)

- Figure 7-6: Sample Prospecting Cover Letter (Bullet Style)

- Figure 7-7: Sample Prospecting Cover Letter (Two-Column, Comparison-List Style)

- Figure 7-8: Sample Email Cover Letter with Resume Inside Message

Kimi Okasaki

148 Barrister Street • Tucson, AZ 85726

(520) 555-0136 • kimi.okasaki@email.com • linkedin.com/in/kimi.okasaki

---

April 20, 20—

Mr. George O'Donnell
Office Manager
MegaMall Property Management Company
P.O. Box 555
Tucson, AZ 85726

Dear Mr. O'Donnell:

EXPERIENCED ADMINISTRATIVE ASSISTANT, JOB #4864

Please accept my application for the administrative assistant position advertised on the *Arizona Bugle* website. As secretary-treasurer of the Valley Elementary School Parent-Teacher Organization, I appreciated MegaMall's offer to let us hold our promotional event in the center of the mall last fall at no charge. I would welcome the chance to work in a civic-minded organization.

I am an energetic, detail-oriented person who has strong administrative and computer skills, retail and community service experience, and the ability to work well with others. I have held positions of responsibility in three community organizations over the last three years.

As you can see from my resume, I thrive in a busy atmosphere that involves many different tasks, the opportunity to work with people, the satisfaction of meeting deadlines, and the chance to excel. I would enjoy the opportunity to talk with you about how I can help MegaMall Property Management with its administrative needs. I will call you next week to request an appointment, or you may call me at your convenience at the number above. Thank you for your consideration.

Sincerely,

Kimi Okasaki

Kimi Okasaki

Enclosure

Figure 7-5 Sample Application Cover Letter

Kate Foresman
2689 Canyon Avenue
Riverside, CA 92502
(951) 555-0179 | kforesman@email.com
linkedin.com/in/katelouiseforesman

June 29, 20—

Ms. Stephanie Nolan
Manager, Auditing Staff
Nolan Henry O'Leary Public Accountants
1410 Granada Avenue, 7th Floor
San Francisco, CA 94115

Dear Ms. Nolan:

Meagan Gerena at Smythe and Associates indicated that you are interested in hiring an experienced accounting graduate. My degree and special interest are in Accounting/Information Systems. Please consider me for a place on your well-respected auditing team, which the *San Francisco Business Reporter* recently named one of the Top 10 auditing firms in the area.

During the last two years, I have worked for a CPA firm where I developed a wide range of accounting and accounting-related skills. My responsibilities included:

- Performing full-charge bookkeeper duties, such as opening, posting, and closing the books; completing federal and state corporate tax returns; and creating templates using Excel.
- Assisting a consultant in upgrading software for a customized accounting system.
- Creating a procedures manual that identified common operating, maintenance, and troubleshooting situations that could occur between the two operating systems and that provided steps for reconciling those problems in a timely and cost-effective way.

During my senior year at the University of Los Angeles, I had the chance to lead an internship research team. We studied the operations of a local accounting firm and assisted its auditors in the audit of several clients. These experiences cemented my interest in auditing as a career.

I am confident in my ability to make a positive contribution to Nolan Henry O'Leary Public Accountants and am enclosing my resume for your review. I will call next week about your interview schedule, or you may reach me at the contact information above. I look forward to meeting you.

Respectfully,

Kate Foresman

Kate Foresman

Enclosure

Figure 7-6 Sample Prospecting Cover Letter (Bullet Style)

TIFFANY WHITAKER

10806 Deleware Avenue | Camden, NJ 08105
(856) 555-0195 | tiffany.whitaker@email.com
Linkedin.com/in/tiffany.whitaker

January 10, 20—

Mr. Gary Whaley
District Sales Manager
Computeriferals Company
1 Computer Way
Camden, NJ 08102

Dear Mr. Whaley:

Computeriferals has earned my respect. I have used and repaired peripherals from most of the leading manufacturers in my studies as a Business Systems/Computer Repair major and in my job as a sales representative at ComputerChoice. I know you build quality products, and I want to sell quality products—Computeriferals.

Careful review of my qualifications and the requirements of a sales representative at Computeriferals suggest that I am well qualified for a sales position with your organization.

Your Requirements	**My Experience**
• Ability to handle multiple prospects	• Expanded customer base from 137 to 183 accounts in the past year—a 34% increase
• Proven ability to meet sales goals	• Increased yearly sales from $743,000 to $1,236,000—exceeded goal by 66%
• Ability to expand sales in existing accounts	• Negotiated a new $250,000 service contract for an existing client with five locations
• Strong communication and follow-up skills	• Attained 100% customer retention through a service-first approach and frequent communication

The expanding market for Computeriferals presents an appealing challenge. Even if you have no current sales openings, I would appreciate meeting with you to discuss your requirements. My resume is enclosed for your convenience. I will call next week to request an appointment, or you may reach me at the contact information above. Thank you for your time.

Respectfully,

Tiffany Whitaker

Tiffany Whitaker

Enclosure

Figure 7-7 Sample Prospecting Cover Letter (Two-Column List)

EXPERIENCED ADMINISTRATIVE ASSISTANT, JOB #4864-10

File Edit View Insert Format Tools Message Help

From: Kimi Okasaki <'kimi.okasaki@email.com'>
To: 'hiring.manager@megamallmanagement.com' <'hiring.manager@megamallmanagement.com'>
Cc:
Subject: EXPERIENCED ADMINISTRATIVE ASSISTANT, JOB #4864-10

Dear Hiring Manager:

Please accept my application for the administrative assistant position advertised on the *Arizona Bugle* website. As secretary-treasurer of the Valley Elementary School Parent-Teacher Organization, I appreciated MegaMall's offer to let us hold our promotional event in the center of the mall last fall at no charge. I would welcome the chance to work in a civic-minded organization.

I am an energetic, detail-oriented person who has strong administrative and computer skills, retail and community service experience, and the ability to work well with others. I have held positions of responsibility in three community organizations over the last three years.

As you can see from my resume below, I thrive in a busy atmosphere that involves many different tasks, the opportunity to work with people, the satisfaction of meeting deadlines, and the chance to excel. I would enjoy the opportunity to talk with you about how I can help MegaMall Property Management with its administrative needs. I will call you next week to request an appointment, or you may call me at your convenience at the number below. Thank you for your consideration.

Sincerely,
Kimi Okasaki
kimi.okasaki@email.com
==
Kimi Okasaki Resume
Kimi Okasaki
148 Barrister Street, Tucson, AZ 85726, (520) 555-0136
kimi.okasaki@email.com, linkedin.com/in/kimi.okasaki

OBJECTIVE
Administrative Assistant position for MegaMall Property Management Inc.

QUALIFICATIONS
– Advanced word processing (Word 2010 for Windows; Word 2011 for Mac)
– Spreadsheet generation with Excel and Apple Numbers
– Database design and maintenance using Access and Oracle
– Experienced in use of PDF files and FTP
– Keyboarding at 75 words per minute
– Write and proofread printed and electronic business correspondence, reports, newsletters
– Presentation preparation using PowerPoint and Presentation software
– Internet research and email correspondence using Outlook and Explorer
– Bookkeeping using QuickBooks Pro and ten-key at 250 strokes per minute
– Proven ability to work successfully with store managers, delivery companies, community organizations, and the general public

EDUCATION
Associate of Applied Science, A.S.A., 2012, Westfield Community College, Tucson, AZ
Major: Administrative Office Technology, GPA 3.6

EXPERIENCE
Community Volunteer, Tucson, AZ. December 2009 to December 2011

National Diabetes Foundation
– Developed and customized Excel spreadsheet report to track three fund-raising activities
– Reduced reporting time by 50%

Secretary-Treasurer, Valley Elementary School Parent-Teacher Organization
– Published electronic newsletters and maintained correspondence
– Tracked budget in QuickBooks Pro; satisfied yearly CPA audits

Meals on Wheels
– Developed and maintained Access database for survey responses from 1,200 participants

Department Supervisor, Part-Time
Katz Department Store. Tucson, AZ. March 2009 to December 2010
– Supervised four salesclerks; trained new salesclerks
– Computed daily cash receipts; balanced two registers
– Attained highest part-time sales volume; had fewest sales returned
– Coordinated weekly deliveries and returns; managed annual inventory

Salesclerk, Floater.
Value Variety. Tucson, AZ. Summers 2008, 2009
– Provided complete customer service in sales and returns
==

Figure 7-8 Sample Email Cover Letter with Resume Inside Message

Chapter Checklist

Underline each action you are already taking and circle the actions you need to work on.

- Fill out employment application forms perfectly. 2

- Tailor my cover letters to specific employers; make sure the cover letters are error-free. 4

- Write a persuasive body of the cover letter that states the position I'm applying for, lists my related abilities, and asks for a meeting or an interview. 4

- Get employers' attention with results-oriented examples in my cover letter. 4

- Ask my network for feedback on and assistance with my cover letters and applications. 4

- Format my electronic cover letters correctly. 5

- Distribute a complete job search paper package; maximize my online job search process. 6

- Demonstrate initiative by calling prospective employers a few days after submitting my cover letter and resume. 6

Critical-Thinking Questions

1. What are the possible consequences of not filling out an employment application completely and according to the instructions? 2

2. Should you mention a salary figure in an application? Explain. 2

3. How is an online application different from a print application? 2

4. Think of a probable employer with whom you would like to interview. How can you learn to whom you should address your cover letter? Write the name, title, and address of the person in your answer. 4

5. What are three features of an electronic cover letter? 4

6. What are three ways to submit a cover letter to an employer? 6

Want access to career resources, study tools, activities, and job information links? Get started at www.cengage.com/career/ yourcareer.

For each of the following cover letter excerpts, explain how it fails to meet the guidelines in the chapter. Rewrite the paragraphs to make them more acceptable for an effective cover letter. (Invent supporting details and evidence as needed.)

- Even though most of my experience is in retail, I think nursing is a field where I could be successful because I am totally into helping people.

- I just love to design computer graphics to enhance specialized publications. It was the only thing I liked about my last job.

- In my volunteer work with Habitat for Humanity, all of my supervisors said that I was one heck of a carpenter. By the age of 5, I was already able to make a wooden birdhouse.

- I'm a talented mechanic, and I really need this job because my rent is expensive.

- Working for Grant Brokerage Company will give me the experience I need to become a certified financial planner. I don't know a lot about the stock market yet, but I'm sure I'll learn quickly on the job.

Working with a partner, use the guidelines in this chapter to create a checklist of 15 criteria for evaluating cover letters. (Use the resume evaluation checklist in the Trial Run in Chapter 6 as a model.) Make sure you include criteria for presentation and content, writing style, addressing letters, formatting, and distribution. Devise a rating scale (for example, 1 to 5) and use your checklist to evaluate a sample cover letter you have written or one from an Internet resource.

CAREER ACTION   7-1 Create an Application Data Sheet ②

A preprinted application form requires information that will not be on your resume. Use this list to collect the information you will need; the product website has a form for recording the information. You will also need your resume and reference list. All forms ask for details about your work history, sometimes for the last five years. Attach additional sheets if necessary—another reason not to fill in the application on the spot.

A completed employment form is an official document, and you can be denied employment or fired if you aren't truthful about the information you supply, including details about previous jobs. (It is acceptable to write *Upon Hiring* in the social security field.) Your signature indicates that the information is complete and accurate.

- Days and hours available to work; hours you can work weekly; if you can work nights; if you want full- or part-time work.

- How you will get to work; driver's license number; type of license, expiration date; number of moving violations and accidents in the last three years.

- If not a U.S. citizen, type of visa and expiration date.

- Armed forces (specialty, date entered, discharge date). You will also be asked if you are a member of the National Guard.

- Criminal history: conviction, nature of offense, state where offense occurred, sentence imposed by the court. (You cannot be denied employment solely because of a conviction record unless the offense is related to the job you are applying for.)

- For every job you have held in the last five years: name of employer, full address, name and phone number of last supervisor, employment dates (month and year), hours per week, starting and ending salary, last job title, reason for leaving (be specific). Forms also have a space for describing duties performed, skills used or learned, and advancements and promotions.

- Many applications have a space where you can summarize your full qualifications for the position you are applying for.

- Names and phone numbers of three personal or professional contacts.

- Emergency contact information.

CAREER ACTION   7-2   **Complete a Paper Employment Application** ③

If possible, obtain an employment application form from an employer in your target industry—even one from your target employer. Using an application from your target industry provides the best preparation and practice. If one is not available, use the application form on the product website or search the Internet for "sample job applications." Many samples are available on websites such as Quintessential Careers and About.com's Job Searching page. Complete the application for practice and use it as a model when you fill out actual applications for employment.

CAREER ACTION   7-3   **Internet Research on Cover Letter Strategies** ④

Visit the websites below and other sites to find five new strategies for writing a successful cover letter. Links are at the product website. Look for new ideas that may be useful to you. Copy or summarize the information and file it in your Career Management Files Tracker. If you find new information or information that varies from that in this textbook, research further and discuss the topic(s) in the classroom, with your school's career services staff, and/or with interview specialists.

- *Career Transitions*
- Monster.com
- Job-Applications.com
- About.com: Job Searching (http://jobsearch.about.com)

- O*NET OnLine (onetonline.org)
- Quintessential Careers
- The Riley Guide

CAREER ACTION 7-4 Draft of Master Cover Letter ④

Part 1: Use this worksheet or the worksheet on the website to organize and outline your master cover letter. Don't try to write a perfect letter at this point; just work on getting the essence of your message on paper. You will refine it later. Use the sample cover letters in Figures 7-5, 7-6, and 7-7 for guidance.

Part 2: Using your cover letter outline and related job target research information, compose a cover letter draft. Make it concise, tailored to the employer's needs, and courteous. Most importantly, make sure it demonstrates how you can benefit the employer. File your draft in your Career Management Files Tracker.

Part 1: Cover Letter Outline

Text for Your Letterhead:
(Name, address, phone
number, email address, and
LinkedIn URL)

_____

_____

_____

Date:

_____

_____

Inside Address:
(Recipient's name, title,
organization, and address)

_____

_____

_____

Salutation: Dear
(Put a colon after the
person's name.)

_____

Paragraph 1 (Opening):
(Include the name
of a referral if you
have one.)

_____

_____

_____

_____

_____

_____

Paragraph 2 (Sales Pitch):
(Tailor it to the job listing. Where appropriate, use bullets or side-by-side columns to highlight strong job-relevant qualifications. See Figure 7-2.)

_____

_____

_____

_____

_____

_____

_____

_____

_____

_____

_____

Paragraph 3 (Closing):
(Mention your attached or enclosed resume and request a meeting or an interview. Include your telephone number and email address. Thank the reader.)

_____

_____

_____

_____

_____

_____

_____

Complimentary Close:
(Leave enough room for your signature and key your name under it.)

Sincerely,

_____

(Key your name here.)

CAREER ACTION   **7-5 Print Version of Master Cover Letter** ④

Working in a Word file, polish the draft of your master cover letter, emphasizing your qualifications and making the content clear and concise. (If you've created your cover letter in *Career Transitions*, save it to your computer and open it in Word.) Use a thesaurus to find words with just the right meaning. As you prepare your final cover letter, remember that, just as with a resume,

IT MUST BE PERFECT!

Review your cover letter carefully. When you think your letter is perfect, ask an outside critic to review it for awkward or unclear wording, looking for even the smallest error. Print the final letter on top-quality paper.

Save the Word file as a .doc file with a new filename. Format the letter as a plain text version (limit lines of text in paragraphs to 65 characters and put a hard return at the end of each line). Save the plain text cover letter as a .txt file.

File printouts of both versions in your Career Management Files Tracker.

For Your Career Management Files Tracker

File your completed Career Action worksheets in your Career Management Files Tracker.

CA 7-1   Additional personal information for employment applications

CA 7-2   Completed employment application(s)

CA 7-3   Internet research on cover letters

CA 7-4   Cover letter outline and draft

CA 7-5   Final print and plain text cover letters and files (also file in Career Portfolio)

The Job Interview

PART 4 teaches you how to ace the most important business meeting you'll ever attend: your job interview.

© Jim Calloway Photography

ADVICE FROM THE EXPERT

D. Lynn Meyers

Producing Artistic Director
Ensemble Theatre of Cincinnati

D. Lynn Meyers has been Producing Artistic Director of the nationally renowned Ensemble Theatre of Cincinnati (ETC) since 1995. The nonprofit ETC, recently celebrating its 25th anniversary, is dedicated to the production and development of new plays and of works new to the region.

Lynn values the opinions of each member of her small staff when hiring. She usually interviews four or five people for a staff position and conducts two interviews. After the preliminary interview determines that an applicant is suitable, she says, "We invite the person back to meet the staff they would have contact with on a daily basis." She has passed on qualified candidates who did not interact well with their prospective coworkers or who did not convince her that they had a strong desire for the job.

Lynn researches job applicants online and on social media sites. "Frankly, if we find unprofessional behavior, we take that into consideration," she says. "We always check references—after we meet the candidate so we know what to ask the person offering the reference."

When faced with two equally qualified candidates, Lynn chooses the person who demonstrates a long-term commitment to be with ETC and a desire to be part of the team. "If we're impressed by someone we can't hire, we keep their application on file. More than once we've called someone back when we added a job opening or needed to replace someone who didn't meet our expectations," says Lynn. She suggests that applicants "should want the job, know why they want it, and be prepared to answer serious questions about their long-term goals."

© Cengage Learning 2013

Interview Essentials

OVERVIEW You have learned how to present yourself well through your resume, cover letters, and job applications. Now it's time for what may be the most important business meeting you ever attend: the job interview. You will learn what happens in the first 30 seconds of the interview and how to create a good first impression by conveying a positive attitude, dressing like a successful professional, using positive body language, speaking well, and following proper business etiquette. You will also learn how to create a 30-Second Commercial for a very important product (you!) and how to assemble your Interview Marketing Kit.

© Photographer/Image Source

CHAPTER **8**

CAREER ACTIONS

TALES FROM THE JOB SEARCH

Billy Callis, Missions Associate

Texas Dental Association Smiles Foundation

Just weeks after moving to Austin, Texas, Billy Callis was weighing three job offers. He credits his strong performance in job interviews to getting to the head of the pack in a tight economy.

"When I got called for an interview," Billy says, "I knew I was only competing against a few other applicants. I researched the company to show the interviewer that I was serious and to help me make sure I really wanted the job. I tried not to overprepare because being comfortable with spontaneity is important to show the interviewer." Billy familiarized himself with the company's websites and checked out the companies through the Better Business Bureau. He also checked Facebook and LinkedIn "because I knew it was likely that they were doing the same."

He prepared for common interview questions "not to give a 'perfect' answer, but to make sure I had an idea of what's coming." To overcome being nervous while knowing that something big was at stake, he reminded himself that "I'm being asked about things I'm an expert on: my past experiences and how I will behave in the future—I'm not being tested on particle physics."

Billy asked interviewers to describe a typical day in the positions he applied for. "Usually, the first response was laughter—many jobs don't have typical days. But I like to be able to imagine what accepting the job would actually mean," he said. "It's important to be keenly aware that while you are being evaluated to determine whether you are the best candidate, the interview is your opportunity to be doing the same for the company."

→ Ready, Set, PLAN

Read the outcomes on the first page of Chapters 8–10 and mark the ones that are most important to you. What do you want to accomplish by reading these chapters and doing the assignments?

How much time is in the syllabus for Chapters 8–10?

List the dates for reading assignments and the dates for turning in homework and projects for this class.

What are your other major commitments in the coming weeks (for other classes, work, home)? For each task, include the estimated time and when you will do it.

If you are doing any group projects, list information that will help the project go smoothly: project goal and due date, each person's assignments and phone number, dates for completing each part of the project, meeting dates, and anything else.

JUMP START
Your Knowledge of Real Job Interviews

Everyone who is working had a successful job interview at some point in his or her career. Ask two friends or relatives about a job interview they had. How did they prepare? Were they dressed appropriately? Where there any surprises?

Talk with two friends or relatives about hiring interviews they have conducted. How do they prepare for interviews? What qualities do they look for in an applicant? What impresses them? What turns them off? Ask them how they rate the importance of attitude, appearance, body language, verbal communication, and job qualifications on a scale of 1 to 10, with 10 being most important.

Ask everyone for his or her top two tips for successful interviews. Organize the information you collect and put it in a format that will be most helpful for your classmates (a PowerPoint® presentation, for example).

akva/Shutterstock.com

Key Elements of Successful Interviews

Outcome 1

No one ever gets a job without having some type of interview. The interview is the doorway that every job seeker must be prepared to walk through on the way to successful employment. Think of it as a very important business meeting—maybe the first one with your new employer. Your goal is to learn about the job and the company, and the interviewer's goal is to learn about your abilities and potential. Both of you are evaluating whether you are a good match.

Before the interview, you "exist" to the interviewer on paper or online. The interviewer has looked at your application documents and has compared your education, work experience, and qualifications with those of other applicants. The interview is your chance to "come alive" as someone who can help the organization achieve its goals and as a person others will want to work with.

A successful interview has many elements, some of which are more important than you may realize. Your attitude is the biggest factor determining your success, and it comes through in many ways, including your appearance, body language, and how you speak. Your job qualifications also count, of course, and you must be able to summarize them well.

Your Attitude—The No. 1 Factor

Attitude is the No. 1 factor that influences an employer to hire. Here are some ways you can exhibit a good attitude:

1. **Concentrate on being likable.** As simple as this may seem, research proves that one of the most essential goals in successful interviewing is to be liked by the interviewer. Interviewers want to hire pleasant people whom others will enjoy working with on a daily basis. To project yourself as highly likable, do these things (these actions are detailed later in this chapter):

   - Be friendly, courteous, and enthusiastic.
   - Speak positively.
   - Use positive body language and smile.
   - Make certain your appearance is appropriate.

2. **Project an air of confidence and pride.** Act as though you want and deserve the job—not as though you are desperate.

3. **Demonstrate enthusiasm.** The applicant who demonstrates little enthusiasm for a job will never be selected for the position.

4. **Demonstrate knowledge of and interest in the employer.** Saying "I really want this job" is not convincing. Explain why you want the position and how it fits into your career plans. You can cite opportunities that may be unique to the company or emphasize your skills and education that are highly relevant to the position.

5. **Perform at your best every moment.** There are no time-outs during an interview. While in the waiting area, treat the assistant or receptionist courteously; learn and use his or her name. (An interviewer often requests this person's opinion of the applicants.)

6. **Understand that an interview is a two-way street.** Project genuine interest in determining whether both you and the employer can benefit from your employment.

2 Dress for Success

By the time you have walked in the room and sat down, the interviewer has decided whether you will be considered for the position. Your image and appearance help determine the all-important first impression you make. Your image and appearance may count for as much as 25% of the employer's positive or negative hiring decision.

Dress Conservatively

Most interviewers expect applicants to wear businesslike clothes when they apply for office or professional positions. For men and women,

---

Find It Fast

STAMIK/iStockphoto.com

An interview can come up fast! Here's a guide to the main topics beginning in Chapter 8:

Develop your 30-Second Commercial, pages 188–189

Assemble your Interview Marketing Kit, pages 189–190

Get interviews:
- Ask for interviews, pages 198–202
- Use indirect strategies to land interviews, pages 203–206

Make a good impression:
- Your appearance, pages 182–183
- Your body language, pages 184–185
- Your verbal skills, pages 185–187
- Your use of business etiquette, page 187

Know what to expect:
- Types of interviews, pages 214–219
- Typical questions (and answers), pages 219–225
- Good questions to ask (and avoid), pages 225–226
- Prepare for your interviews, pages 236–238

During the interview:
- Use items in your portfolio, pages 237–238
- Close the interview in your favor, pages 238–240

After the interview:
- Good follow-up strategies, pages 240–244
- If you don't get interviews, pages 268–269
- If you don't get job offers, pages 269–270
- Strategies for achieving better outcomes, pages 270–271

a conservative suit of dark quality fabric is the best choice. For women, a tailored dress or coordinated skirt or slacks and blouse with matching jacket are also appropriate. Strengthen your image by using your best colors in your accessories—scarves, ties, shirts, blouses, etc.

Base your clothing choice on your research about the career field and the employer. Whenever possible, visit your target employer before the interview to observe the work environment and dress code. A word of caution: Even if an employer permits casual dress on the job or if employees wear uniforms or safety gear, you should still dress formally for an interview to show that you take the opportunity seriously. Never dress too casually. T-shirts, jeans, tennis shoes, and other casual or faddish items may cost you the job.

Try on the outfit before your interview and appraise yourself honestly. Do you come across as the professional, competent, qualified person the employer is looking for? Consider the entire event, not just the conversation with the interviewer. For example, if you're riding a motorcycle or bike, what will you do with your helmet? If there's two feet of snow on the ground, what will you carry your shoes in and where will you put your boots?

Be Perfectly Groomed

Make sure your clothes fit well and are clean and pressed. Shine your shoes and, ladies, leave behind that beloved ancient handbag you take everywhere. If it looks like rain, take an umbrella and wear a raincoat—you do not want to walk into an interview dripping wet! Wear effective deodorant, but go easy on the after-shave lotion, cologne, or perfume. Be immaculately groomed from head to toe.

Look the Part

If you try to make a bold statement against business world conformity with a nose ring and pink hair, you can probably kiss the job good-bye. People who sport visible tattoos or body piercings; unnatural hair or makeup styles; ball caps and baggy pants; or too many earrings, bracelets, or rings to an interview might as well stay home. Many organizations have policies that prohibit radical hairstyles, low-cut blouses or shirts that don't cover the waist, and even open-toed shoes. Show employers that you conduct yourself professionally and dress accordingly.

> **COMPLETE** **CAREER ACTION 8-1**
>
> Internet Research on Dressing for Job Interviews, p. 193

The First 30 Seconds Count

wragg/istockphoto.com

People often form opinions about others within 30 seconds of first meeting them! For this reason, the first 30 seconds can make or break an interview.

Interview and interpersonal communications experts have studied what applicants can do to make a favorable first impression and project professionalism and competence during interviews.

Area	Impact on Interview
Attitude	40%
Image and Appearance	25%
Verbal and Nonverbal Communication	25%
Job Qualifications	10%

MAKE IT A HABIT

Communicate That You Are Trustworthy

During an interview, it is essential to come across as a trustworthy and believable person. Conveying trust is almost entirely a nonverbal function.

Trust is an emotional response that is learned in infancy and childhood and remains embedded in the brain. As children, we learned to trust people who projected caring, competence, warmth, and self-confidence through their body language.

As adults, we evaluate trustworthiness in the same way—through positive nonverbal messages that convince our emotional brain center that a person can be trusted. Looking someone in the eye when speaking to them is the single most important thing you can do to build confidence in what you are saying. A good handshake and good posture; a pleasant facial expression; and an energetic, pleasant tone of voice also affect believability.

Digital Vision/Getty Images

Outcome 3 Use Positive Body Language

Through our life experiences, we become experts at sending and interpreting nonverbal messages. Your nonverbal communication, or body language, actually carries more influence than the words you say. You may be speaking persuasively, but body language that conveys arrogance, lack of enthusiasm, excessive nervousness, or other negative messages will drown out your words.

Appear Relaxed

Your body language will immediately notify an employer if you are overly tense. Be well rested before an interview so that you will be alert and, if possible, exercise by running, stretching, or doing yoga on the day of the interview. Exercise is one of nature's best techniques for relaxing your body and your mind. Try to allocate adequate time in your day—especially during your job search—to do some form of exercise. And be sure to eat something light and healthy before your interview so that you don't feel hungry or tired.

During the interview, occasionally change your position in your seat; this relaxes muscular body tension and breaks the rigid feeling that nervousness can cause. Breathe deeply and don't hurry your movements; this will project confidence and will reduce your anxiety. If possible, give a genuine smile! It's an effective tension breaker for both you and the interviewer.

Develop Assertive Body Language

Concentrate on sending assertive messages with your body language. Assertive body language is relaxed, open, and confident. Your posture and gestures support your words and convey credibility and self-assurance.

- **When you meet the interviewer, give a firm handshake and make eye contact.** This immediately communicates intelligence, competence, and honesty.

- **Walk briskly.** You'll look confident and show that you're ready for the meeting.

- **Sit, stand, and walk with your head up and your back straight.** Good posture conveys that you're composed, respectable, alert, and strong. Slouching conveys that you're bored,

"If you think you don't have any physical mannerisms or don't know what they are, spend a day watching the body language of the people you interact with."

disinterested, lazy, or unintelligent. Crossing your arms and legs may be interpreted as being closed or stubborn.

- **Make eye contact.** Making good eye contact is essential to achieving effective communication. It conveys that you really care about what the person has to say. It also conveys confidence, intelligence, competence, and honesty. This doesn't mean that you should glue your eyes to the interviewer; it means that you should look at the interviewer, especially when he or she is talking. Break eye contact at natural points in the discussion. If you are extremely uncomfortable looking directly into the eyes of the interviewer, look at his or her forehead. This gives the impression of looking into his or her eyes. In a group interview, periodically make eye contact with each person. Avoid letting your eyes dart back and forth around the room.

- **Aim for a pleasant, uplifted facial expression.** Occasionally nod your head and gesture to convey agreement and emphasis. Avoid frowning, clenching your jaw, and making other negative expressions.

- **Don't fidget.** Fidgeting is distracting and makes you look nervous, self-conscious, and unsure of your ability to get the job. Keep your hands apart to avoid fidgeting. Rest them on the arms of the chair and keep them still. Keep your hands relaxed, not in tight fists.

- **Watch the interviewer's body language.** The interviewer may lean forward, signaling you to expand on what you are saying. If the interviewer shuffles papers, looks around the room, or gives other nonverbal cues that you should finish speaking, heed the signal. Continue listening and watching to determine whether what you are saying is clearly understood. Retreat from a subject if you observe that it's not being well received.

- **Subtly mirror the interviewer's communication behaviors.** Some people have intense, highly energetic body language and voice qualities, while others are more relaxed. Subtly match your interviewer's style, speed, and tone of voice—but don't overdo it. Do not mirror negative behavior.

COMPLETE **CAREER ACTION 8-2**

Body Language Self-Assessment, p. 193

Outcome 4 | Speak Well for Yourself

You're dressed for the part; your positive attitude is shining through; and your body language shows that you're confident, relaxed, and enthusiastic. What's next? Speaking, of course. Even though research shows that body language can carry more influence than words can, you need good verbal communication skills to make a strong case for yourself and to get the information you need.

It's How You Say It

Follow these general tips about voice quality to build on the great first impression you made.

- **Start off right by greeting the interviewer by name.** This conveys respect, which enhances your likability. If more than one person is conducting the interview, learn and use everyone's name.

- **State your name and the position you're seeking.** Begin with a friendly greeting and state the position you're interviewing for: "Hello, Ms. Ong. I'm Bella Reyna. I'm here to interview for the accounting position." Identifying the position is important because interviewers often interview for many different positions. If someone has already introduced you to the interviewer, simply say, "Good morning, Ms. Ong."

- **Use an energetic, pleasant tone of voice** to convey a positive attitude and to enhance your likability.

- **Modulate your voice.** Don't speak in a monotone or speak too slowly or too rapidly. Speak loud enough to be heard, but not too loudly.

- **Don't slur your words.** Speak distinctly and clearly. No one likes to ask a person to repeat something.

- **Use positive words and phrases.** One of the most important interview goals is to keep the content positive so that the interviewer's final impression is "Yes, this is the person for the job." Use a positive vocabulary and eliminate all negative terms.

- **Use proper grammar.** Grammatical errors can cost applicants a job. Use correct grammar, word choice, and a businesslike vocabulary, not an informal, chatty one. Avoid slang and never use profanity or derogatory terms. When under stress, people often use pet phrases (such as "like" and "you know") too often. Ask a friend or family member to help you identify any speech weaknesses you have. Begin eliminating these poor speech habits now.

It's What You Say

Speak professionally during your interview.

- **Emphasize how you fit the job.** Near the beginning of an interview, as soon as it seems appropriate, ask a question similar

WATCH OUT

Choose Your Words Carefully

Avoid using words and phrases that make you sound indecisive or unbelievable. Eliminate the following credibility robbers from your vocabulary:

- *Just or only.* Used as follows, "I just worked as a waiter" or "I only worked there on a part-time basis" implies that you are not proud of your work or that you don't consider the work meaningful. All work is meaningful; it demonstrates initiative. Leave out these credibility robbers.

- *I guess.* This makes you sound uncertain.

- *Little.* Don't belittle your accomplishments, as in "This is a little report/project I wrote/developed."

- *Probably.* This suggests unnecessary doubt: "The technique I developed would probably be useful in your department." This statement sounds more convincing: "I believe the technique I developed would be useful in your department."

This is a small sample of words and phrases that can diminish your image. Ask members of your support system to help you identify other verbal credibility robbers and to remind you when you use them.

to this: "Could you describe the scope of the job and tell me what capabilities are most important in filling the position?" The interviewer's response will help you focus on emphasizing your qualifications that best match the needs of the employer.

- **Keep the interview businesslike.** Do not discuss personal, domestic, or financial problems.

- **Don't ramble.** Be concise—but not curt—with your replies. Answer questions with required information, adding anything you think is relevant or especially important; then stop talking or ask your own question.

- **Concentrate.** An interview isn't just about talking. Listen to the interviewer carefully to learn important details about the job requirements, the organization, and the department so that you can respond appropriately. See "Be a Good Listener" on page 220.

- **Try to demonstrate a sense of humor.** Humor is an important factor in working well with other people and is a sign of intelligence. Use humor only when appropriate, however, and don't tell jokes; they're not suitable for an interview. Never use profanity or off-color humor. Making yourself the subject of the humor is usually safe, but be careful not to make yourself look bad.

- **Emphasize your strengths—even when discussing an error you made.** Emphasize your strengths and abilities that are relevant to the job. Although you want to avoid bringing up past shortcomings, do not try to dodge one that comes out during an interview. Face it head-on and explain what you learned from the experience. If the interviewer asks you about the circumstances, explain briefly; don't make excuses or blame others. You will create a better impression by being honest, candid, and sincere. Remember: The interviewer is human too and has made his or her share of mistakes.

- **Do not lie during an interview.**

- **Be prepared to state why you left a previous job if you're asked.** Do not speak unfavorably about your former supervisor or firm. Interviewers may believe that you would do the same after leaving their companies. Maintain your business and professional integrity throughout the interview.

- **Focus on your goal.** Keep coming back to the main purpose of the interview: determining how both you and the employer can benefit from your employment. If the conversation strays too far from this subject, bring it back in the right direction. Get feedback from the interviewer to determine how you're coming across. Stop and ask: "Do you think my skills in that area would be helpful to you?" If the answer is yes, you know you're on the right track. If the answer is no or unclear, clarify how you are qualified for the job.

Outcome 5 Be Aware of Business Etiquette

Business etiquette is the expected professional behavior in the workplace, and it is based on common courtesy, manners, and cultural and societal norms. Etiquette blunders include leaving your cell phone ringer on during a business meeting and using your napkin to wipe your nose during a business lunch.

Your behavior in an interview gives your prospective employer clues to how you will treat clients and customers.

Culturally appropriate business etiquette is important in conducting global business successfully. An unintentional etiquette breach can quickly squash a delicate international transaction. For example, in Asia, presenting a business card using only one hand is considered rude.

COMPLETE **CAREER ACTION 8-3**

Internet Research on Interview Etiquette, p. 195

Outcome 6 Prepare Your 30-Second Commercial

You need to convince the interviewer that you are the best qualified person for the job. If you don't, you won't be hired. At some point in every interview, you will have an opportunity to deliver a prepared "clincher" speech highlighting your best qualities and showing how they will benefit your employer.

Getting hired can be compared to making a sale. In this case, you and your capabilities are the product. You complete the "sale" by emphasizing how your capabilities can benefit the employer. To help make the sale, develop a 30-Second Commercial, a power-packed summary of the benefits you offer.

As a starting point, think of times you provided benefits to an employer or some other organization. Employers are persuaded to hire the person who can offer advantages in one or more of these areas: increasing sales, increasing profits, increasing productivity, as well as:

- Decreasing costs
- Saving time
- Solving problems or resolving conflicts
- Increasing convenience
- Enhancing image and/or improving relationships
- Increasing accuracy or efficiency

Do not use vague language. Provide evidence of your capabilities with specific examples. Use numbers to boost your credibility when you can. ("I developed a processing system that reduced processing time by 20 percent.")

Because employers are looking for flexible employees who can adapt to new situations, you should also emphasize your transferable competencies, such as your ability to handle diverse responsibilities, manage yourself (attendance, punctuality, problem solving), and work well with others. Transferable competencies were introduced in Chapter 3.

Your "master" 30-Second Commercial will be useful in many situations, such as direct requests for interviews, phone requests, networking, practice and real interviews, and thank-you letters. You can draw from it for 45-second and even 15-second "spots."

Show That You Can Work with Others

Be able to give examples that emphasize your ability to work successfully with others. Be prepared to explain what contributions you made to a group and how you were able to solve a problem or resolve group conflicts. Identify any particularly complex projects you handled in past jobs. Be ready to explain what tasks you performed and how you managed multiple priorities at the same time.

Be Convincing

Follow these additional tips to develop and deliver a convincing 30-Second Commercial:

- **Be authentic.** Make sure your 30-Second Commercial represents you authentically. Don't "sell" what you can't deliver.

- **Create an opening for your commercial.** Ask the interviewer to review the scope of the job responsibilities and the reason for the job opening. Pay attention to the answers. If necessary, probe further to clarify what the employer really needs and then discuss the benefits you can offer to meet those needs. An untrained interviewer may not ask you directly about your qualifications. Be sure you present them in the interview.

- **Include measurable accomplishments.** The key to an effective 30-Second Commercial is to provide examples of your capabilities. Pick the items that best fit the needs expressed by the interviewer. Example: "I can see that xyz is the most crucial challenge to your organization. My skills can alleviate those problem areas because of my specific xyz experience."

- **Be concise.** Your interview commercial must be short, relevant, and convincing. Thirty seconds is a very long time for a monologue, so practice presenting your commercial in a conversation.

- **Focus and polish the content.** Your aim is to prepare a brief, polished summary of your qualifications. The heart of your message should emphasize how you can benefit the employer. It is your interview "billboard" saying "Here's what I can do for you." This helps the interviewer focus on the strengths you have to offer.

- **Be ready for any situation.** Practice delivering the 30-second version, a 45-second version, and a 15-second version. Weave your commercial into the interview—perhaps a longer version first, followed later by a shorter one. Don't overdo it, however; twice is probably enough.

- **Tailor your 30-Second Commercial to each employer.** Vary your commercial slightly to match the requirements of each job. If the job description lists computer skills first, talk about your computer skills first. Use the wording and terms used in the job requirements.

- **Don't bore your audience.** Observe the situation so that you know when to stop talking. Watch for signals that the interviewer wants to ask a question or move on to a different topic.

Figure 8-1, on the next page, shows the outline of a 30-Second Commercial and shows how Shane, the author, delivered his commercial at a professional meeting. Shane's conversation with Lillian probably lasted more than 30 seconds, but notice how Shane uses

examples that focus on employer benefits and emphasize his results-oriented accomplishments and his transferable competencies (abilities he can apply in various work situations). Because his outline is short and to the point, he can hone in on the information that will interest his listener and convince her to take a closer look.

COMPLETE **CAREER ACTION 8-4**

Create Your 30-Second Commercial, p. 195

Outcome 7 Prepare Your Interview Marketing Kit

Job applicants who prepare well for interviews have a decided advantage over those who don't: they perform better during the interview. By performing well, you will project professionalism and organization skills and increase your own sense of readiness.

Before each interview, assemble your Interview Marketing Kit. Select the items that are most appropriate for the current job target from your Career Portfolio (see Chapter 1). Put these items in a professional-looking binder or small attaché case. A regular briefcase is not recommended because interviewers may view it as overkill. Include these items in your Interview Marketing Kit:

- **Items from your Career Portfolio** that pertain to the interview:
  - Job-related samples of your work if applicable
  - Required certificates, licenses, transcripts, and related documents
  - Extra copies of your resume
  - Letters of recommendation
  - Lists of references appropriate for the job

- **A copy of your 30-Second Commercial** (for your use only)

- **A notebook with questions** you can ask during the interview (see Chapter 10). Bring a businesslike, middle-of-the-road pen—not too expensive, too flashy, or too quirky.

- **Your appointment calendar.** If you keep your calendar in your smartphone, turn off the phone before you even walk in the building.

Arrange the portfolio items in the order that best shows how your abilities relate to the employer's needs. Chapter 11 has tips for using items from your Career Portfolio during interviews.

COMPLETE   **CAREER ACTION 8-5**

Action Plan for Core Areas of Successful Interviewing, p. 196

Outline	Delivery
Job Target: Sales representative with Axion Group, an office technology company	**Shane (reading Lillian's name tag with her company name):** Hi, I'm Shane Bradley. You're with Axion Group? I read about the opening for a sales representative in the office technology solutions group, and I think I'd be a good fit.
Experience Credentials: Two years developing small business solutions at Computer Logistics, Inc.	**Lillian:** Nice to meet you, Shane. What's your background? **Shane:** I've been with Computer Logistics' small business solutions group for two years. I have hands-on experience in customized solutions, and I have a B.S. in sales and marketing from DePauw University.
Education Credentials: B.S. in sales and marketing from DePauw University	
Proof of Benefits Provided • Received "excellent" customer performance ratings for both years at Computer Logistics • Voted "Most Helpful Clerk" by customers in Service Excellence contest at Ralston Pharmacy • Increased school newspaper revenues by 20% as advertising assistant	**Lillian:** Do you think you can make the transition from small business to consulting with Fortune 1000 customers on enterprise-wide solutions? **Shane:** I do. I recognize that there are differences, and I've wanted to move to larger-scale solutions for a while. I keep up with the industry, and I'm strong on the technical side and the sales side. Selling any technical solution is a team effort, and I've been called the ultimate utility player. **Lillian:** That group has a reputation for being tough on new hires. They throw you into the deep end, and it's up to you to sink or swim. But I know they're trying to grow the business and get back some accounts they lost in the recession.
Related Job Skills/Preferences • Strong organizational skills • Highly skilled in business computing (hardware, networking, data storage, cloud computing, off-the-shelf and proprietary software) and business math • Enjoy travel; open to relocation	**Shane:** The listing says that the reps are on the road about 25% of the time, and that sounds great. My family has gradually moved away from this area, and I'd jump at the chance to relocate to help turn around an underperforming district. **Lillian:** Do you have a business card? **Shane:** Here it is. My LinkedIn profile has more details. May I give you a copy of my resume?
Transferable Competencies: Strong communication skills; strong interpersonal relations skills	**Lillian:** My hands are pretty full, so why don't you email it to me? Here's my card. It was nice meeting you, Shane. **Shane:** Likewise. You'll have my resume tomorrow, Lillian. It was great talking with you.

Figure 8-1 30-Second Commercial—Outline and Delivery

Chapter Checklist

Underline each action you are already taking and circle the actions you need to work on.

- Project enthusiasm and a positive attitude in interviews. 1

- Project professionalism; smile, dress neatly and appropriately, and be well groomed. 2

- Use positive body language to project trust and credibility. 3

- Use positive verbal communication; use positive terms and avoid grammatical errors and slang. 4

- Follow accepted business etiquette for interviews. 5

- Make the sale by delivering a polished "30-Second Commercial" that emphasizes my qualifications and includes measurable accomplishments whenever possible. 6

- Prepare an Interview Marketing Kit that contains appropriate items from my Career Portfolio. 7

Critical-Thinking Questions

1. Which aspects of the job applicant do interviewers focus on the most? Why? 1

2. How can a job applicant demonstrate a positive attitude during an interview? 1

3. Why do interviewers respond positively to assertive body language? How can a job candidate demonstrate assertive body language? 3

4. What negative nonverbal habits are most important for you to eliminate to improve your interview abilities? 3

5. Why would an interviewer respond positively to a job applicant who has a sense of humor? What should you avoid when using humor? 4

6. What could happen during an interview if a job applicant hadn't prepared a 30-Second Commercial? 6

Want access to career resources, study tools, activities, and job information links? Get started at www.cengage.com/career/yourcareer.

TRIAL RUN

To keep current with interview styles, trends, and expectations, conduct interviews of your own with hiring managers and human resource directors across a variety of fields. When you request the interview, tell the person that you are conducting research for a class assignment. Be sure to follow the advice in this chapter and in Chapter 4 for acting professionally in these meetings.

Copy this form and use it to conduct at least two interviews with employers in different fields. File the completed forms in your Career Management Files Tracker.

Name of Person Interviewed _____

Name of Company _____ Position _____

Who in your company is responsible for interviewing job candidates?

How are new employees recruited?

What skills are you looking for? What types of questions do you ask in interviews to evaluate candidates?

How important are skills and education as compared to enthusiasm, reliability, and communication skills?

What advice would you give someone seeking a job and an interview in your field?

CAREER ACTION   8-1   **Internet Research on Dressing for Job Interviews** [2]

Read different experts' tips for looking your best at job interviews. You can use the Interviewing & Applying Help feature of *Career Transitions* for advice. Take an honest look in the mirror. Where can you enhance the first impression you will make? Record the most helpful advice you find and plan your outfit.

Tips for dressing for success:

Ideas for my interview outfit:

I already have these items:

I need to buy or borrow these items:

Member of support network who will give an honest opinion and good advice _____

CAREER ACTION   8-2   **Body Language Self-Assessment** [3]

Part 1. Review the descriptions of nonverbal behaviors and voice qualities and check the box for each item that describes your body language habits. You also can do this Career Action with a partner. Definitions:

- Assertive body language is relaxed, open, and confident. It supports your words and conveys competence, self-assurance, caring, and credibility.

- Passive body language looks nonenergetic and diminishes your credibility by conveying insecurity, weakness, anxiety, and a lack of self-assurance and competence.

- Aggressive body language appears brash and overbearing and sends offensive messages that convey hostility, pushiness, intimidation, and a domineering attitude.

Review your answers and highlight your aggressive or passive habits. In Part 2, list the habits you think are most important to change. Finally, take action to correct these habits and ask others to remind you when you exhibit them.

POSTURE

❏ Comfortably upright	Assertive	❏ Overbearing, intimidating	Aggressive
❏ Relaxed, balanced	Assertive	❏ Wooden, tight	Passive
❏ Open, not constricted	Assertive	❏ Slumped shoulders	Passive
❏ Overly stiff	Aggressive	❏ Slumped back/spine	Passive
❏ Arms/legs crossed	Aggressive		

HANDSHAKE

❑ Appropriately firm	Assertive	❑ Held for too long	Aggressive
❑ Connect between thumb and first finger	Assertive	❑ Limp	Passive
❑ Shake from elbow through hand	Assertive	❑ Shake from wrist through hand	Passive
❑ Held for appropriate length of time	Assertive	❑ Hold too briefly	Passive
❑ "Bone-crushing" grip	Aggressive	❑ Grasping fingers only	Passive

FACIAL EXPRESSION

❑ Open, relaxed, pleasant	Assertive	❑ Clenched jaw	Aggressive
❑ Frowning	Aggressive	❑ Wrinkling forehead	Passive
❑ Moody, sulking	Aggressive	❑ Biting or licking lips	Passive
❑ Tight upper lip, pursed mouth	Aggressive	❑ Continual smile	Passive

EYE CONTACT

❑ Comfortably direct	Assertive	❑ Constantly looking down	Passive
❑ Staring off; bored expression	Aggressive	❑ Blinking rapidly	Passive
❑ Sneering, looking down nose	Aggressive	❑ Frequently shifting focus	Passive
❑ Direct stare	Aggressive	❑ No eye contact; avoidance	Passive

VOICE QUALITIES

❑ Distinct and clear	Assertive	❑ Too loud	Aggressive
❑ Controlled but relaxed	Assertive	❑ Arrogant or sarcastic	Aggressive
❑ Warm, pleasant tone	Assertive	❑ Dull or monotone	Passive
❑ Energized; suitable emphasis	Assertive	❑ Whiny tone	Passive
❑ Too rapid	Aggressive	❑ Too soft or too low	Passive
❑ Too demanding or urgent	Aggressive	❑ Too nasal	Passive

GESTURES

❑ Natural, not erratic	Assertive	❑ Hands on hips	Aggressive
❑ Occasional gestures to emphasize	Assertive	❑ Wooden gestures	Passive
❑ Occasional positive head nodding	Assertive	❑ Tilting head to one side	Passive
❑ Open hand (conveys trust)	Assertive	❑ Bringing hand to face	Passive
❑ Leaning toward speaker	Assertive	❑ Nodding head too much	Passive
❑ Pointing finger	Aggressive	❑ Fidgeting	Passive

DISTRACTING NONVERBAL HABITS

❑ Drumming fingers	Passive	❑ Fiddling with an object	Passive
❑ Use of fillers (*um, uh, you know*)	Passive	❑ Rubbing beard or mustache	Passive
❑ Jiggling leg/arm	Passive	❑ Biting nails	Passive
❑ Fiddling with hair or glasses	Passive	❑ Scratching	Passive

Part 2. In order of importance, list the negative nonverbal habits you plan to change.

My Goals for Improving My Nonverbal Communication and Voice Qualities

1. _____

2. _____

3. _____

CAREER ACTION   8-3   **Internet Research on Interview Etiquette** ⑤

Part 1. Read about expected business etiquette for job interviews.

List the most important things you learned.

What behaviors do you need to improve?

How will you practice the new behaviors before an interview?

Part 2. Different cultures have different business etiquette rules. Record some things you learned about business etiquette in other cultures. Be sure to note the culture.

CAREER ACTION   8-4   **Create Your 30-Second Commercial** ⑥

Follow these instructions to create your own 30-Second Commercial. File copies of your commercial in your Career Management Files Tracker and your Interview Marketing Kit.

1. **Prepare a rough draft.** On a separate sheet of paper, prepare a rough draft of your basic list.

2. **Use short phrases, not full sentences.** The goal is to say the most about your qualifications in the fewest possible words.

3. **Name your target job position and employer.**

4. **Briefly summarize your education and training.** Use your resume and Career Action 3-1 (Education, Training, and Activities Inventory) as references.

5. **Focus on "proof of benefits provided."** Provide relevant examples of your work performance and accomplishments and successful use of your job-specific skills. Whenever possible, use numbers or percentages to describe your successes. Also emphasize the benefits you can provide for the employer.

6. **List your job skills and transferrable competencies that are most relevant to the job target.** Refer to Career Actions 3-2 and 3-7 to review your job-specific skills and qualifications.

7. **Tailor each list.** Use your draft as a base and tailor it to each target employer. Practice delivering your commercial aloud, but don't memorize it word for word. (You don't want to sound as though you are reading a script or that you lack the energy to talk enthusiastically about your qualifications.) Take a copy of your commercial with you to an interview. If you have a momentary memory lapse, quickly scan the list, but don't read from it directly.

CAREER ACTION   8-5   **Action Plan for Core Areas of Successful Interviewing** [7]

Develop an action plan for strengthening the interview strategies presented in Chapter 8 and applying them in your own job search.

Attitude:

Image and Appearance:

Nonverbal Communication:

Verbal Communication:

Business Etiquette:

30-Second Commercial:

For Your Career Management Files Tracker

File your completed Career Action worksheets in your Career Management Files Tracker.

CA 8-1   Tips and plans for dressing for job interviews

CA 8-2   Body language assessment and plans for improvement

CA 8-3   Plans for improving specific areas of business etiquette

CA 8-4   30-Second Commercial

CA 8-5   Action plan for successful interviewing

Ask for—and Get— the Interview

Outcomes

1 Explain the importance of taking the initiative and asking for interviews.

2 Develop skills and strategies for making a direct request for an interview.

3 Explain when and how to make an indirect request for an interview.

4 Develop a backup plan if your target employer isn't hiring.

OVERVIEW In Chapter 9, you will be challenged to step outside your comfort zone and take a proactive approach to landing an interview. You will research and practice strategies for getting that all-important meeting with a target employer. You will learn the skills and styles—direct or indirect, in person, or on the phone— necessary to get the opportunity you need—and use it to your advantage. In this chapter, you also will see the importance of taking a less-than-perfect job while you continue looking for the right one.

CHAPTER 9

© Photographer/Image Source

JUMP START

Asking for an Interview

Your success when asking for an interview is related to the type of work and career you are targeting. Some employers might view a direct request for an interview as aggressive, while other businesses would be grateful to find a qualified applicant.

What is the business etiquette in your field or at your target employer? Remember what you read in Chapter 8: the most important business meeting you will ever have with your employer is your job interview. Don't get off on the wrong foot or have the door slammed in your face because you broke the unspoken rules.

Ask people who work in your target career field how they were selected for their interviews. Do they think a direct request via telephone or email is acceptable? Or do they recommend asking someone in your support network to try to open a door for you?

akva/Shutterstock.com

 Getting an Interview
Outcome 1

In the best of all worlds, you apply for your dream job, the employer reads your resume and cover letter or application, and he or she contacts you to schedule an interview. This happy scenario is not far-fetched, but you also need to know how to take the initiative and ask prospective employers for a job interview.

- You can contact an employer directly—in person, by telephone, or through a standard letter or an email—to ask for an interview.

- You can use an indirect strategy to create opportunities to be asked to interview for a position.

You should be prepared to use direct and indirect strategies to get through the interview doorway. Indirect requests for interviews are especially important when job competition is high.

Every opportunity you have to meet with employers, whether for a formal interview or an informational survey, gives you important practice and keeps your job search active.

 Direct Requests for Interviews
Outcome 2

Once you have identified a promising employer prospect, your goal is to get an interview. It's best to meet face-to-face or over the telephone. Don't write when you can call and don't call when you can make a personal visit. If you can't visit or call, a standard letter or an email is appropriate. Tailor your request for an interview to each prospective employer by emphasizing your strengths and experience that are most relevant to the employer's needs.

Apply Your Verbal Skills to Interview Requests

To increase your chance of getting an interview, focus on being courteous, likable, persuasive, and resourceful. As always, act professionally because your interview begins at the time of that first contact. You will be judged as to whether you are a potential candidate based on the first impression you make.

On the phone and in person, use a friendly tone and correct grammar. Write out a practice script or outline beforehand if it helps you feel more confident. Speak distinctly and confidently and eliminate slang and filler expressions such as *um, uh,* and *you know.*

Be courteous and respect the person's time. Most businesspeople will have only a few minutes for your visit or call. If you sense that this is not a good time, say, "I would be glad to call (visit) at a more convenient time." Remain composed and professional. Do not act inconvenienced or become irritated.

Focus Your Interview Request

The focus of an effective interview request should be on how your abilities can help—or even be essential to—the employer. Identify the advantages of your qualifications and translate them into benefits for the employer. Communicate your message clearly and concisely and emphasize your qualifications before requesting an interview.

Conducting employer research is vital and should include finding out who is in charge of the department that could benefit most from your abilities. This is the target person for your interview request.

Request an Interview in Person

Requesting an interview by making a personal visit is the most successful method of getting an interview. It is difficult for people to ignore you when you are standing in front of them. If you make a good impression, you have already achieved a major goal in the interview process. Follow these guidelines:

1. **Research the firm** thoroughly beforehand.
2. **Dress for the part**. Dress and groom yourself as though you are going to an actual interview.
3. **Be prepared**. Take your Interview Marketing Kit (see Chapter 8) with your 30-Second Commercial and your resume.
4. **Pay special attention to the gatekeeper** (the person standing between you and the

MAKE IT A HABIT

Do Your Homework before Every Interview

Learn as much as you can about an organization before you walk through the door.

- Formal name, address, locations, and contact information, and hours of operation
- Industry; products and/or services
- Advertised job openings (with salary ranges)
- Number of employees
- Departments and managers
- Competitors and customers
- Corporate culture
- Reputation
- History (past successes and challenges)

slidezero_com/iStockphoto.com

employer). This may be a front-line staff member, an administrative assistant, a supervisor, or a human resources staff member. Actively and courteously seek that person's help.

5. **Present the most concise, action-packed version of your 30-Second Commercial;** then request an interview.
6. **Thank your contact by name** for his or her time and consideration.

If you don't get an interview, ask for a referral to another department or company that may need your abilities. Remain courteous and professional throughout the conversation.

Study the following example of a request for an interview made during a personal visit to an employer. The applicant is applying for an administrative support position in a medical center. Note how he highlights his qualifications, demonstrates his knowledge of the employer and the industry, and expresses his interest in a job—just the right approach.

Sample In-Person Request for an Interview

The Opening. "Hello, Mr. Washington. My name is Stephen Rogowski. My instructor Phyllis Johnston recommends your Information Services Department at St. Mary's Hospital for its well-organized systems design. I recently completed my education at Mesa College, earning two A.S. degrees—one in Information Management Technology and another in Medical Administrative Assisting."

The 30-Second Commercial Excerpt. "I worked for 18 months as a clerical assistant in the Business Office at Lewis State College while attending school. I'm proficient in Office 2010 and SharePoint software and have my MOUS certification in Office 2010. I operate personal computers, networks, and general office equipment. I also key 70 words per minute and am skilled in English usage."

The Request. "I've developed time-saving methods for creating templates and macros that may be appropriate for your department. Would you have time today for me to review them with you, or would a day next week be more convenient?"

The Close. "Next Tuesday at 10 a.m.? I appreciate your willingness to meet with me so soon, Mr. Washington. I look forward to meeting with you then. Thank you. Good-bye."

COMPLETE **CAREER ACTION 9-1**

Develop Your In-Person Request for an Interview, p. 210

Request an Interview over the Phone

The telephone can be a powerful ally. Because it is "live," it demands immediate attention from the person who answers it. Because it allows for two-way communication, you can respond immediately to the person's questions and he or she can respond to yours. Use the telephone to create a short list of employers who are viable targets for employment. Follow up with personal visits to the most likely prospects.

Using the Telephone Persuasively

Your telephone communication skills will affect your success throughout your career. You can develop these skills just as you develop any other skill.

Your voice is your personality over the telephone. You want to use your voice to project confidence and enthusiasm and make a positive impression. Follow these guidelines:

1. **Know why you are calling.** Is your purpose to get the name of the hiring individual? Is it to request information about the position? Is it to request an interview?

2. **Research the firm thoroughly beforehand.** Get the name of the person you need to contact before you call to request an interview. You may need to make a preliminary call to get this information.

3. **Write a script or an outline before you call.** Know what you want to say before you make an important phone call. A script or an outline helps you organize your message, making you sound intelligent and well prepared. You also can refer to it if you forget something. Summarize the key points you need to cover before placing the call, including the information you need to obtain from your contact. Pattern your

script after the samples in this chapter and refer to your 30-Second Commercial.

4. **Don't read from the script during the call.** Not using the script during the call is just as important as writing a script or an outline in the first place. Practice what you want to say before the call until you become comfortable saying it. During the call, use your script or outline to guide you from one idea to the next.

5. **Speak clearly and get to the point.** Any long pauses could cause you to be put on hold or transferred to voice mail before you have had a chance to make your pitch.

6. **Don't do anything else.** Listen and respond to the person on the other end of the line. Give the phone call your complete attention. Don't chew gum or drink while talking on the phone.

7. **Stand up, speak directly into the mouthpiece, and smile while you talk.** The muscles used to smile relax your vocal cords and create a pleasant tone of voice. Standing up gives your voice more energy.

Study the following telephone request for an interview and note how the applicant incorporates her qualifications, knowledge of the employer and the industry, and interest in the employer.

Sample Telephone Request for an Interview

The Opening. "Hello, Ms. Hope. This is Jaleesa Williams. I recently completed research comparing the product quality and service records of computer network manufacturers. I'm impressed with the results XYZ Company has achieved, and I'm interested in learning about a possible sales representative position."

The 30-Second Commercial Excerpt. "I'm completing my degree in sales and marketing at Fairmount State College and have two years of successful retail sales experience. I also was the advertising assistant for our school paper and increased sales by 18 percent this year."

The Request. "Would it be possible to arrange a meeting with you to discuss your sales goals and how I might contribute to them?"

The Close. "Thank you, Ms. Hope. I look forward to meeting with you next Tuesday, the 18th, at 2:30. Good-bye."

Research and Social Media

Social networking sites can be invaluable for researching the companies you are interested in. In the last few years, establishing a presence on all the three big social networking sites—Facebook, Twitter, and LinkedIn—has become normal practice for businesses. Some companies are more involved than others, but chances are you'll at least find a presence there.

- An active Twitter feed can tell you a lot about a company's values and current projects. Follow posted links to articles or press releases and search for mention of the company in others' feeds.
- A Facebook profile or Fan Page often features pictures, comments, and status updates that can offer insights into the company and its public perception.
- On LinkedIn, a "Companies" search can yield interesting statistics about a company. Look through the list of employees who have LinkedIn profiles and find the top players. You can also look for first-, second-, and third-degree connections who might give you an introduction to an employee who can then give you firsthand information.

COMPLETE   **CAREER ACTION 9-2**

Develop and Practice Your Telephone
Interview Request, p. 211

Write a Letter to Request an Interview

If you are relying on your cover letter and
resume to get interviews and you have prepared these documents well, you are ready to
make an interview request. Review the guidelines for preparing and distributing a cover
letter in Chapter 7. You may want to use email
and a letter. By using both media, you give
extra emphasis to your message and increase
the likelihood that your request will be read.

If you don't receive responses from your
cover letter and resume within a week to ten
days, reinforce the request through a telephone
call or personal visit.

If you call, say that you mailed a letter on
a specific date and that you are calling to see
if the letter was received and who received it.
Then ask to speak to that person to discuss
your letter. You can also ask about company
hiring policies or openings.

Respond to a Job Posting on the Internet

When you apply for a job on a general job listing site or a specific employer's website, follow
the instructions exactly. Often employers want
you to email or fax your resume and a cover
letter. They may use a special code to identify

Please Leave a *Good* Message

DrGrounds/iStockphoto.com

- **Make notes about what you want to say** before you place the call.
- **Have a backup plan for a conversation in case the person answers the phone.**
- **Listen carefully to the person's voice mail greet-ing.** The person you are trying to reach may be on vacation or may ask callers to send an email instead of leaving a message.
- **Use a pleasant, profes-sional speaking voice.** When a person you have not met listens to your message, your voice is you. Avoid sounding ingratiating, needy, pushy, or anything else that will make the speaker not want to call you back.
- **Speak slowly.** Speak more slowly than you ordinarily do so that the person can take notes without having

to listen to your message more than once.
- **Pronounce your name clearly.** Speak clearly when you say your name, espe-cially if it is an unusual one. Spell your name slowly if necessary.
- **Say your phone number clearly and slowly.** Your listener is writing down your number, so don't mumble or rush.
- **Leave *yourself* the mes-sage before you make the real call.** Call yourself from another phone and leave the message on your own voice mail.
- **If you speak English with an accent,** ask a friend to listen to your message and tell you if any parts of it were hard to understand.
- **Repeat your name and phone number** at the end of the message.

a specific job opening; be sure to include any such code in your cover letter.

They may also have an online resume form for you to fill out or a text block into which you can paste your resume or letter. All of these options become your "request for an interview."

Indirect Strategies for Landing Interviews

Outcome 3

To reach an employer, to bypass a gatekeeper, to find the hidden job market, or to get around the office receptionist, you may need to use an indirect strategy to land an interview.

Get Through to an Employer

When job competition is high, many employers are flooded with applicants. In response, they may issue a temporary no-hire policy, which makes personal contact difficult because employees are instructed to notify applicants that no interviews are being scheduled at that time.

In a situation like this, you need to use initiative and persistence. Develop a persuasive reason to contact the person with hiring authority in your target organization.

Using an indirect strategy can create opportunities to meet people in your target organization who can arrange an interview for you. While you should not make a direct request for a job during a meeting that is arranged indirectly, you can discuss your experience and abilities. By doing so, you may convince your contact that you would be an asset to the organization, which is exactly your intention. Also ask whether the employer may need your skills in the future or if your contact could suggest another organization or department that may need someone with your qualifications.

Ask for Professional Advice

One effective indirect strategy is to arrange a brief meeting or telephone call with a prospective employer to discuss professional issues and to ask for advice about additional preparation to make you more employable.

Sound Impressive by Sounding Prepared

Felix Mizioznikov/Shutterstock.com

- **Identify yourself.** "Hello, this is Brenda Bernstein." Personnel who screen calls are suspicious of callers who don't give their names or state why they are calling. Be straightforward to eliminate any suspicions instantly.

- **Explain why you are calling.** Emphasize your qualifications before you make a request so that your listener has a reason to answer yes. Ask for an interview or use a practiced indirect strategy for getting through to the employer.

- **Get the name of the person who answers.** Ask, "Could I please have your name in case I need to talk with you again?" Write down the name. Using this person's name may make him or her more receptive to helping you.

- **Ask whether it's a good time to talk.**

- **Clarify the details.** Clarify any follow-up activities you are instructed to complete (for example, pick up an application, supply additional information or references, or keep an appointment). Verify the time and place of any meetings and get the correct spelling and pronunciation of the names of the people you will meet.

- **Thank the person you speak to by name.**

Ask about Professional Organizations

Ask for recommendations about professional associations, industry trade groups, and publications in your field. Consider asking the following questions:

- What professional association(s) would keep me informed of industry developments, technological advances in the field, and emerging trends?

- Which professional publications or Internet resources deal specifically with our field?

- Who else could I speak to for further advice on this topic?

Ask for Help with Career Planning

If you have not completed your education or have limited experience related to your target job, ask for help in choosing your course work or with career planning. Your conversation could be similar to this example.

Sample Request for Career Advice

"Hello, Mr. Cuervo. This is Cecilia Lee. I'm completing an assignment for a career planning course and would appreciate your assistance with some of my research. I'm seeking opinions from people who are recognized and experienced in the field of (your field).

"My skills lie in the area(s) of _____. Could you please help me identify positions in (your career field) for which these skills would be most useful?

"I'd also appreciate your recommendations about any additional course work and preparation I may need."

Ask for Help with Your Resume

If you are seeking help in developing your resume into one that employers will not pass over, you can place a telephone call to an employer and ask for his or her help in a manner similar to this.

Sample Request for Resume Advice

"Hello, Ms. Pappas. This is Nhon Tran. You've been highly recommended to me by Dr. Ivarsen of the Computer Information Systems Department of Nevada College. I'm developing a professional resume and would very much appreciate your critiquing it."

Develop a Relationship with Your Target Organization

The **gatekeeper** (the administrative support person, receptionist, or human resources staff member) who must screen all job applicants can help, hinder, or ruin your chances of obtaining a job with the organization. Because this person's influence on your job campaign can be considerable, you need to use good diplomacy skills when communicating with him or her. Follow these guidelines:

- Express respect for the organization, perhaps referring to its reputation for professionalism, reliability, or leadership.

- Find common ground in an effort to establish a good rapport with the gatekeeper. If he or she likes and trusts you, you may learn valuable information about what it is like to work for the company and whether you will fit in.

- If it seems feasible, ask for the person's help in arranging a meeting with the appropriate staff member. Indicate your awareness of everyone's busy schedules and ask the gatekeeper the best time to contact the employer. Ask if you could speak with someone else who can tell you more about your areas of interest.

- Before leaving, thank the person by name for his or her time and assistance.

When making the first contact with a target employer, remember that if you are successful in your job search, you will be working with the people you meet. You cannot afford to be ill-mannered, unprofessional, or overbearing with anyone you encounter during the first phone call or step through the door.

Uncover the Hidden Job Market

Numerous studies emphasize that 80 to 85 percent of job openings are never published and that personal searching is required to uncover them. This is the **hidden job market**. It's up to you to make an employer aware of your potential and possibly create a job in the process.

The first step to uncovering the hidden job market is researching target employers thoroughly. See the feature "Do Your Homework before Every Interview" on page 199 for what you should learn. Find out who is in charge of the department that can use your assets. Then analyze how your qualifications can be useful— or even essential—to the employer. The key is to identify how you can provide a useful service or save or make money for the organization.

Practice and polish your 30-Second Commercial. Ask a member of your support system to help you by playing the role of your contact and critiquing your presentation. Then present your qualifications for the job or service so convincingly that an employer is motivated to create a job for you. The hidden job market is uncovered through your own ingenuity.

Other Indirect Strategies

Try these tried and true strategies for getting interviews. Refer to additional sources of job leads in Chapter 5.

Go Through the Human Resources Department

If your target employer has a strict policy requiring all applicants to be processed through the human resources department, follow the required procedure. You can expect the first step to be submitting an application, a resume, and a cover letter. If you are selected, you will be invited to a screening interview with a member of the human resources staff. This interview may be in person or over the telephone. (The screening interview is covered in Chapter 10.)

WATCH OUT!

Don't Overlook People at Your School

When you are considering indirect strategies for getting interviews, don't overlook people at your school.

- Visit your college career center. As you learned in Chapter 5, your school's career center is a gold mine of information and professional advice. Ask a staff member for advice about getting interviews.

- Ask your instructors for advice and leads for interviews. Don't limit yourself to current teachers or even teachers at your current institution.

- Ask successful alumni for help. If you haven't already done so, join your college or university alumni association and participate in the social events, outings, and guest speaker engagements that it sponsors. Ask for the names of alumni who are successful in your field and request a career information survey with them or with someone else in their company.

- Don't forget your classmates as possible resources for leads for interviews.

MAKE IT A HABIT

Apply Your Networking Techniques

By far the most effective indirect strategy for getting an interview is through the continuous process of networking. Let everyone you know, even if only casually, that you want to get a job, change your career, or get back to work.

Employers are flooded with resumes of highly skilled individuals. If they do not immediately call qualified applicants to arrange an interview, what are they looking for? The answer is a personal referral.

Employers would rather take a chance on an individual whose name has been passed on to them by someone they know, socially or professionally, than interview a stranger.

iofoto/Shutterstock.com

If you perform well during a screening interview and you appear to be qualified, you may be scheduled for a departmental interview. If the employer doesn't have an opening in your area, find out how to keep your file active and how you can stay informed about the hiring status for the position.

Use a Private Employment Agency

If you plan to use employment agencies, staffing agencies, or employment contractors in your job search, they will arrange your job interviews. Read the agency's agreement thoroughly to be certain you are satisfied—and comfortable—with their procedures, including interviews. Clarify all of the procedures carefully before agreeing to them, as advised in Chapter 5.

Request Interviews at Career Fairs

Employers use job fairs to show off their businesses and to actively seek resumes and contacts. Job seekers can meet dozens of potential employers in one location, so bring several copies of your resume. Ask company representatives about hiring procedures, their opinion of industry trends, and the types of employees they typically hire. Try to arrange a follow-up career information survey meeting with an employer, using the name of the person you meet as your contact. Keep your contact's business card and use it to follow up within the week with a thank-you note or phone call.

COMPLETE **CAREER ACTION 9-3**

Internet Research Strategies for Getting Interviews, p. 212

Show the interviewer the type of employee you will be. Give solid, to-the-point answers. Ask thoughtful questions and never interrupt.

While You're Waiting for the Interview

Outcome 4

You should develop a contingency plan to fall back on if your strategies for getting interviews are taking longer than you expected. Look back at the suggestions about internships, cooperative jobs, and volunteer work in "Try Before You Buy" in Chapter 5, page 91, and consider these additional options.

Take Another Job

You may need to take another job while you wait for a position to become available. This work experience can increase your value. Use the experience to polish your current skills, develop new ones, and establish a reputation as a valuable employee.

Follow Up

Call your target employer when you have been in your interim job for some time and when you think employment opportunities may have improved. Ask whether the employer would consider reevaluating your qualifications in light of your new experience.

Check Back Periodically

Call the human resources department to remain informed of the hiring status and to reaffirm your interest. This may help you be first in line for openings.

If you consider more than one organization to be a prime employer, don't let one discouragement slow you down. Review the techniques in this chapter and rally your efforts toward your next target. Preparation, practice, action, and perseverance will pay off.

COMPLETE **CAREER ACTION 9-4**

Develop a Contingency Plan, p. 212

Chapter Checklist

Underline each action you are already taking and circle the actions you need to work on.

- Emphasize my qualifications before I ask for an interview, giving the listener a reason to answer yes. [1]

- Prepare for an in-person request for an interview as though it were an actual interview, knowing that a first impression can influence the outcome. [2]

- Prepare a written script or an outline and practice asking for an interview before doing it in person. [2]

- Treat gatekeepers and other staff members courteously and professionally because I know they are often the key to connecting with the hiring authority. [2]

- Create my own opportunities for employment by exploring the hidden job market. [3]

- Develop a backup plan in case my strategies for getting interviews take longer than expected. [4]

Critical-Thinking Questions

1. What method of making a request for an interview do you think will be most effective in your job search? Why? [1]

2. What are some advantages to requesting interviews by telephone rather than by letter? [1]

3. Why is it important to establish a good relationship with the gatekeeper and other people you meet while you wait to be interviewed? List several strategies you can use to establish good rapport. [2]

4. Get creative. Think of an employer you could realistically target for a hidden job market position. What are the needs of this employer based on your research? What special skills and knowledge do you have that represent a hidden job you could perform to meet the employer's needs? [3]

Want access to career resources, study tools, activities, and job information links? Get started at www.cengage.com/career/yourcareer.

TRIAL RUN

You need to be proactive and confident to use the strategies in this chapter successfully. Before you try your approach on strangers, practice with your classmates and support team. Most of these approaches are new, so review the basic advice as a class to make sure you understand when to apply each suggestion.

Divide into teams of three or four students. Each team creates an interview request scenario and presents it to the class. Discuss types of employers, types of approaches, possible pitfalls, and follow-up. One student can play the role of the employer on the phone or in person, reacting to the request for an interview.

Use this checklist to evaluate each team:

- In-person verbal skills
- Telephone skills
- Written skills
- 30-Second Commercial applicable to job
- Request style appropriate to employment target
- Reaction to rejection

Team's Strengths:

Suggestions for Improvement:

CAREER ACTION   9-1   **Develop Your In-Person Request for an Interview** [2]

Read the sample request for an interview on page 201 and write a script or an outline that would be appropriate to use when requesting an interview with your prospective job target(s). File a copy in your Career Management Files Tracker.

The Opening:

The 30-Second Commercial Excerpt:

The Request:

The Close:

CAREER ACTION

9-2 Develop and Practice Your Telephone Interview Request ②

Part 1: Write a script or an outline that would be appropriate when using the telephone to request an interview with your prospective job target(s). File a copy in your Career Management Files Tracker.

The Opening:

The 30-Second Commercial Excerpt:

The Request:

The Close:

Part 2: Turn to your support system for assistance. Do some role-playing, following the guidelines below. Deliver your telephone request for an interview to someone in your support system.

1. Record your delivery, play it back, critique it, and improve on it as necessary.

2. Have your helper ask you questions that require more information about your qualifications.

3. Practice responding when your helper makes excuses for not scheduling an interview.

4. Practice presenting your qualifications persuasively.

5. Practice turning objections into acceptance.

CAREER ACTION   9-3   Internet Research Strategies for Getting Interviews [3]

Search the Internet or *Career Transitions* for additional tips for getting job interviews. You may want to look for tips on using social networking sites in your job search. Look for new ideas that you find especially useful. Summarize your findings and file your research in your Career Management Files Tracker.

CAREER ACTION   9-4   Develop a Contingency Plan [4]

Use this worksheet to discover what types of jobs you are qualified for that may not be your target career. Refer to your completed Career Actions 3-6 and 3-7 to complete the form below.

List three jobs that you are currently qualified or overqualified to do:

List the benefits of working in a field related to your target career:

Describe your action plan for finding a backup job through indirect interview requests:

For Your Career Management Files Tracker

CA 9-1   Script or outline for in-person interview request

CA 9-2   Script or outline for telephone interview request

CA 9-3   Internet research findings about strategies for getting interviews

CA 9-4   Contingency plan while waiting for interviews

Interview Styles and Questions

Outcomes

1 Prepare for the most common interview styles.

2 Prepare answers to typical interview questions.

3 Plan the questions that you will ask during interviews.

© Photographer/Image Source

OVERVIEW Job interviews are either structured (the interviewer asks each job candidate the same questions with the goal of comparing candidates) or unstructured (the interviewer guides the interview based on the candidate's responses). You can improve your chance of success in an interview if you are prepared for different styles of interviews. Use the information in this chapter to help make the best impression in your interviews by understanding different interview styles, practicing answering interview questions, asking appropriate questions of your own, and practicing good listening skills.

CHAPTER 10

CAREER ACTIONS

10-1: Research Interview Styles

10-2: Internet Research on Question-and-Answer Tips

10-3: Create a Question-and-Answer Planning Sheet

JUMP START
Your Interview Performance

Job interviews are like other situations you find yourself managing in daily life. You intuitively know how to act and speak in formal and less formal situations. For example, your style of speaking with your friend's grandparents at his formal wedding is probably quite different from the way you talk with your nieces and nephews at a backyard barbecue.

Interviews call for your best performance, and part of that means matching your behavior to the structure and style of the interview. With a partner, practice giving the most persuasive excerpt of your 30-Second Commercial in two situations: (a) a structured interview conducted by a trained interviewer from the human resources department and (b) the close of an unstructured interview with a small business owner who did not directly ask about your qualifications for the job. Record these sessions and meet with another group. Listen to all four commercials. Identify the type of interview the person was in, point out the strongest parts of each Commercial, and offer tips for improvement.

Outcome **1**

Inside the Interview

Have you ever had a job where you had all the time in the world to finish each assignment or where your department could choose the deadline for an important project? Of course not. Hiring a new employee is no different—the people in charge of finding the perfect person need to work efficiently to fill the empty position. Chances are high that for most jobs, you are competing against a handful of applicants—the very few whose cover letter and resume made the cut.

You will be nervous—everyone is—but less so if you know what to expect during the interview and have practiced your answers to the most likely questions. There are two basic styles of interviews:

- In a structured interview, the interviewer asks each job candidate the same questions (often factual) with the goal of comparing candidates objectively after all of the interviews have been conducted.

- In an unstructured interview, the interviewer seeks to learn about each person being interviewed as an individual: background, skills, personality, etc. The interviewer changes the questions or the direction of the interview based on the candidate's responses.

You should be prepared for both styles of interviews. You should also be prepared for both styles in the same interview. The interviewer may start by asking more factual questions and then ask more open-ended questions that give you opportunities to reveal the type of employee you would be.

As a rule, you should expect to have no fewer than two interviews with an employer before a hiring decision is made. If you are scheduled for a follow-up interview, you are definitely in the running; so review and polish your interviewing skills.

The Structured Interview

The **structured interview** is often used by professional interviewers who work in the human resources department or are part of a corporate interview team. The interviewer typically asks a predetermined set of questions, sometimes noting the applicant's responses on an interview rating form or a checklist. Many interviewers use the same list of questions for each job applicant to ensure fairness. The approach is formal and focuses on obtaining factual information.

Because it is highly structured, this approach may not give the interviewer adequate information about the applicant's personality and attitudes. Applicants who impress the interviewer and the hiring committee favorably are typically called back for a second interview.

Screening Interview

Large organizations often require applicants to be interviewed first through the human resources department. The **screening interview** is used to identify qualified applicants for the next level of interviews and to screen out applicants who do not have the basic qualifications for the job.

Some employers conduct screening interviews by telephone. Also, some screening interviews are outsourced, especially by small companies with limited human resources staff. In these cases, the interviewers may not actually work for the employer and may not be able to answer all of your questions. The interviewer may use a rating sheet to evaluate each applicant.

Your goal in a screening interview is to be scheduled for the next required interview. Make sure you state your qualifications clearly and concisely. Ask what to expect next, who is responsible for making a hiring decision, and when this decision will be made.

Behavioral Interview

The behavioral interview, which is widely used today, is based on the premise that past performance is the best predictor of future behavior. In a **behavioral interview**, the interviewer asks questions aimed at getting the applicant to provide specific examples of how he or she has successfully used the skills required for the target job. This helps the interviewer evaluate the candidate's experience and predict future on-the-job behavior in the following areas:

- **Content skills**—work-specific skills such as computer programming, CAD, and medical transcription.
- **Functional or transferable skills**—skills used with people, things, or information, such as good communication, organizational, or planning skills. These skills are valuable from one job to another.
- **Self-management skills**—personal characteristics such as being a dependable person, a team player, a self-directed worker, a problem solver, or a decision maker.

If you have completed the activities in Chapter 8, you are ready to handle a behavioral interview. Your 30-Second Commercial contains the proof-by-example descriptions of your capabilities that are most relevant to the target job. This is what an interviewer is looking for in a behavioral interview.

To prepare for behavioral interviews, recall scenarios from your experiences that illustrate how you have performed or behaved on the job. Write out examples that demonstrate good performance. Also be ready to describe how you have handled difficult situations. Students with little work experience should focus on class projects and group situations that illustrate their task performance and interpersonal behavior. These four steps provide a good model for your answers to behavioral questions:

1. Describe the situation.
2. Explain the actions you took.
3. Describe the outcomes.
4. Summarize what you learned from the experience.

    Example: Describe an accomplishment that demonstrates your initiative.

    Suggested Answer: "While I was working part-time as a computer lab technician for Seattle Technology College, our department received several complaints about service response time. I set a personal goal of answering all troubleshooting calls within 90 minutes. I recorded the exact response time for each call and maintained the goal of a 90-minute response time for one full semester. I was awarded the Customer Service Certificate for this performance."

Whenever possible, give positive examples that demonstrate measurable achievements. Or when describing a less positive experience, emphasize what actions you took to correct weaknesses or poor performance. By giving specific examples, you establish credibility and believability that can translate into a job offer. See additional examples of behavioral interview questions in the section "Behavioral Questions" on pages 220–221.

Campus Interview

Campus interviews are generally scheduled through a school's career center. These prearranged screening interviews are usually structured. The average campus interview is 20 to 30 minutes, and the schedule is closely observed.

Because the interviewer must evaluate each candidate quickly, you should keep your remarks concise and to the point. Most interviewers are professionally trained and know how to guide applicants through the fact-finding process. Let the interviewer take the lead and respond as briefly as possible without omitting pertinent information about your qualifications.

Panel Interview

In a **panel interview** (also called a *board interview*), you talk with more than one person at a time. Focus on the person questioning you at the moment, but don't ignore the others. Appearing relaxed and projecting a self-assured attitude is important. Before a board, or panel, interview, try to obtain and memorize the names of the panel members. During the interview, draw a diagram of the seating arrangement and label seats with interviewers' names. At the close of the interview, shake hands and thank each interviewer by name as you leave.

Team Interview

A **team interview** may be given by a group of three to five employees. The applicant meets individually with each person; the team and the applicant do not meet together at one time. (If an employee will work directly with several managers, a few team members may conduct a panel interview.)

Employees who conduct team interviews are usually trained in interviewing techniques. They meet before the interview to determine the subject areas each team member will cover. The team members may ask a few common questions to give the applicant more than one opportunity to cover a particular topic. After the interview, the team members meet to discuss the applicant's performance. Using common criteria, they assess the information from

The Stress Interview

Marcin Balcerzak/Shutterstock.com

Stress interviews are generally reserved for jobs that involve regular pressure. They are designed to test the applicant's behavior, logic, and emotional control under pressure.

A skilled interviewer may combine some stress techniques with an unstructured interview approach to get a well-rounded picture of your personality. Some techniques used in stress interviewing include (a) remaining silent following one of your remarks, (b) questioning you rapidly, (c) placing you on the defensive with irritating questions or remarks, and (d) criticizing your responses or remarks.

Some stress questions are routinely asked in other types of job interviews—even informal ones. Every job has an occasional crisis situation. An interviewer may also use a stress technique unintentionally. Do not react negatively. Take a deep breath, demonstrate control, and be courteous.

the individual sessions and their reactions before identifying the best candidate.

Team interviews give applicants a chance to meet with several people who may be their peers or supervisors on the job. This type of interview ensures a personality fit and increases the applicant's chances of establishing rapport with one or more members of the team.

Before a team interview, learn the names of the members and, if possible, learn something about their areas of expertise. Use this information to enhance your performance. Be sure to give consistent answers to the individual members' questions.

Telephone Interview

A telephone interview is a cost-effective screening technique. If you expect to be interviewed by telephone, ask a member of your network to role-play the interviewer. Practice delivering a short version of your commercial and answering typical interview questions.

Expect to receive a call at any time to schedule an interview. Make sure you have a businesslike outgoing voicemail message that includes your name and phone number and make sure anyone who may answer the phone knows to answer professionally and take a complete message. Return calls promptly and be prepared to interview immediately or to leave a message with your contact information and availability. Using these tips will help you succeed in a telephone interview:

1. **Be prepared to take an interview call at any time.** Have a copy of your resume and Commercial where you can refer to them easily. Keep paper and pen handy so that you can write down names and information and keep a log of your calls. If you need a moment to collect yourself, politely ask the interviewer to hold for a moment while you move to a quiet location. Eliminate all distractions and background noise.

MAKE IT A HABIT

Focus on Your Job Qualifications

It takes planning and preparation to be able to discuss your strengths persuasively and explain how they can benefit an employer. Consider the positive capabilities and personal qualities your coworkers, supervisors, instructors, and others have recognized in you.

Look through your resume and your 30-Second Commercial for examples of your positive performance that are related to requirements of the target job. Look too for examples that showcase what you can do for any employer:

- Examples that demonstrate your organizational skills and orderly mind
- Examples of improved methods of performing tasks
- Examples of motivating people successfully
- Examples of leading a team or being an effective team member
- Examples of effective problem solving
- Examples that demonstrate your creativity
- Examples of handling detailed assignments carefully and accurately
- Examples of being dependable and flexible
- Examples of working independently without regular supervision

Robert Kneschke/Shutterstock.com

2. **Focus on why you are interested in working for the prospective employer** on the basis of your research and understanding of the employer's products or services, current developments, philosophies, etc.

3. **Be professional, courteous, and friendly;** let the caller lead the conversation but ask questions of your own.

4. **Stand up, speak directly into the mouthpiece, and smile while you talk.** This gives your voice more energy and a pleasant tone. Never smoke, eat, or chew gum while on the telephone.

5. **Be factual in your answers; be brief yet thorough.** Avoid yes/no answers; they give no real information about your abilities.

6. **If you need time to think about a question, avoid using repetitive phrases to buy time.** Instead, simply say, "Let me think about that."

7. **Ask what skills, knowledge, and qualities the employer is looking for in filling the position.** While the interviewer answers, jot down the qualities you have that match; then describe them to emphasize how you meet the employer's needs.

8. **As you wrap up the interview, ask what the next steps are.** Tell the interviewer that you are available for a face-to-face interview at his or her earliest convenience.

9. **Follow up.** Call back one or two days later, thank the interviewer for his or her time, and restate your interest in the position. If necessary, leave this message by voicemail or send an email.

Computer-Based Interview

Some companies use **computer-based interviews** to screen applicants. The applicant logs onto a password-protected website with instructions on how to complete the interview. The interview typically consists of 50 to 100 multiple-choice and true/false questions. Interviews are usually timed, and you cannot start and stop once you have begun.

Some programs search for contradictions by asking you the same question several times in different forms; so be consistent in your answers.

For the employer, the benefits of computer-based interviews include ease and cost effectiveness of data collection, consistent gathering of information from all applicants, and avoidance of any slant the interviewer may, consciously or unconsciously, give to a particular applicant. The primary drawback is that computers are not capable of assessing personal qualities such as attitude and enthusiasm. These qualities can be observed in follow-up interviews, however.

Some computer-based interviews include open-ended questions that are reviewed by recruitment specialists or managers. Answer questions just as you would in a face-to-face interview. Emphasize your related skills but don't exaggerate. Be concise, avoiding overly long responses or a negative focus on a topic.

Video Interview

A video interview uses two-way video to conduct a "face-to-face" interview over the Internet. Video interviews are used to save money and time for organizations.

To succeed in a video interview, follow the guidelines for standard face-to-face interviews outlined in Chapter 8. Dress appropriately, project energy, and maintain eye contact with the camera. Use positive body language and good posture and avoid fidgeting.

The Unstructured Interview

The **unstructured interview** approach is generally taken by people who are not professionally trained in interviewing. It tends to be more informal and conversational in tone than a structured interview approach. The unstructured approach is often used by the owners or managers of small businesses and not-for-profit organizations. Interviewing job applicants is just one of many responsibilities of the interviewer, unlike a human resources specialist in a large organization.

In writing, answer every question you think you may be asked—and every question you hope you won't be asked. **"**

The questions in unstructured interviews are usually open-ended to encourage the interviewees to express their personalities, background, and goals. Success or failure in this type of interview may be based more on the ability of the job seeker to communicate well than on the content of the answers.

An untrained interviewer may not be skilled in discussing job qualifications, so the conversation may get bogged down by unimportant details. In this situation, you need to be the "professional interviewee." You can help the interviewer, and yourself, by asking questions to learn about the full scope of the job and by communicating all of your skills, experience, and attributes that apply to it.

COMPLETE	**CAREER ACTION 10-1**

Research Interview Styles, p. 229

Typical Interview Questions

The core of a job interview is the question-and-answer period. Generally, you should let the interviewer take the lead. Interviewers usually consider an applicant's effort to control the interview to be rude or aggressive.

Questions asked by interviewers generally fall into four categories:

- General information questions
- Behavioral questions
- Character questions
- Stress questions

Study the following lists of the most common questions and suggested answers.

General Information Questions

General information questions are asked to obtain factual information. They usually cover your skills, work experience, etc.

1. **Why do you want this job?** (Be prepared; every employer wants to know the answer to this question.)
   Suggested answer: "My skills and experience are directly related to this position, and I'm very interested in this field." If applicable, relate examples of your experience, education, and/or training that relate to the job you are seeking. Never say that you want the job because of the pay and benefits.

2. **What type of work do you enjoy most?**
   Suggested answer: Play your research card; name the types of tasks that are involved in the job and demonstrate how you are qualified for the position.

3. **What are your strongest skills?**
   Suggested answer: Review your abilities and accomplishments and your 30-Second Commercial to develop your answer. Relate your skills directly to those required for the position.

4. **Are you a team player?**
   Suggested answer: Teamwork is highly valued in today's workplace, so a positive answer is usually a plus. Give examples of your successful team roles (as a leader, a member, or a partner) from school, previous jobs, volunteer work, or sports.

5. **What are your long-term career goals, and how do you plan to achieve them?**
   Suggested answer: Emphasize your strengths, state that your goal is to make a strong contribution in your job, and explain that you look forward to developing the experience necessary for career growth.

Employers are impressed with employees who show initiative because they perform better than those who have no plans for self-improvement. Mention your plans to continue your education and expand your knowledge to become a more valuable employee.

6. **Do you have a geographic preference? Are you willing to relocate?**
Suggested answer: If the job requires relocation, this question is important. If you have no objection to relocating, make this perfectly clear. If you do have objections, this could be a stress question. Be honest in your answer. If you don't like being mobile, say so; otherwise, you will no doubt be unhappy in the job.

7. **With what type of supervisor have you had the best relationships?**
Suggested answer: "I've had good relationships with all of my supervisors. Communication is so important; I make sure I understand what I'm supposed to do. That's especially important when I've been

given new responsibilities so that we can get off to a good start. I think supervisors appreciate someone who takes responsibility for his or her job." (Be prepared to give an example of a "new responsibility" you were given and what you did to "get off to a good start.")

Behavioral Questions

Behavioral questions probe the applicant's specific past performance and behaviors. The interviewer wants details of experiences that illustrate how you perform or behave on a job or in stressful environments. You can expect questions such as "Describe the most challenging assignments you've had. How did you handle it?" This may be followed by several more in-depth probes such as "Explain what problems you encountered. How did you overcome them?"

Some behavioral questions probe for negative experiences. In responding to these, use the SAR technique to frame your

Become a Good Listener

peepo/iStockphoto.com

You may think of the interview primarily in terms of talking, but listening carefully is just as important. So that you can respond appropriately, you need to listen to the interviewer carefully to learn important details about the job requirements, the organization, and the department.

Follow these tips to become a more effective listener:

- Give each question your undivided attention. Don't formulate your response while you are listening.
- Nod as appropriate.
- Repeat or summarize the main ideas.
- Ask questions when you need to clarify what the

interviewer means. If you don't understand a question, ask for clarification instead of talking and hoping you answered correctly.

- Listen "between the lines" for the underlying messages.
- Don't argue or interrupt.
- Maintain eye contact (but not too intensely).
- Maintain an "open" position (don't cross your arms or legs; keep your hands unclenched).
- Maintain the same eye level as the interviewer (sit or stand as appropriate).

answer: **S**ituation–**A**ction–**R**esults. What happened? What did you do? What were the results? Be thorough but keep your answer short. Focus on what you learned from the experience or what actions you took to improve the situation.

1. **Tell me specifically about a time when you worked under great stress.**
   Suggested answer: Be careful to choose a relevant example that would be considered stressful in a work environment. Quickly describe the elements that made it stressful for you and how you maintained your cool and got the job done. If you don't have a good example, describe what you would do or how you would handle the situation better this time.

2. **Describe an experience when you dealt with an angry customer or coworker.**
   Suggested answer: Give an answer that highlights how you value communication and know that conflict can lead to personal growth and opportunity. Your reply also should include how you resolved the situation and what you would do differently in the future.

3. **Give me an example of your ability to adapt to change.**
   Suggested answer: "When the new firm took over management of our site, I focused on the positive outcomes rather than looking back and comparing management styles. I encouraged my coworkers to remain flexible and patient." This shows your leadership and maturity.

4. **Explain what problems you have encountered. How did you overcome them?**
   Suggested answer: Some behavioral questions probe for negative experiences. In responding to these, focus on what you learned from the experience or what actions you took to improve the situation.

Character Questions

Character questions are asked to learn about your personal attributes, such as integrity, personality, attitudes, and motivation.

1. **How would you describe yourself?**
   Suggested answer: Emphasize your strongest personal attributes and focus on those that are relevant to your target job. Review

Be Prepared for Silence

Creatas/JupiterImages

Be prepared to handle silence. The interviewer asks you a question, you answer, and the interviewer does not respond.

Interviewers sometimes use this technique to test applicants' confidence and ability to handle stress or uncertainty. Do not retract your statement; just wait calmly. You have no obligation to continue talking if you answered adequately. By doing this, you will pass the "test" and project a mature, confident image. Break a long silence by asking whether the interviewer needs more information or by asking a related question.

You also can use silence. If you are asked a difficult question, answering too quickly without enough thought can be detrimental. You're entitled to think carefully about a question and to prepare a response. The employer wouldn't want you to solve problems on the job without adequate thought and planning.

Avoid long pauses in a telephone or video interview, however. When the interviewer has fewer "clues" about you as a person, long pauses may be perceived as slow thinking abilities.

your capabilities and accomplishments. Examples: "I'm punctual and dependable. At my current job, I haven't been late or missed one day in the last two years." "I get along well with others; in fact, my coworkers chose me to represent them in our company's monthly staff meetings."

Give specific examples of your strengths. Don't just say "I'm a hard worker" or "I'm dependable." Other leads include "I learn quickly," "I like solving problems; for example . . . ," "I like contributing to a team," and "I like managing people." Use a relevant example that shows that you know what is important in a work environment.

2. **What rewards do you look for in your career?**
   Suggested answer: Don't make financial rewards your prime motivator. Emphasize your desire to improve your skills, make a valuable contribution to the field, and become better educated. These answers show initiative, interest, and professionalism.

3. **What accomplishment are you most proud of, particularly as it relates to your field?**
   Suggested answer: Relate an accomplishment that shows special effort and initiative. "I recognized the need to improve communications [between two departments]. I designed a questionnaire that was completed by representatives from each department. Management made several of the changes, and communications were improved in those areas."

4. **Do you work well under pressure?**
   Suggested answer: You may be tempted to answer with a simple yes or no, but don't. Yes and no answers reveal nothing specific about you. Don't miss an opportunity to sell yourself.

   Be honest in your answer. If you prefer to work at a well-defined job in an organized, calm atmosphere (rather than one that involves constant decision making and pressure), say so. Otherwise, you may end up in a job that is a constant source of tension. If you enjoy the challenge of pressure,

WATCH OUT!

"Tell Me about Yourself"

Sometimes an employer will start an interview by taking a few minutes to establish rapport or make small talk and then say, "Tell me about yourself."

Be prepared to handle this type of interview effectively. Once the interviewer makes this request, he or she comments just enough to encourage you to keep talking. The purpose is to see whether you focus on your qualifications for the job and how the employer would benefit by hiring you. Do not ramble on about your life history; this is a sure way to disqualify yourself on the spot. Ask questions such as "What exactly do you want to know about [my work experience, educational experience, skills, or extracurricular and community activities]?"

Your objective is to highlight your positive qualities (personal attributes, accomplishments, skills, pertinent training, work experience, etc.). After you think you have covered these topics, ask, "Would you like me to clarify or expand on any area for you?" This helps you focus on the information the interviewer wants.

Kemter/iStockphoto.com

either in decision making or in dealing with people, make this fact clear.

Keep in mind that a large company may have more than one working environment. For instance, an administrative support job in the customer relations department would likely involve more interactive pressure with the public than a support job in the data processing department.

Stress Questions

Stress questions are asked to determine how you perform under pressure (controlled and composed or nervous and unsettled). They are also used to find out whether you are good at making decisions, solving problems, and thinking under stress.

Some questions may be aimed at clarifying issues the interviewer perceives as possible problems, such as being overqualified or underqualified or lacking dependability (if your resume shows many different jobs).

Preparing Answers to Stress Questions

Prepare to answer any stress questions that are based on your resume or personal circumstances. Look at a stress question as an opportunity to prove that a situation is not a problem as it relates to your ability to do the job. Career Action 10-3 will help you prepare by having you write out responses to possible stress questions. Rehearse your responses. Either record yourself giving the question(s) and prepared response(s) or ask a member of your support network to help you role-play the interview. Revise your responses based on the feedback you receive.

Remaining Cool under Stress

Keep your cool. Take three to five calming deep breaths and tell yourself, "I can do this."

If you are asked a question that you are totally unprepared for, don't ramble through an answer. Use the "that's a good question, let me think about it for a minute" technique. This can buy you time to prepare a well-thought-out response. Your goal is to demonstrate that you can handle stress—that you don't just react, but instead think through the situation and remain composed.

Whenever possible, give positive examples that demonstrate measureable achievements. When describing a less positive experience, emphasize what actions you took to correct weaknesses or poor performance. Specific examples help to establish credibility and believability.

1. **Why do you think you are the best candidate for the job? or Why should I hire you?**
   Suggested answer: Ask the interviewer to highlight the important objectives and challenges of the job. Then explain how you can handle them. Focus on how you can benefit the employer, citing examples of increasing productivity, saving money, increasing sales, etc. Summarize your accomplishment, skills, and experience that are pertinent to the job. Then ask, "How does that fit your requirements?" This shifts the focus from you to the interviewer, helping reduce stress for you.

2. **Why do you want to leave your current job?**
   Suggested answer: This question will likely be posed to determine whether you have a problem with your current job. Accentuate the positive—for example, you are seeking a new challenge, you have mastered your present job and are seeking advancement, or you want to work for a company with stability. If you have a problem with your current job or boss, avoid discussing it. If you feel you must, describe the situation briefly and unemotionally, then return the tone to a positive one.

3. **Why have you held so many jobs?**
   Suggested answer: Employers like to see a work history that implies stability and dependability. People often have valid reasons for holding numerous jobs that don't necessarily imply immaturity or an inability to commit. Some jobs are seasonal (agriculture and recreation), some jobs require frequent relocation (construction), and some jobs are profoundly affected by

MAKE IT A HABIT

Savvy Q&A Strategies

- **Be enthusiastic.** Enthusiasm is a quality that employers look for when hiring.

- **Pause to think before you reply.** If you're uncomfortable with a question, go back to the familiar. Stress your assets. Use a "thinking pause" to buy time to answer the question well. For example, "Could we return to this question? I'd like to think about it for a moment" or "That's a good question" or "Let me see . . ." (This works if you need only a little extra time.)

- **Be candid and honest.** Be realistic when expressing your preferences and dislikes. You won't be happy in a job that isn't a good fit.

- **Do not use canned responses.** Tailor your answers to fit your goals, objectives, and personality as well as the goals and needs of the employer.

- **Be concise.** Keep your responses to the point but avoid being curt or too brief.

- **Answer in complete sentences and speak correctly.** Avoid using slang, bad grammar, or repetitive terms. Speak clearly.

- **Be positive.** Positive thinking promotes positive behavior and speech, a positive image, positive responses, and a positive atmosphere. It also projects enthusiasm, self-confidence, and initiative.

- **Fill in the gaps.** If you sense that the interviewer thinks you have an area of weakness, communicate how you plan to eliminate the weakness or round out your qualifications—perhaps by completing research or course work in the area.

Digital Vision/JupiterImages

the economy. You may have held a variety of summer jobs while completing your education. Capitalize on this fact; it shows initiative and provides you with broad working experience. Whatever the case, emphasize that while you may previously have wanted to obtain a broad base of experience, your goal now is to apply yourself to long-term employment and the development of a career.

4. **What is your greatest weakness?**
   Suggested answer: "My weakest area is accounting, so I am taking a course in beginning accounting at the community college. It's going well, and I plan to take the advance course next semester." The objective is to acknowledge a weakness that is low on the employer's list and to explain your steps to improve the weakness (through practice, education, planning, etc.).

5. **Have you ever been fired from a job?**
   Suggested answer: If you have been fired, use terms such as *laid off*, *let go*, or *employment ended*; they sound less negative. Be honest about the reason for your termination. Briefly describe the situation; explain what you learned from the experience and how you could have handled the experience differently. Take responsibility for past mistakes but end your response on a positive note.

6. **Does your current employer know you are planning to leave?**
   Suggested answer: If your current employer is aware of this fact, say so. If not—and especially if you depend on your current income—make this clear. Say that you prefer your current employer not be informed of your job search until a firm offer is made and that you will give two weeks' notice before leaving. Consider it a good sign that the interviewer is asking this question—you are probably close to being offered a position.

Inappropriate Questions

The interview is going along well, and then it happens: "Do you have any children?" or "How long has your family been in this country?"

On the surface, questions such as these seem innocent enough. Yet the structure and format of the questions may be illegal or, at the very least, inappropriate. When you are in a situation where the person asking the question has the power to decide whether you will get the job, this information can be used to discriminate against you or other candidates.

Questions that focus on age, gender, race, marital status, language, children, criminal record, national origin, religion, or disability are inappropriate in a job interview.

So you've just been asked an inappropriate question. What do you do? How do you respond? The risk here is that refusing to answer can count against you, even though the question was illegal. If you complain about a question being illegal or unfair, you probably won't be offered the job. You certainly have the right to refuse, but first weigh the situation. Is it worth jeopardizing the job over this question? If it is an offensive question, the answer may be "Yes, the job is worth risking because I'm not sure I want to work for this company." Or does the interviewer appear nonthreatening and unaware that the question was inappropriate? Only you can decide.

The most effective approach is to answer the question in a polite, honest manner. Don't offer detailed personal information. Instead, steer the conversation back to your ability to meet the employer's expectations, as in the following examples:

Interviewer: Do you have any children?

Applicant: Yes, and I'm thorough in arranging dependable child care. It pays off; I've never had to miss a day of work for child care purposes (emphasizing planning and management skills). *Or* I am available to work the hours required of this position, including overtime and travel with advance notice.

Interviewer: Where you born in the United States?

Applicant: I have the legal right to work in the United States, and my English language abilities are more than ample to meet the requirements of the job.

Outcome 3 Your Questions Count

Making the interview an instance of effective two-way communication is important. Prepare to ask three to five well-chosen questions. Outline a list of questions that will help you learn what you need to know about the employer, organizational culture, and position.

Don't ask all of your questions at the end of the interview. Interject them naturally at appropriate intervals throughout the meeting. Keep your questions positive and avoid asking anything that could elicit a negative reaction. Also, do not discuss salary until a job offer has been made.

Good Questions to Ask

Asking appropriate questions demonstrates interest and confidence, showcases your knowledge, and gives you an active role in the interview. Study the following sample questions carefully; then write your own questions as part of Career Action 10-2.

1. **Do you have a training program for this position? If so, will you describe it?**
   Why it works: This question demonstrates interest in the job and a desire to perform it well.

2. **Can you tell me about the duties and tasks of this position in a typical workday?**
   Why it works: The answer to this question will help you better understand the scope of the job. The job may be just what you want, or you may learn that it's not the type of work you are seeking. The information you receive will be important to you in considering a job offer.

3. **May I have a copy of the written job description?**
   Why it works: Getting a job description can help you tie your qualifications to those required for the job.

4. **Will the responsibilities of this position expand with time and experience on the job? Can good performance in this job lead to opportunities for career growth?**

Why it works: Answers to these questions will help you determine whether this is a dead-end job or whether employee career growth is encouraged.

5. **Can you tell me about the people I would work with? To whom does this position report?**
   Why it works: These answers can help you assess company structure and how you might fit into the organization.

6. **Do you need any more information about my qualifications or experience?**
   Why it works: If the interviewer wants more information, you have an opportunity to clear up any misunderstanding or lack of information. It also gives you another chance to run your 30-Second Commercial, once again emphasizing just how well qualified you are.

7. **When will you be making your hiring decision? May I call you if I have additional questions?**
   Why it works: These types of questions help you judge when to follow up and will keep the door open for further communication.

Turnoff Questions to Avoid

Following are some questions that are most disliked by employers. Do not ask them; they will make you sound uninformed and diminish your likability.

1. **What does this company do?**
   Why to avoid: You should have done your research well enough to know what the company does. Asking this question will make you appear uninformed and unqualified. Employers are not looking for employees who know nothing about their business.

2. **How much sick leave and vacation time will I get?**
   Why to avoid: Do not ask this question during a first interview. Although employee benefits are important, asking specifically about vacation time or sick leave projects a negative attitude. You should ask this question before making a final decision about a job offer, however. Employers understand the importance of major benefits to prospective employees.

3. **Will I have an office?**
   Why to avoid: This suggests that you care more about where you will work than about what you will do.

4. **What time do I have to be at work in the morning? How long do you allow for lunch?**
   Why to avoid: These questions sound immature and do not project an enthusiastic interest in the work.

5. **How long do I have to work before I am eligible for a raise?**
   Why to avoid: This question tells the employer that you are more interested in the salary than the job.

COMPLETE   **CAREER ACTION 10-2**

Internet Research on Question-and-Answer Tips, p. 229

COMPLETE   **CAREER ACTION 10-3**

Create a Question-and-Answer Planning Sheet, p. 230

Chapter Checklist

Underline each action you are already taking and circle the actions you need to work on.

- Prepare for different types of interviews. [1]

- Focus on responding persuasively to questions about my qualifications and abilities; cite examples of applying my abilities in work, school, and other activities. [2]

- Prepare and rehearse responses to typical interview questions. [2]

- Anticipate the stress of inappropriate interview questions and practice careful responses. [2]

- Prepare and practice responses to stress questions; think through the question and remain composed. [2]

- Prepare and ask appropriate questions. [3]

- Avoid asking questions that diminish my likability, including questions that are too direct, questions that my research should have answered, and questions that make me appear immature or uncommitted to the job. [3]

Critical-Thinking Questions

1. How will you benefit from knowing what style of interview your target employer typically uses? [1]

2. What style(s) of interviewing do you expect to be most prevalent in your job search? What techniques do you plan to use to maximize your performance in these types of interviews? [1]

3. What are the job applicant's main objectives during the question-and-answer portion of the interview? [2]

4. What specific types of questions do you most need to prepare for to be ready for your interviews? List two examples and include the answers you plan to give. [2]

5. How will you handle an illegal or inappropriate question from an interviewer? [2]

6. Why is it important for an applicant to ask some questions during an interview? [3]

Want access to career resources, study tools, activities, and job information links? Get started at www.cengage.com/career/yourcareer.

TRIAL RUN

Divide into teams of four and make sure you have a sheet of paper.

Each person selects a type of interview question (general information, behavioral, character, or stress) and uses a sheet of paper to write two questions from the lists in this chapter:

- One question on side A.
- One question on side B.

Pass the sheets to the left.

- Take two minutes to write an answer to the interview question on side A.
- When time is up, pass the sheets to the left again and answer the second question on side A.
- Do this until each person on the team has answered all four interview questions on side A.

Repeat the exercise with the questions on side B.

Read each question and the four suggested answers aloud. Critique the answers and decide which one is the best choice or how a combination of the answers would be most appropriate. Be creative.

If possible, have someone record all of the questions and answers and distribute them to the group.

CAREER ACTION 10-1 **Research Interview Styles** [1]

Part 1. Using Your Personal Contacts for Research.

Contact at least two organizations in your field that are similar to your target employer and arrange a brief meeting with someone at each place to research his or her interview style. Make sure the person understands that this is not a request for an interview. Follow the guidelines for conducting a successful career information survey in Chapter 4, as well as these steps.

1. During your meetings, ask your contacts to describe the style of interviewing they use to evaluate applicants for positions similar to the one you are targeting.

2. Ask what criteria (skills, experience, education, personal qualities) they use to evaluate applicants.

3. Ask for specific examples of applicants' positive and negative actions and comments.

4. Take notes of any information you find useful.

5. As always, act professionally and thank the people who help you. Follow up by sending thank-you notes.

Part 2. Internet Research.

Use these sites and others to search for information on the interview styles you expect to be most prevalent in your field (links are on the product website). Summarize the key points you find useful or print relevant articles. File your research in your Career Management Files Tracker.

- AARP
- CareerJournal.com
- Quintessential Careers
- The Riley Guide
- WomensJobList
- jobsearch.about.com

CAREER ACTION 10-2 **Internet Research on Question-and-Answer Tips** [2]

Use *Career Transitions* and the Internet to search for additional tips about interview questions and answers. Summarize the key points or print the relevant articles that you find. Be sure to use many sources, including sponsored links on newspaper and media sites, the links on the product website and Career Transitions, and other career information sites. If you want to know more about handling inappropriate questions, include this topic in your search directly from a search engine.

CAREER ACTION

10-3   Create a Question-and-Answer Planning Sheet ②

Record the answers to typical questions you can expect to be asked during job interviews. Also write sample questions you can ask during interviews. Use the suggestions in this chapter and in previous interview chapters as well as your 30-Second Commercial. Tailor your answers to your target job. Emphasize your qualifications for the job at every opportunity. Use positive, action-oriented words. Save the completed worksheet in your Career Management Files Tracker.

General Information Questions

Why do you want this job?

What type of work do you enjoy doing the most?

What are your strongest skills?

What are your long-term career goals? How do you plan to achieve them?

Do you think of yourself as a team player? If so, give examples.

Do you have a geographic preference? Are you willing to relocate?

Under what management style do you work most productively?

What is important to you in a company? What do you look for in an organization?

Behavioral and Character Questions

What have you accomplished that demonstrates your initiative?

How do you deal with an angry customer or coworker? Describe an experience you've had.

How are you able to adapt to change? Give an example.

How would you describe yourself?

What rewards do you look for in your career?

What accomplishment are you most proud of, particularly as it relates to your field?

What do you think are the most important characteristics and abilities a person must possess to be successful? How do you rate yourself in those areas?

Stress Questions

Why do you think you are the best candidate for this job? Why should I hire you?

Why do you want to leave your current job?

Why have you held so many jobs?

What is your greatest weakness?

Have you ever been fired from a job?

Does your current employer know you are planning to leave?

What kinds of decisions are most difficult for you?

What is your salary range? (Although this is not strictly a stress question, being asked about salary expectations is awkward. Chapter 12 has advice about handling this common question. Hint: Avoid giving a direct answer.)

Questions and Topics to Avoid

List several questions to avoid asking during an interview and explain why the questions are inappropriate.

Q&A Savvy Strategies

Review "Savvy Q&A Strategies" on page 224. List the strategies that are most applicable to your job search. Add others you found through your Internet research.

Your Questions

Review the sample questions in "Your Questions Count" on pages 225–226. In your own words, write the questions you want to ask during your interviews. If necessary, ask for help from a member of your support system. Add questions that are pertinent to your job search and goals.

For Your Career Management Files Tracker

File your completed Career Action worksheets in your Career Management Files Tracker.

CA 10-1   Types of interview styles

CA 10-2   Interview Q&A tips from the Internet

CA 10-3   Interview Q&A planning sheet

CHAPTER 11

Interview Like a Pro

Outcomes

1. Develop confidence by participating in practice interviews.
2. Prepare for job interviews.
3. Close a job interview in your favor.
4. Develop effective strategies for following up after an interview.
5. Be prepared to take pre-employment tests.

© Photographer/Image Source

OVERVIEW Chapter 11 covers vital interview rehearsal activities, including a practice interview with a member of your support network and a dress rehearsal interview with an employer in your field. You will learn important strategies to prepare for interviews, sharpen your skills, boost your confidence, and close interviews in your favor. You will also learn about pre-employment tests an employer may require if you are being considered for a job.

JUMP START
Your Interview Success

Because an interview is a dynamic exchange between two people, there will never be a list of "Interview Do's and Don'ts" that works in every situation. There are, however, three gifts you can give yourself to be at your best in interviews:

- Plenty of time to prepare so that you aren't rushed or stressed right before the interview
- Diligent, focused preparation and practice
- The self-confidence you will gain from feeling ready for the interview

Go online and search on the phrase *job interview advice*. Read a few articles in depth or gather tidbits from several sites. Look for guidelines about standard business etiquette and see if you can find specific expectations for your career field. The Internet has the power to set standards and establish cultural norms by judging or rewarding certain behaviors; so it's important to know what's being said. For fun, read about the worst interview blunders to make sure you don't repeat someone else's.

Outcome 1 Gain a Competitive Advantage

While some people may claim that they can walk into an interview and "wing it," do not try be one of them.

If you get an email or a telephone call asking you to come to a job interview, the employer is interested in *you*. You are the focus of the interview. You will be evaluated on your past successes and mistakes and on your future goals and potential. You will be expected to give concrete examples of your skills and explain how they relate to the requirements for this job.

Any nervousness that you feel about an upcoming job interview is an appropriate response to a situation that will test your interpersonal, social, professional, and verbal and nonverbal skills. Preparation and practice can help you relax and give you a genuine competitive advantage over the other people who are interviewing for "your" position.

Users of *Your Career: How to Make It Happen* emphasize that the practice interviews improve their actual interview performance by as much as 100 percent. They say that this valuable practice enhances their preparation, increases their self-confidence, improves the image of competence they project, and reduces their anxiety about the process—all of which improve their performance in actual interviews.

Gain these valuable advantages yourself by doing practice interviews.

Interview with Someone in Your Support Network

Schedule a practice interview with a friend, a family member, or an acquaintance in your support network, preferably someone experienced in interviewing who knows you personally. Ask someone to observe the practice interview and get recommendations from both people for improving your performance.

If possible, video-record the practice interview. This firsthand review may be the most valuable performance feedback you can get. Reread the tips in Chapter 8. Listen to your tone of voice and look at your body language.

- Did you speak too fast or too slowly? Practice improving your speaking and above all, aim to speak in a warm, energetic tone.

- Using your body language self-inventory in Career Action 8-2, watch for negative, passive, or aggressive body language and try to improve it.

COMPLETE | **CAREER ACTION 11-1**

Arrange a Practice Interview, p. 249

Interview with Someone in Your Career Field

Once you feel comfortable with your performance in the practice interview with your support team, schedule a dress rehearsal interview with an employer in your field.

Some people receive job offers as a result of dress rehearsal practice interviews; others obtain leads that result in jobs. Everyone gains helpful interview experience. When making an appointment for a dress rehearsal interview, do the following:

- Explain that the interview is a course assignment and that you would appreciate the employer's help in completing it.

- Say that you would like the interview to be as realistic as possible.

- Ask what the protocol is for real applicants and follow each step. If there is an application form, pick it up ahead of time and complete it carefully.

- Take your Interview Marketing Kit (Chapter 8) and use it appropriately.

MAKE IT A HABIT

Manage Your Schedule

Limit the number of interviews you schedule for the same day. After two interviews, an applicant's performance level typically drops. Don't jeopardize your chances of getting a job because you are tired.

Never be late for an interview. If you know where you are going, you will have one less thing to worry about. If the interview is in an unfamiliar area, be sure you have directions and know how long it will take to get there.

If possible, go to the location a few days before, at the same time of day, to look for construction delays and traffic jams. Alternatively, take public transportation and use the time to relax and rehearse. Take your cell phone so that you can call the interviewer if you will be late. (Be sure to turn it off during the interview.)

Plan your commute to arrive about ten minutes before the interview in case something goes wrong. If you are early, sit in your car or find someplace else to wait until a few minutes before it's time to go in. (Being too early for an appointment may create some awkwardness with the receptionist and/or the interviewer, who may be busy until the time of the interview.)

prodaksyn/Shutterstock.com

Remember that any job offer during a practice interview should come spontaneously from the employer. Asking directly for a job contradicts your request for help in practicing your interviewing skills. If your contact makes an offer or provides leads or suggestions, however, follow up immediately if you are interested.

Ask everyone who interviews you to evaluate your performance and give them a copy of the Interview Critique Form in Career Action 11-4.

Be sure to follow up with a thank-you note like the one in Figure 11-2 on page 242.

COMPLETE **CAREER ACTION 11-2**

Participate in a Dress Rehearsal Interview, p. 249

Outcome 2 Prepare for the Interview

The tips in this section apply to all of your job interviews. To get the most benefit from your practice interviews, prepare for them as if they were real interviews.

- Reduce your stress level by learning as much as possible about the interview in advance,

such as the name and job title of the person with whom you will meet.

- Study the job description or ad and match your qualifications and experience with every job requirement. Say these things aloud. Practice what you will say about your plans to fill any gaps between the job requirements and your qualifications.

- Pick five likely questions and five questions you hope aren't asked. Prepare your answers and practice saying them in front of a mirror or with friends. Practice "thinking on your feet" in response to tough questions (Chapter 10).

- Review and practice your 30-Second Commercial (Chapter 8).

- Assemble your Interview Marketing Kit (Chapter 8) and Interview Survival Pack (next page).

- Have you heard the advice to "make up your mind to have a good time and *then* go to the party"? Approach your interviews the same way and see how a positive attitude can strengthen your performance (Chapter 1 and Chapter 8). Try positive visualization and other techniques for managing stress (Chapter 1).

Practice Using Your Marketing Materials

Anton Gvozdikov/Shutterstock.com

To capture an interviewer's attention, refer first to an item that represents one of your most outstanding accomplishments. Save another exceptional item to use toward the end of the interview to leave a favorable last impression.

Practice using your Interview Marketing Kit items so that the actual delivery will be smooth. Have a friend give you a mock interview and practice referring to your portfolio items at key points during the interview.

Suppose an interviewer asks, "How important do you think it is to keep up with changing technology?" To this you can reply "I think it is very important, and I have taken several classes to update my software skills." You can then provide an appropriate example of how you have kept up to date with technology in your field. By rehearsing, you will be able to work the portfolio items into an interview naturally.

❝Show portfolio items that highlight your hands-on experience in the areas that count the most. Do not use every item for every interview.**❞**

- Look at the Interview Critique Form in Career Action 11-4 to remind yourself how you will be judged.
- Call someone on your support team for a last-minute morale boost before heading to the interview.
- On the day of the interview, take the time to look your best. Eat well and be rested, immaculately groomed, and appropriately dressed (Chapter 8).
- Use positive, assertive body language (Chapter 8).
- Use your voice well—what you say and how you say it (Chapter 8).
- Learn how to wrap up an interview in your favor (next page).

Prepare an Interview Survival Pack

Feeling in control is one way to keep your cool in stressful interviewing situations. If you can anticipate uncomfortable situations ahead of time, you can more effectively manage the stress they cause. With a little planning, you can avoid an interview-sabotaging experience.

Prepare a survival pack that contains items such as these:

- Personal hygiene items (toothpaste and toothbrush, comb, deodorant, tissues)
- Spare stockings or tie (in case of snags or stains)
- Whatever else you need to look, smell, and be your best no matter what happens

Put your gear in a zippered pouch that fits neatly in your Interview Marketing Kit. If you travel by car, store it there.

Organize Your "Props" before the Interview

Organize the physical items you will have with you so that you don't have to fumble with them during the interview.

- Review the recommended contents of the Interview Marketing Kit on pages 189–190 and put your portfolio items in the order in which you will use them.
- Bring a businesslike pen—and make sure it works before the meeting.
- Open your notebook to your questions and open your appointment calendar to the current week or month.

Using Items in Your Portfolio

Use your portfolio items wisely. Before an interview, arrange the portfolio items in the order that best demonstrates how your abilities relate specifically to the employer's needs. Ask if the interviewer would like to see samples from your portfolio before you display anything. Even if the interviewer prefers not to review them, having a portfolio with you makes a good impression and conveys that you are professional and organized.

During the interview, you may still have an opportunity to offer a portfolio sample if the topic suggests it. Simply turn to (or take out) the appropriate portfolio items that demonstrate your qualifications. This tangible evidence of abilities often gives candidates a winning edge in competing for a job. When employers ask questions about your resume, you can use your portfolio items to support your responses. Do not misrepresent yourself in the portfolio items; the work must be your own. Be prepared to provide copies of the work if requested to do so.

It's a mistake to rely only on your portfolio items to convince an interviewer of your qualifications. The focus of the interview is still on you. Your personal appearance, your body language, and your verbal communication skills are essential. The portfolio items are visual aids to support your qualifications. For each interview, select the items to match the specific employer and job. Do not use every item for every interview.

Some interviewers may not want to review your portfolio items while they meet with you. Ask permission before you show any portfolio items and before you take any notes.

Referring to your appointment calendar is an exception to this rule. If you need to schedule a follow-up meeting or activity, having your appointment book handy is essential so that you can confirm any further appointments immediately. Doing so later could result in a lost opportunity; an interviewer may want to schedule an appointment while you're still in the interview.

Wrap Up the Interview in Your Favor

Outcome 3

Whether it's a practice interview or the real thing, be proactive and professional by influencing how the interview ends. For your own sake, clarify what to expect next in the process. Leave a positive impression by restating your qualifications and by closing the interview skillfully.

Clarify What to Expect Next

Before you leave the interview, clarify:

- What, if anything, you should do to follow up.
- When a decision will be made.
- How the interviewer prefers you to follow up (by telephone, by letter, or in person).

The following sample dialogue shows how to get this information:

WATCH OUT!

Avoid Interview Disqualifiers

Any one of these blunders during an interview could cost you the job:

1. Don't be late. It's hard to count all of the negative messages that being late sends: lack of respect, lack of genuine interest, personal disorganization, and on and on.
2. Don't be abrupt or discourteous to anyone you meet.
3. Don't sit down until the interviewer invites you to; waiting is courteous.
4. Don't bring anyone else to the interview; it makes you look immature and insecure.
5. Don't invade the interviewer's personal space by reading anything on the desk or putting anything on it.

wavebreakmedia ltd/Shutterstock.com

You: When should I expect to hear whether I am selected for the position?

Interviewer: We'll notify all applicants of our decision within two weeks.

You: Do you mind if I check back with you?

Interviewer: I prefer that you don't until we notify you.

or

Interviewer: No, I don't mind.

You: How would you prefer I contact you?

Interviewer: Please call my assistant.

Clarifying these details underscores your image as a professional who understands the importance of following through after important meetings.

Use Your Clincher

As you near the close of an interview, make a point of leaving your interviewer with a clear picture of how you fit the job. Bring the interview full circle by asking a question similar to this example in a courteous tone: "Would you please summarize the most important qualifications you're looking for in filling this position?"

Run the short version of your 30-Second Commercial to restate your skills, experience, and other assets that meet the employer's needs. This important clincher gives you one last chance to market yourself and your qualifications. People remember best what they hear first and last.

Close the Interview Skillfully

Some applicants lose the race for a job by not clearing the final hurdle: closing the interview skillfully. Don't let your posture, attitude, or verbal and nonverbal communication slip for even a moment. Use the following techniques to close an interview skillfully:

- Watch for signs from the interviewer that it's time to wrap up the interview. Signs include asking whether you have any further questions, tidying up papers on the desk, pushing the chair back, or simply sitting back in the chair. Heed the cue. Don't make the interviewer impatient by droning on at this point.

- If the interviewer is not skilled at interviewing, help wrap things up smoothly by asking, "Is there anything else you need to discuss with me? I know you are busy, and I appreciate the time you have given me for this interview."

- Request a commitment from the interviewer to notify you when an applicant has been selected. Imply that this is not the only job you are considering: "By what date will you make your decision on this position? I'd appreciate knowing within the next two weeks so that I can finalize my plans."

- Before you leave, determine any follow-up activities the interviewer expects from you. If a second interview is arranged, write down the date, time, place, and names of all of the people who will be interviewing you. If you are expected to provide additional information, credentials, references, or work samples, make a note and verify what you are supposed to do before you leave.

- If you're seriously interested in the job, say so! Just as in effective sales, the person who asks is the most likely to receive. Interviewers are impressed by applicants' expressions of interest; candidates who directly express their interest strengthen their position. Offer a simple statement—for example, "I'd be pleased to be a part of this organization" or "After talking with you, I'm convinced that this is the job I want, and I believe my qualifications would be an asset to the Acme Corporation. Please consider me seriously for this position."

- Finally, as you leave, remember to use the interviewer's name: "Thank you for interviewing me, Ms. Carpenter."

- If you haven't been given one, ask the interviewer for a business card. You'll need it for your thank-you note.

- Be conscious of using positive body language. Keep your shoulders back and your head up when you stand and give a warm smile and a firm handshake. Once you leave the interviewer's office, you are still interviewing. Thank the receptionist or assistant by name and add a brief parting greeting.

Review Figure 11-1 to reinforce your understanding of the areas that employers consider most important during an interview.

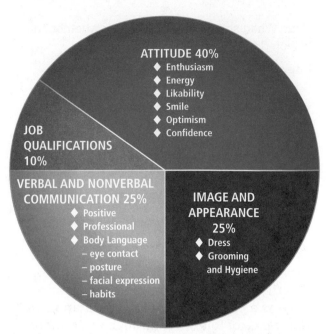

Figure 11-1 How You Are Rated during an Interview

Outcome 4 Good Interview Follow-up Moves

Interview follow-up can increase your chances of getting the job by 30 percent or more because many applicants don't bother to do it! Interviewers see follow-up by a job seeker as a proactive step that shows initiative and interest.

Good follow-up reinforces your qualifications and helps you stand out favorably from the competition. Be patient during this stage of the job search. The hiring process often takes longer than the employer expects.

The key to follow-up is action: evaluate your interview performance and send a follow-up message to the interviewer.

Evaluate the Interview

At the earliest possible time, summarize and evaluate your own interview performance in writing. Ask and answer the following questions:

- What positive impressions did I make? Why did I make these impressions?

- What negative impressions might I have left with the interviewer? Why did I make these impressions?

- Was there anything I should have said but didn't?

- What other questions would I have liked to ask?

- What questions would I have answered differently? How would I have answered them differently?

- How did I feel about the interview immediately after it concluded? How do I feel about the interview now?

- What behaviors or habits of speech distracted from my professionalism?

- Did my appearance give the impression I hoped it would?

Give everyone who conducts or observes a practice interview a copy of the Interview Critique Form (pages 251–252). Ask each person to evaluate your performance, identify your strengths and weaknesses, and suggest ways you can improve your performance. Work on your areas of weakness before you have an actual interview.

COMPLETE **CAREER ACTION 11-3**

Summarize and Evaluate Your
Interviews, p. 249

COMPLETE **CAREER ACTION 11-4**

Interview Critique Form, p. 251

Plan Your Follow-up Strategies

Look at your completed Career Action 11-3 and circle in red any notes that require follow-up (information you need to clarify or reinforce with the employer, questions you want answered, areas of weak performance and suggestions for improving them, and specific actions you need to take).

Determine what method of follow-up is most appropriate. If you remembered to ask the interviewer how he or she wanted you to follow up, the decision has been made for you. If you forgot to ask, send a follow-up letter or email rather than make a telephone call. If the interviewer approves of follow-up telephone calls, use that method. A telephone call is more personal and lively and gives you quicker feedback. If you call, you should also follow up with a letter or an email because it serves as a reminder of you.

Outline Your Follow-up Message

Regardless of the method you choose for follow-up, outline the message first:

- List any questions you need to ask.
- Summarize pertinent information you omitted or covered inadequately in your interview.
- State specifically how the organization could benefit by hiring you (a brief rerun of or an excerpt from your 30-Second Commercial).

Make your follow-up message brief and polished. Include only the most important questions or information.

Time Your Call

Make your follow-up call within two days of your interview, while your name and the interview are still fresh in the interviewer's mind. Keep the following points in mind:

- Mondays and Fridays are the busiest business days, so call on another day.
- Just before lunch and just before the end of the workday are usually inconvenient times as well.

Send a Brief Thank-You Note Too

Even if you make your initial follow-up by telephone, you should send a brief thank-you letter or email message within 48 hours of your interview to be sure your message is received during the decision-making stage. (The body of a thank-you email is similar to that of a thank-you letter.)

You should write a thank-you note to every person who interviewed you. The letters can be basically the same, but try to vary each one in case the recipients compare notes. If you've already made a telephone call, do not restate your qualifications in this message; just thank the interviewer.

Send a thank-you note even if you're sure the job is not for you. The thank-you letter brings your name before the interviewer in a favorable light one more time, reinforcing your name in his or her mind. It also provides a positive written record of you in the employer's files.

Review the brief thank-you letter in Figure 11-2 on page 242.

When to Send a More Complete Follow-up Letter

If the interviewer wants you to follow up in writing or if you think follow-up is important to getting hired, send a more complete letter similar to the one in Figure 11-3 on page 243. Include the following:

- A reference to your interview and the position you are seeking
- Clarification of any pertinent information omitted during your interview
- A brief version of your 30-Second Commercial

Max Wu

626 Sally Lane   •   Reno, NV 89511

(775) 555-1537   •   MaxWu@email.com   •   linkedin.com/in/MaxWu

July 2, 20—

Ms. Stephanie Nolan
Manager, Auditing Staff
Wyatt & Berkowitz Pubic Accountants
1410 Quarrier Street, Suite 700
Reno, NV 89503

Dear Ms. Nolan:

Thank you for the opportunity to interview for the position of Staff Auditor I with you and your team. Your invitation to join the first hour of the weekly staff meeting made me feel especially welcome—and sent me to the library to brush up on the finer points of the state's tax credit program for employers who train welfare recipients!

I feel I have a good understanding of the requirements for the position, and I am very interested in joining your team. I look forward to the possibility of working with you. Please call me any time this week at 775-555-1537.

Sincerely,

Max Wu

Max Wu

Figure 11-2 Brief Thank-You Letter

FRANCESCA VALDEZ

3493 Huntington Heights, Denver, CO 80204   (720) 555-2871
Francesca.Valdez@email.com   linkedin.com/in/Francesca.Valdez

August 23, 20—

Mr. Frederick J. Gray Wolf
Normandy Copiers, Inc.
3500 Main Street
Boulder, CO 80301

Dear Mr. Gray Wolf:

The enthusiasm you shared this afternoon for the customer-centered philosophy behind the new Normandy Print Center is contagious! I know from experience how satisfying it is to break new ground and to achieve results that exceed all expectations. The Normandy management system sounds unique, innovative, and challenging.

During our meeting, we discussed how I could contribute to your marketing plan, but we didn't have time to talk about store operations. While I managed the parts and service operations of Renaissance Business Systems, our team achieved and maintained a production efficiency rate that consistently placed us in the top 5 percent of the 160 shops nationwide. Sales of maintenance contracts increased every year I was in charge, and we had the lowest return rate for products of all the centers.

Thank you for talking with me about the new opportunities at Normandy Print Center. The company will be a great success in Boulder, and I would like to contribute to that success. As we agreed, I will call you next Thursday, but you can reach me before that at 303-555-0171.

Sincerely,

Francesca Valdez

Francesca Valdez

Figure 11-3 Longer Thank-You Letter

- A thank-you for the interviewer's time
- A statement of enthusiasm for the job

The follow-up letter provides a permanent written record of your qualifications and professional courtesy. The employer can review it any time, making it an effective way to keep your "commercial" running.

Connect with Your Support Network Again

If a member of your support network is influential with your prospective employer, contact him or her to ask for additional support. A friendly follow-up call from this person to the employer could tip the scales in your favor.

An alternative to the follow-up call by a network member is a letter of recommendation from one or more people who can confirm your qualifications. Some employers routinely request letters of recommendation from former employers, managers, or supervisors of applicants. Arranging to have such letters sent on your own demonstrates initiative—another benefit for you.

COMPLETE **CAREER ACTION 11-5**

Interview Follow-up Tips, p. 253

COMPLETE **CAREER ACTION 11-6**

Follow-up Telephone Call and Letter or Email, p. 253

Successful Follow-up Phone Call

oliveromg/Shutterstock.com

If your interviewer gave the go-ahead for a follow-up call, you can set yourself apart from the competition with a well-timed, well-prepared telephone call.

- **Demonstrate courtesy.** "Is this a good time for you to talk?"
- **Begin with a greeting and self-introduction.** "Hello, Ms. Nabavi. This is Greg Bell."
- **Identify the position for which you interviewed and the date.** "I want to thank you for meeting with me yesterday to discuss the Data Processing Systems Analyst I position."
- **Provide important information you omitted.** "After reviewing our meeting, I realized that I hadn't mentioned some pertinent information regarding my (education, work experience, qualifications, certification, other)."

Concisely give the specifics.

- **Reemphasize your qualifications.** If necessary, give a short, targeted version of your 30-Second Commercial, emphasizing precisely how your qualifications can benefit the employer.
- **If necessary, ask questions to clarify any points that were not covered adequately.** For example, a clearer description of the job responsibilities or clarification of work relationships.
- **Thank the interviewer, express your interest, and encourage a speedy hiring decision.** "Thank you again for the interview. I look forward to learning of your hiring decision soon. I believe we could benefit each other, and I'd be pleased to be a part of Mississippi Central Power Company."

5 Ace Employment Tests

You may be asked to take a pre-employment screening test before you are considered for a job. Doing your homework is a sure way to improve your test scores in school, and it helps you succeed in employment tests. As part of your research, find out if you will be asked to take any tests. Many employers don't use pre-employment testing, but you may apply for a job that does.

If a test is involved, find out whether it's a written, oral, computerized, or combination test. Does it test technical knowledge, skills, manual dexterity, personality, special abilities, or other job-related capabilities? Try to find out what will be tested and how.

The Personality Test

The **personality test** is the exception to the "do your homework" rule. Because this type of test is usually designed to determine whether your personal and behavioral preferences are well matched to the work involved, advance study doesn't apply. Technically, there are no wrong answers in these tests. Most personality tests measure, for example, your solitary or social tendencies, your relative need for stability, your preference for efficiency or creativity, your style of goal achievement (flexible or fixed), and your tendency to accept others' ideas or stick to your own. Answer all questions honestly. If your personality doesn't match the job, you won't be happy in it.

The Skills Test

If you will be taking a **skills test**, start to review, practice, and improve your skills today. No matter how good your skills are, you can improve them with practice, which increases your employability. Another benefit of polishing your skills is that you'll be able to start your new job with more confidence. However, stop preparing one or two days before you take a skills test. Cramming until the last minute increases anxiety and often results in poorer performance.

The Technical Test

If you will be required to take an oral or written test for a professional position, try to get samples of the technical questions that may be asked. Resources for learning about the types of questions are the employer's human resources department, other employees in the company, people who have taken the test, and people who have taken similar tests in your field. Libraries and bookstores also have sample tests.

If you can find sample questions or even general topics that will be covered in the technical test, write out answers to the questions. The important thing is to be as complete as possible in your answers. The purpose of a technical test is to find out how much you know about the subject.

The Computerized Test

The computerized pre-employment test is useful for screening large numbers of applicants because it saves time and other expenses. The test may be general in content, or it may be a skills or personality test.

Typically, you take this test at the employer's site or at an employment agency. You may also be asked to log on to an employer's website and take the test online. You receive instructions on how to use the computerized test program and are given a specific amount of time to complete it. The results are usually scored electronically and generated in a report. They are then analyzed by human resources personnel. The best advice for performing well on a computerized pre-employment test is to do your best; don't try to outwit the test. Also avoid using absolutes such as *never* and *always*. These words can signal an extreme personality or lying. For a skills test, practicing ahead of time can help improve your score.

Taking Employment Tests

Employment testing may be an important factor in an employer's hiring decision. Follow these guidelines to perform at your best:

- Eat properly before the test and be well rested. A sluggish body and brain can diminish your performance.

- Do some physical exercise or yoga before the test to improve your circulation and your ability to relax and concentrate.

- Arrive ten minutes early to avoid feeling rushed or tense.

- Ask exactly how much time is allotted for the test. Take your time and don't rush into poor performance.

- Read the test carefully to clarify the instructions and to determine how many points are assigned to each question. If the points aren't indicated, ask the person monitoring the test how the questions are weighted.

- Ask whether points will be deducted for questions you don't answer. If they will, answer every question. If not, don't spend a lot of time on questions you can't answer easily. (Save those for last.)

- Many tests are objective, often including multiple-choice questions. In true-false questions, extreme statements are frequently false (for example, choices that contain the words *all*, *never*, or *always*). Moderate statements are often true.

- Double-check to be sure you didn't skip any questions. Because your first response is usually the correct one, don't change answers unless you made a careless mistake.

- On general math tests, expect some simple addition, subtraction, multiplication, division, fraction, percentage, and decimal problems. Many math tests also include word problems.

- Advanced math tests will be geared to your field (engineering and statistical analysis, for instance). Consult others who have taken similar tests to determine what you should review. Your education and work experience are your primary preparation for advanced math tests.

WATCH OUT!

Take Drug Screening Seriously

Applicants who test positively for drug use or who admit to using illegal drugs may be screened out of the job immediately. Never give flippant answers to questions about drug use. They could be interpreted negatively.

Policies for drug screening vary considerably from one employer to the next. As part of your employer research, find out the drug screening procedures and requirements. Check with employers directly and with people who work for them. Schools' career services counselors often have information about drug testing procedures and may be familiar with the procedures that local employers use.

To protect yourself, before you are tested, report to the employer any prescription or over-the-counter drugs you are taking. Some of these can result in a false-positive test.

jhorrocks/iStockphoto.com

Chapter Checklist

Underline each action you are already taking and circle the actions you need to work on.

- Schedule two practice interviews to improve my performance and confidence (an interview with someone in my support network and an interview with an employer in my target field). [1]

- Prepare for interviews carefully to reduce my stress level and to avoid appearing disorganized. [2]

- Use strategies to wrap up interviews in my favor. [3]

- Ask interviewers to evaluate my practice interviews. [4]

- Summarize every interview and evaluate my performance. [4]

- Prepare a written script for a follow-up telephone call (if the interviewer said that calling is appropriate). [4]

- Thank every interviewer with a thank-you note or an email message. [4]

- Send a more complete follow-up letter if I need to clarify something or add information. [4]

- Find out if an employer requires pre-employment testing. [5]

Critical-Thinking Questions

1. How have you used the success strategies described in Chapter 1 (maintaining a positive outlook, setting goals, managing your time, being proactive, and being assertive) to prepare for and participate in a practice interview? Which strategies are most useful?

2. Why is it important to prepare for and perform in a practice interview as if it were the real thing? [1]

3. What would you tell your friend to do to reduce his or her stress level the day before an interview? The day of the interview? [2]

4. What advice would you give your friend about wrapping up the interview skillfully? [3]

5. What steps should you take to follow up after an interview? [4]

6. What are the important topics to include in follow-up communications? [4]

7. What strategies can you use while you wait to hear about a hiring decision? [4]

8. Are employment tests common in your career field? How do you know? [5]

Want access to career resources, study tools, activities, and job information links? Get started at www.cengage.com/career/yourcareer.

TRIAL RUN

If you are using the chapters in order, you are likely to have found some job leads, applied for jobs, and had at least one practice and/or real interview. In this Trial Run, you take stock of your job search strategies.

Set aside at least two hours for this look-back and assessment. You will need this book, your Career Management Files Tracker, your Career Portfolio, and some blank paper (or the worksheet on the product website). Find a quiet place to do this work. You can also work with a partner or in groups of three. Spend at least one hour evaluating each person's materials and progress and planning the next steps.

Remind yourself of the key points in Chapters 1–11 by looking at the end-of-chapter checklists and your Career Action worksheets. Evaluate each area of your own job search thoughtfully and honestly.

	What have I accomplished?	What advice or activity in the book has been most helpful?	Where are the gaps?	What advice or activity in the book (that I haven't done) could I apply?
Example: Find job leads (Chapters 4 & 5)	Everyone knows I'm looking for a job Contacts in Ashland & Paducah	Very prepared for meeting with Ms. Owens-Garcia; sent her thank-you note	Need job leads in small businesses Ask Anil & Jean how they found their jobs	Look at trade group sites & Chamber of Commerce sites
Prepare (Chapters 1–3)				
Find job leads (Chapters 4 and 5)				
Apply for jobs (Chapters 6 and 7)				
Interviews (Chapters 8–11)				

Develop a plan for each area:

	What is the most important activity(s) I could do in this area?	What is my plan?
Example: Find job leads	Attend spring job fair at Campus Career Center	• Research companies @ fair • Post resume at CCC job fair page • Ask Mrs. Heldman about portfolio; more samples? • Ask Mrs. H if I should schedule 2nd practice interview • Look for job fairs @ convention center website
Prepare		
Find job leads		
Apply for jobs		
Interviews		

CAREER ACTION   11-1   **Arrange a Practice Interview** 1

Schedule a practice interview with your support network members (an interviewer and an observer if possible). Use the sample questions in Chapter 10 as a guide for your practice session. You can make a copy of them for the "interviewer" and add any stress (or other) questions that you want to rehearse. Encourage the interviewer to expand on the questions, if possible, tailoring them to your job target to give you relevant interview practice. If possible, arrange to have the practice interview video-recorded.

CAREER ACTION   11-2   **Participate in a Dress Rehearsal Interview** 1

Contact an employer in your career field and ask for help with a course assignment. Ask the employer to conduct a practice interview and complete the Interview Critique Form (Career Action 11-4).

1. Dress appropriately.

2. Take a copy of the Interview Critique Form with you and ask the interviewer to evaluate your performance by completing the form during or after the interview.

3. After the dress-rehearsal interview, evaluate your performance using Career Actions 11-3 and 11-4.

4. Within two days of the dress rehearsal, send a thank-you letter to the person who gave you the interview.

CAREER ACTION   11-3   **Summarize and Evaluate Your Interviews** 4

Summarize every practice and real interview as soon as possible to avoid forgetting important details. Duplicate and use Career Action 11-3 for your own evaluation and follow-up plans. Answer the questions as completely as possible.

Name of Organization _____ Date of Interview _____

Name(s) and Title(s) of Interviewer(s) _____

_____

Telephone _____ Email _____

Summary Activities and Questions

On a separate sheet of paper, write every question you can remember being asked during the interview. Take your time and be thorough. Do this before answering the following questions.

1. Based on the knowledge you gained in your interview and research, which of your qualifications would be the greatest asset in this job? Which of these qualifications should be reinforced with the prospective employer in your follow-up?

2. List any questions you think you answered inadequately. Write out the best possible answer to each question. Use additional paper as needed.

3. Did you forget to provide important information that demonstrates your qualifications for the job? Explain in detail.

4. What questions did you intend to ask but forgot or didn't have a chance to ask? Write them out now.

5. How could you have presented yourself more effectively?

6. In what area(s) do you think you performed the best in your interview? Why?

7. In what area(s) do you think you performed poorly? What steps can you take to improve?

8. Describe information you learned about the interviewer that may be helpful in establishing greater rapport in the future (for example, philosophy, current working projects, personal interests or hobbies, or mutual goals).

9. Is there any point of confusion that needs to be clarified for the employer? Explain.

10. Are you scheduled for another interview with the organization? If so, record the date, time, place, and name(s) of the interviewer(s).

11. Record any other activities you offered to follow up on or were specifically asked to follow up on by the interviewer (for example, provide references, transcripts, certificates, or examples of work).

12. How does the interviewer prefer you to follow up (by telephone, by letter, in person)?

13. When did the interviewer indicate the hiring decision would be made?

CAREER ACTION   11-4 **Interview Critique Form** 4

Give copies of the Interview Critique Form to the people who help you in practice interviews. You can also ask them to look at your completed Career Action 11-3 and offer suggestions. Before you give this form to someone, complete the first two lines below.

Name of Interviewee _____ Date _____

Position Applied for _____

Interviewer: Check the appropriate rating in each category. If desired, add any comments for each category.

Documentation (Resume, cover letter, employment application)

Excellent _____ Very Good _____ Good _____ Needs Improvement _____

Comments or suggestions (optional)

Attitude (Interested in position, self-confident, likable, pleasant tone of voice, smiling)

Excellent _____ Very Good _____ Good _____ Needs Improvement _____

Comments or suggestions (optional)

Appearance (Generally neat and tidy, appropriately dressed, alert, good hygiene)

Excellent _____   Very Good _____   Good _____   Needs Improvement _____

Comments or suggestions (optional)

Job Qualifications (Education, skills, and experience suitable for position; good personal attributes; human relations capability; dependable; punctual; industrious)

Excellent _____   Very Good _____   Good _____   Needs Improvement _____

Comments or suggestions (optional)

Verbal Communication (Speaks clearly with positive tone, uses proper English, avoids slang or repetitive words, emphasizes assets, is courteous, uses name of the interviewer)

Excellent _____   Very Good _____   Good _____   Needs Improvement _____

Comments or suggestions (optional)

Nonverbal Communication (Positive, assertive body language, good eye contact, does not fidget)

Excellent _____   Very Good _____   Good _____   Needs Improvement _____

Comments or suggestions (optional)

Listening (Does not interrupt or respond too quickly, asks to have a question repeated if necessary, takes time to think through important questions, calmly endures silence)

Excellent _____   Very Good _____   Good _____   Needs Improvement _____

Comments or suggestions (optional)

Enthusiasm (Demonstrates interest and energy through verbal and nonverbal communication)

Excellent _____   Very Good _____   Good _____   Needs Improvement _____

Comments or suggestions (optional)

Please summarize any other observations you made during the interview. Note any favorable behavior and provide suggestions for improvement.

CAREER ACTION   11-5   Interview Follow-up Tips 4

Search *Career Transitions* (or other Internet sites) for additional tips on interview follow-up that could be useful. File your research in your Career Management Files Binder. Try searching on *interview thank-you letter* and *interview follow-up letter*.

CAREER ACTION   11-6   Follow-up Telephone Call and Letter or Email 4

Write a script for your follow-up telephone call, letter, or email message. File the completed worksheet and final documents in your Career Management Files Binder.

For Your Career Management Files Tracker

File your completed Career Action worksheets in your Career Management Files Tracker.

CA 11-1   Plans for a practice interview with a member of your support network

CA 11-2   Plans for a dress rehearsal interview with an employer in your field

CA 11-3   Interview summary and evaluation

CA 11-4   Interview Critique Form

CA 11-5   Interview follow-up tips

CA 11-6   Interview follow-up communication

Next Steps

PART 5 provides tips for negotiating the best job offers and then succeeding in your new job.

ADVICE FROM THE EXPERT

Margaret Friedman-Vaughan

Director of Education and Administration, Rockdale Temple

Margaret Friedman-Vaughan has her hands full supervising 7 full-time staff members, 15 part-time teachers, and 18 high school student assistants.

"Soft skills are important in every job," says Margaret. "I've interviewed people who didn't have the exact skills I thought the position needed, but who had a strong work ethic, energy, raw knowledge, and passion. For some positions, I look for personal attributes like these as much as actual skills.

"I ask a lot of 'how would you handle this situation' questions in interviews. I depend a lot on references: Can the person manage stressful situations? Can they multitask? Do they accept supervision and grow with it?"

Margaret cautions employees not to assume that their supervisor is too busy to notice small things such as "who comes in late, leaves early, takes too long for lunch, who is on the phone with family or personal business, who is playing games on their computer, and who seems bored." She can also list the fastest ways to alienate one's coworkers: "Gossiping about co-workers, not pulling your weight, being negative, and not showing up for work."

Margaret's advice for new employees is to "Do your best. You applied for the position because it was of interest to you; you were hired because they believed you were a good fit. Challenge yourself and be open to growing and learning. Don't listen to the rumor factory: talk to someone in authority if you have a problem."

Molly Cramer

Sophomore, University of Richmond
Psychology and Leadership
Studies Major

Molly Cramer's major in Leadership Studies required an internship experience, and she learned of an ideal opportunity through word of mouth. She says, "A family friend had participated in the internship program and raved about the experiences he had. I then searched online to learn how I could apply." Her proactive approach led to her paid internship at the JVS Cincinnati Career Network, helping members of the community search for sustainable employment.

Molly prepared for her first "real" interview by researching the organization and reading about its staff on LinkedIn. She then "did a quick brainstorming session of questions I thought the interviewer would ask me. I enlisted a friend to ask me the questions, listen to my responses, and give me feedback."

Molly's professional behavior and work habits had a positive effect on her workplace. She says, "I think I contributed to the organization because I brought a can-do attitude and executed a task—organizing a job fair—that would not have been accomplished without a capable intern."

Molly's advice to others is to "establish positive relationships with your supervisors, coworkers, and other personnel. You never know whether an internship could turn into a job down the line, so make every effort to be friendly and professional with everyone."

She now believes "there is nothing more fulfilling than helping others." Helping others find employment was deeply satisfying for Molly. "I know that whichever path my career takes, I will find a way to help others in the process," she says.

© Cengage Learning 2013

Photo courtesy of Molly Cramer

→ Ready, Set, PLAN

Read the objectives on the first page of Chapters 12–14 and mark the ones that are most important to you. What do you want to accomplish by reading these chapters and doing the assignments?

How much time is in the syllabus for Chapters 12–14?

List the dates for reading assignments and the dates for turning in homework and projects for this class.

What are your other major commitments in the coming weeks (for other classes, work, home)? For each task, include the estimated time and when you will do it.

If you are doing any group projects, list information that will help the project go smoothly: project goal and due date, each person's assignments and phone number, dates for completing each part of the project, meeting dates, and anything else.

Following Up and Negotiating Offers

Outcomes

1 Evaluate job offers.

2 Prepare for salary negotiations.

3 Respond to a job offer professionally.

OVERVIEW Accepting a job is an important career—and life—decision. You will be more comfortable making this decision if you understand the conditions of the job and the terms of employment before you decide what to do. In Chapter 12, you will learn how to evaluate job offers, how to research salaries and benefit packages, how to negotiate a fair compensation package, and how to accept or reject a job offer professionally.

© Photographer/Image Source

CHAPTER 12

CAREER ACTIONS

12-1: Internet Research on Salary Information

12-2: Salary and Benefits Planning Sheet

12-3: Plan for Dealing with Job Offers

JUMP START

Your Knowledge of Healthcare Benefits

The high cost of healthcare is on everyone's mind these days. You can't watch television without seeing a news story or a commercial about the cost of prescription drugs or individuals going bankrupt after trying to pay for a catastrophic illness or emergency.

Most Americans get their healthcare coverage through their employer, but this situation is not as stable as it was in the past. More Americans work in the service sector, where fewer employers offer health insurance. Many employees are part-time workers or contractors who are not eligible to participate in employer-sponsored health insurance.

Ask five people you know about their healthcare benefits. If they are comfortable talking with you for this report, ask how and why their situation has changed in the last three years. What do they expect in the future? What are their suggestions for changing the system? Try to reach a cross section of people, such as a government employee, a self-employed friend, and a retiree. With a partner, present your findings to the class. Recommend changes.

akva/Shutterstock.com

Outcome 1

Evaluate a Job Offer

"We'd like to offer you the job." Those are the words every job seeker wants to hear. Because the decision to accept or reject a job offer affects your lifetime career plans, you must consider this important decision carefully.

Consider the following factors when you evaluate a job offer:

- **The job itself:** Is the scope acceptable? Is the work interesting to you? Will you work in teams or alone?

- **The organization and personnel:** Do you feel comfortable with the organizational structure and the people you met?

- **The salary and benefits:** Does the salary match your education and abilities, and is it comparable with that of the competition? Does the potential for increases exist?

- **Career development opportunities:** Will you have adequate opportunities for professional growth (through training, increased responsibilities, and opportunities for advancement)?

- **The values and philosophies of management:** Are they compatible with your own?

- **Expense considerations:** If you have to relocate, will the company pay all or part of the moving cost? What is the cost of living in the new location?

- **How the job meets your goals:** Consider carefully how the job fits into your long-term career goals.

- **The job market:** Are jobs in your field plentiful or in short supply?

The company expects you to have questions and may have a standard process for giving you the information you need to make an informed decision. You may be given access to a website for job candidates, or a member of the hiring committee or the human resources department may contact you.

Be sure you understand all of the conditions of the job before you decide whether to accept the offer.

Negotiate for Top Salary and Benefits

Outcome 2

To optimize your ability to negotiate for the best possible salary and benefits, you must become as knowledgeable as possible about the going salary ranges and the types of benefits being offered in your field. You significantly reduce your salary and benefits bargaining power if you omit this research step.

The Compensation Package

Salary is not the only factor you should consider when assessing the value of a job. The complete compensation package includes salary, potential for earnings growth, and all other benefits. All of these are important. Base your compensation considerations on the following:

- The trends in your field (based on research)
- Your worth (the value you can offer the employer)

- The benefits that are most important to you: health/life insurance, retirement programs, flextime, dependent care, reimbursement for education or training, etc.

Research Compensation Trends in Your Field

Research the going rate. Increase your chances of being offered the best compensation package by including this topic in your employer and industry research. Talk with leaders in your field, people who hold positions that are similar to your target job, and area placement specialists. Also search the Internet for salary and benefits information.

Some employers provide printed job descriptions that include a fixed salary listing, while others offer salary information on their websites. A job notice may include a salary range, or the salary may be open. You may be able to find the range or approximate salary for a position from the employer's human resources department. Some employers, however, don't

---

Take Stock of Your Situation

Accepting a job or changing jobs is a big decision! On average, Americans who are fully employed spend 2,000 hours per year at work. When you consider a job offer, think about your current situation and your goals for the future.

If you have a job:
- Are you sure you want to change jobs?
- Why do you think the new job is a better opportunity?
- Does the work sound as interesting as you thought it would?
- Is the new job in a more stable company or industry?
- Will you have more opportunities for advancement or more interesting work?
- Do you like your future manager and future coworkers?
- Does the new job have better benefits?

- Have you hit a plateau in your current job?

If you are not working:
- How long have you been looking for a job?
- How much longer can you afford to look for a job?
- How many jobs have you applied for without getting an interview?
- How many interviews have you had without getting a job offer?
- What is the job market like where you live?
- Are you willing to take the risk of declining the job?
- What is your backup plan if you decline the job?

Ask a career professional and a trusted member of your network (or both) for help weighing the pros and cons of the decision.

"Before you accept the job offer is the best time to negotiate the terms of your employment.**"**

give out this information. They may give you only the bottom of the range—rarely the top figure. Having a general idea of the range is better than having no idea. Your school's career services office can help you research salary and benefits packages.

If the salary is fixed, as it may be in some union or government jobs, you must decide whether it's acceptable to you. Research salary and benefits information online. Check the websites of associations in your career field.

If you learn that the salary is negotiable, try for a salary at the top of the range. (You can agree to accept a salary that is lower than the top level, but if you offer to take the lowest end of the range first, that's probably what you will get.)

> **COMPLETE** **CAREER ACTION 12-1**
>
> Internet Research on Salary Information, p. 264

Salary Negotiation Tips

To obtain the strongest bargaining position, try to postpone any discussion of compensation until you receive a job offer. Bringing up the topic of compensation too soon could shift the focus away from your qualifications and cost you the job. Concentrate on what the employer will gain (your skills, experience, personal strengths, etc.) before focusing on the price (your compensation). Review and apply the following strategies:

- **Whenever possible, let the interviewer bring up the topic of salary and benefits.**

- **Do not accept a job offer without discussing the salary and benefits.** You can bring up the

topic by asking, "What salary range do you have in mind for the job?"

- **Aim for a salary that equals the peak of your qualifications.** The higher you start, the higher the offer is likely to be. State your requirement in a range (upper twenties, midthirties), making it broad enough to negotiate. Don't specify a low end; if you do, the employer will likely select it.

- **If the interviewer asks what salary you want, a good response is "What figure or range is the company planning to pay?"** This gives you a starting point for negotiation. If it's higher than you expected, you help yourself by not stating a lower figure first. If it's lower, you now have a place to begin negotiations.

- **If the interviewer presses for your salary requirement, refer to your research.** "The national average for a person with my experience, education, and training is $_____. Considering the cost-of-living factors, I would expect a salary in the range of _____."

- **If the interviewer brings up the subject of salary before you adequately cover your qualifications,** delay the topic by saying, "Actually, the position itself is more important to me than the salary. Could we discuss the position a little more?"

- **While discussing salary, return to your assets.** Review all of the benefits and qualifications you have to offer the company.

- **Once you state your salary range, do not back down,** particularly if you think it is equal to your qualifications. Base your range on careful research. The employer will respect your confidence in the quality and worth of your work.

- **Do not discuss any other sources of income and do not whine about your expenses.** Stay focused on the negotiation.

- **Discuss the benefits package** (insurance coverage, paid vacations, etc.) during the discussion of salary.

- **Ask about the criteria used to determine compensation increases and the frequency of salary reviews.** Good benefits and salary increases can offset a lower starting salary.

- **If the salary offer is made in a letter and the salary is too low, arrange an appointment to discuss it right away.** Bargaining power is far greater in person than it is by letter or telephone.

- **If the salary isn't acceptable, state the salary you would accept** and close by reaffirming your interest in the company and the job. If the interviewer says, "I'll have to think about your requirements," wait one week; then call back. You may receive a higher or compromise offer. If the interviewer gives you a flat "no," express regret that you were unable to work out a compromise. Restate your interest in the job and organization; then send a follow-up thank-you letter within two days. This could swing the decision in your favor.

COMPLETE   **CAREER ACTION 12-2**

Salary and Benefits Planning Sheet, p. 264

Outcome 3 Respond to a Job Offer Professionally

A job offer may be made by telephone, by letter, or in person. If the offer is made by letter, you have more time to think it over carefully and less emotionally than you do if it's made by telephone or in person. Respond to the offer quickly so that you don't jeopardize it in any way.

If the offer is made by telephone or in the interviewer's office, request time to think it over. You may want to discuss the job offer conditions with a member of your support system, a family member, a career specialist, or all of these people.

Occasionally, interviewers will offer to increase the salary or benefits if that appears to be your main concern. This is particularly

drbimages/iStockphoto.com

WATCH OUT!

Background Checks

A background check is a consumer report that employers use to screen potential employees. In addition to confirming your education and work history, employers may request a consumer report from a credit reporting bureau to check your Social Security number, credit payment record, driving record, or criminal history.

This type of background check is common for jobs that require government security clearance, but it may be used for any job.

Before employers can get your consumer report, they must have your written consent, however. You always have the option of withdrawing your application if there is information you do not want to disclose.

The best way to prepare for a background check is to be truthful on all employment forms, maintain good credit, know what your references are going to say about you, and obtain copies of your personnel files from past employers. If necessary, get a copy of your credit report from a credit bureau and dispute any incorrect information.

true if they believe you are the right person for the job and they don't want to interview other applicants. But even if this doesn't happen, it's still in your best interest to take at least one day to consider the advantages and disadvantages of the job offer.

Important: Be sure that waiting one day won't be an imposition or affect the job offer. Don't put yourself in the position of returning the next day to accept the offer only to find that someone else has the job.

If you have absolutely no doubts or objections about the job offer, accept the offer on the spot with enthusiasm. This will reinforce the employer's confidence in your suitability for the job.

When the Answer Is Yes

If you accept the job offer verbally, follow up immediately in writing. Summarize your understanding of the conditions of the offer and state the position title, starting date, salary, and other pertinent items. (Your employer may do the same, but this helps ensure mutual agreement about all of the conditions of the offer.)

If you are waiting to hear about more than one offer, tell the other organizations you interviewed with that you have accepted a job. You may deal with these people in your new job, or you may want to contact them in the future regarding employment.

Contact your references and other people who helped with your job search to tell them about your new job and thank them for their help. People you thank are more likely to help in the future when you seek a new position or advancement in your career.

When the Answer Is No Thanks

If you decide this is not the job for you, first notify the employer by telephone if possible. Then politely decline the offer in a letter, thank the employer for the job offer, and wish the employer future success.

MAKE IT A HABIT

Be a Gracious Winner

A job search certainly takes a lot of work, but it is not a paying job. The time will come when you need to stop looking for a job and start working at one. Your final decision about accepting a particular job may well be influenced by economics—the need to earn a living.

If a job offer meets most of your requirements but is not your first choice or is not a perfectly logical career step, you may still decide to accept it. If so, take the job with a determination to excel. It is an opportunity for you to establish your reputation—while at the same time taking home a regular salary.

Accept the challenge and view it as preparation for the next step in your career development.

nyul/iStockphoto.com

COMPLETE **CAREER ACTION 12-3**

Plan for Dealing with Job Offers, p. 265

Chapter Checklist

Underline each action you are already taking and circle the actions you need to work on.

- Consider all aspects of a job offer—the job and company, the compensation package (salary and benefits), growth opportunities, etc. [1]

- Conduct research about salary ranges and trends. [2]

- Develop a strategy for salary negotiations. [2]

- Accept or decline a job offer professionally. [3]

Critical-Thinking Questions

1. If economic conditions require you to accept a job that is not exactly what you are aiming for, how can you best approach the new job? What are the benefits of doing so? [1]

2. Is it more advantageous for the applicant or the interviewer to bring up the subject of salary first? Why? [2]

3. What is an appropriate response when an interviewer asks what salary you are looking for? [2]

4. Base your answers to the following questions on your salary research: (a) What is the entry-level salary for the job you are seeking? (b) What salary range do you plan to seek in your job search? (c) What is this range based on? [2]

5. Why is it important to act professionally when turning down a job offer? [3]

Want access to career resources, study tools, activities, and job information links? Get started at www.cengage.com/career/yourcareer.

TRIAL RUN

Pay scales and benefit packages are affected by larger economic issues. Divide into four teams and research the employment conditions in your area. Use anecdotal information and your own observations and check the websites of the local newspaper, business journal, chamber of commerce, and television stations.

Start by having a class discussion about what you want to learn from your research. For example:

- How have the students in this class been affected by economic changes?

- What can older workers tell you about past economic downturns or economic bubbles?

- What is the relative impact of national and local factors?

- What is the local unemployment rate? How has it changed in the last two years?

- How long do people report taking to find a new job in their field? Are people changing fields or taking contingency jobs?

- What are the elected officials predicting? What are business leaders predicting?

- What advice do you have for your community leaders?

Team 1. Research the two or three largest employers in your area. How have they been affected by the national economic downturn? Have there been layoffs? If so, have these jobs been shifted to other parts of the country or to other countries or eliminated altogether?

Team 2. Research the local stores or branch offices of national companies. What is the reason behind any closures; for example, did the national company close low-performing stores, or did it go bankrupt and close all of its stores? Have any national chains opened new stores in your area? Have any openings been postponed? How many people have lost their jobs? How many new jobs have been created?

Team 3. Research small, locally owned retail businesses. Have any small businesses near your school closed? What about the neighborhoods you live in? Have new businesses opened?

Team 4. Research locally owned service businesses. Include companies that provide services to consumers (such as dry cleaners and nail salons) and business-to-business companies (such as janitorial services and restaurant supply companies).

CAREER ACTION   12-1   Internet Research on Salary Information ②

Part 1. Compare the websites Homefair.com and Salary.com. Use one site's salary calculator to compute the cost-of-living differences between two cities in which you would consider working. What are some other factors to consider? Print the results.

Part 2. Visit the *Occupational Outlook Handbook* at the Bureau of Labor Statistics site and complete the following steps.

1. Select the title of your occupational cluster.

2. Choose the title of your field (and a subtitle if necessary) and then click "Earnings."

3. Print or summarize in writing the wage ranges listed for the occupation.

4. Find the wage ranges for at least five more occupational clusters and career fields you have been interested in at one time.

Part 3. For additional salary information, check out the valuable "Salary Info" section at the JobStar website. Take at least one quiz or read one article.

CAREER ACTION   12-2   Salary and Benefits Planning Sheet ②

Contact two employers in your field to learn about the salary ranges and benefits they offer for the type of job you are seeking. Ask the following questions.

Part 1: Negotiating Salary and Benefits

Does this position have a fixed salary or a salary range?

If the salary is fixed, would you tell me the amount?

If the salary is in a range, would you tell me the range?

Is the salary negotiable?

What criteria are used for determining the salary for this position?

Are salary raises awarded for excellent job performance? If so, what criteria are used in this process?

What is included in the typical complete compensation package (salary and benefits)?

Part 2: Summary of Strategies for Negotiating Compensation

Review the strategies in the section "Negotiate for Top Salary and Benefits." Use a separate sheet of paper to summarize, in your own words, the tactics you plan to use when negotiating a compensation package (salary and benefits). List any additional tips you have found in your Internet or other research.

CAREER ACTION   12-3   **Plan for Dealing with Job Offers** ③

Respond to the following.

1. List every factor you should consider when evaluating a job offer. Be thorough in your answer. You may want to talk with a member of your support system network, a placement counselor, or both. Address the factors that are specific to your personal job search, as well as general factors.

2. Explain how you can best respond to a job offer made in person:

   a. If you think you want the job

b. If you are sure you want the job

c. If you don't want the job

3. How can you best respond to a job offer made by telephone?

4. List the follow-up steps you should take when accepting a job offer.

5. What should you do to reject a job offer in a professional manner?

For Your Career Management Files Tracker

File your completed Career Action worksheets in your Career Management Files Tracker.

CA 12-1   Internet research on salary information

CA 12-2   Salary and benefits planning sheet

CA 12-3   Plan for dealing with job offers

Outcomes

1 Develop strategies for increasing your chances of getting interviews.

2 Develop strategies for improving your interview performance.

3 Explain strategies for reversing a rejection notice.

© Photographer/Image Source

Dealing with Disappointment

OVERVIEW Getting a good job often requires more than one interview; it may take several tries before you land the job you want. Getting a rejection notice is not a great ego booster, but it's not a reason to stop your job search campaign either. Think of it as a learning experience and continue with your job search activities. Chapter 13 highlights practical strategies for recharging your motivation, reversing a rejection notice, and trying new angles to land a top job.

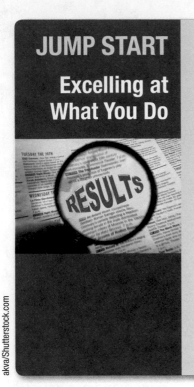

JUMP START

Excelling at What You Do

If you are reading this book, chances are high that you want to improve your employment situation. If the process is taking longer than you hoped, renew your career by using the opportunities available in your current place of employment. Brainstorm how you can apply the following strategies:

- Observe how the managers and the more senior people do their jobs. What can you learn for your own career?
- What are the most important technical skills in your workplace? What is your plan for acquiring these skills?
- Who are the most "popular" employees? How can you become a more positive and energetic force in your workplace?
- What does each department do? What do the departments need from your group?
- How can you help your organization succeed?

Persevere for Success

No one is right for every job. The right person for a job doesn't always get the job. The best prepared and most determined person often does, however. While you may be partly responsible for an initial rejection, you have the power to turn the situation to your favor. All of the strategies in this chapter have been used successfully by other job seekers to win a job offer after having been rejected for a job.

If You Don't Get Interviews

Outcome **1**

You may not be finding the best jobs to apply for. The Bureau of Labor Statistics has compiled data showing that people who use many resources for finding job leads find jobs faster than people who use only one or two resources. If you are relying on Monster and Craigslist for job leads, look at the many sources of leads in Chapter 5 and expand your search options. In a 2010 survey of people who had been laid off in the last year, 21% found jobs through job sites and 22% found jobs through "personal referrals." Reconnect with your network—or risk not applying for a full 50% of jobs you may be qualified for. Remember, people hire people they have a connection with. Do not sound discouraged or describe your job search woes in detail. An excellent strategy for getting the person's attention is to mention a job lead that you are not using.

You may be applying for the wrong jobs. You may be aiming too high and applying for jobs that you aren't qualified for. Look carefully at the required qualifications and skills for several jobs you have applied for. If your skills and qualifications are at the low end of the requirements, you probably won't get an interview.

You may be applying for too many jobs. Job sites make it easy to respond to job listings, and employers get more applications than they need to consider. If you find it easy to apply, so do all of the people you are competing against.

You may need to give your resume a facelift. Print a copy of your master resume and compare it with sample resumes online. Try using a different format or different fonts (see Figure 6-9 on page 126 for an example). Highlight and count the action verbs and keywords and make sure you are using them effectively (Chapter 6).

You may need to spend more time customizing your resume and cover letter to match the requirements in the job listing. Convince the hiring committee that you are interested in *this* job and *this* company.

To address these issues and reenergize your job search, make an appointment with a career counselor to get a professional appraisal of your job search strategy and recommendations for new strategies. Work with a resume adviser to make sure your resume stands out in appearance and content.

Finally, keep in mind that most job listings do not yield a miniscule number of qualified applicants. Even if you did everything right, you may not be one of the top two or three candidates who are interviewed.

Outcome 2 If Interviews Don't Lead to Job Offers

Getting an interview indicates that you were one of the top applicants for the job. Most people have several interviews before they are offered a good job. Keep your positive attitude after a bad interview; take what you learned to the next interview and use it in your favor. Getting a top-notch job is a full-time job that usually requires several interviews and some rejections.

Nevertheless, your immediate priority must be to improve your performance the next time. How many of these roadblocks to a job offer apply to you?

- You didn't prepare for the interview. You hesitated over your answers, or your answers (or questions) showed that you weren't aware of the company's current situation or industry issues.

- You didn't convince the interviewer that your qualifications match the specific job requirements in the job listing.

MAKE IT A HABIT

Counter Rejection with Success Strategies

To counter natural feelings of rejection, the best approach is taking immediate positive action.

- Maintain a positive attitude.
- Evaluate your performance and your self-marketing package.
- Connect with your network for support and rework your contacts.
- Plan your next job search steps and follow through.

Taking a short breather helps renew your energy and enthusiasm. Allow yourself one day—but no longer—to do something you enjoy and to relax. And don't use rejection as an excuse for giving up. Regroup and rework your action plans.

Reread the success strategies in Chapter 1, focusing on the strategies that project competence and strengthen self-esteem. Visualize yourself performing successfully in your next interview and on your new job. Make a conscious effort to think and act positively and to use positive self-talk and affirmation statements.

Review your self-analysis forms from Chapters 2 and 3 (your talents, skills, qualifications, special accomplishments, and personal attributes).

Comstock/Jupiter Images

"Winners in all fields agree: Perseverance is a major factor in their success. When they meet an obstacle, they find a way around it.**"**

- You didn't give well thought out examples that showed in concrete, measurable ways how your work helped your previous employer.

- You didn't convince the interviewer that your qualifications match the specific job requirements in the job listing.

- Your physical appearance was "off" (clothing, jewelry, fidgeting, posture, facial expressions, body language, etc.).

- You didn't sell yourself well. The interviewer was not convinced that you understand the job or have the qualifications to be productive quickly. You did not convince the interviewer that *you are a person who gets things done.*

- Your answers were too long or rambling.

- You gave too many details or said something negative about a previous employer.

- You didn't send the interviewer a thank-you letter.

Take *all* of the actions below to improve your interview performance.

- If you haven't already done so, use Career Action worksheets 11-3 and 11-4 to evaluate your performance and recall interview details.

- Make notes about the ideal answer to each question you were asked. Video-record yourself answering the questions.

- Ask at least one person you do not know well to give you a mock interview.

- Follow the advice in Chapter 10 to prepare for different types of interviews and interview questions.

- Remember what you learned from interviews and use it the next time.

- Do your homework before the next interview!

The rest of the chapter has more details about bad interviews and unsuccessful interviews as well as advice for improving your performance.

The Bad Interview

Some interviews are not good; in fact, some are grim. After learning the details of a job, you may be convinced that you don't want it. The interviewer may be inept at interviewing, making it difficult for you to perform well.

Do not stop trying. Do your best to be professional in every interview. You can always learn something beneficial or use the opportunity to polish your interviewing skills.

Never give up *during* an interview. Besides being unprofessional, it could cost you a future reference or a good job lead from the interviewer.

Outcome 3 Strategies for Better Outcomes

After receiving a rejection notice, if you're not sure where you fell short, call the interviewer and ask for an honest evaluation. If you are aware of the perceived shortcoming though, prepare a strong written clarification that you can refer to while making this follow-up call.

The interviewer may be willing to tell you if he or she considers you to be lacking in any area of skill, training, or experience. Attaining this information may be the starting point for an update of your skills or interviewing technique before your next interview.

Some employers are reluctant to offer specific opinions and are justifiably cautious about being sued by job applicants for unfair hiring practices. Even if you don't get concrete help, express your thanks.

Prepare and Respond

If the interviewer is willing to evaluate your performance and make suggestions for improvement, listen carefully and take notes. Accept the concerns expressed. Their validity is irrelevant. The important point is that they represent problem areas in the interviewer's perception of you.

If you like the organization and you want the job, be prepared to *briefly* clarify your qualifications or clear up any misunderstanding. Use a friendly tone and do not react defensively. Remember that you asked for the opinion. If the interviewer seems receptive, explain that you didn't convey your qualifications as completely as you had planned and suggest that you meet once more to review them. Handled well, this approach demonstrates confidence, competence, and assertiveness.

Consider Other Departments

If your rejection response doesn't land you the job, emphasize your enthusiasm for working for the employer and ask whether you are more qualified to fill another position. This strategy encourages the interviewer to give you more consideration and may land a "hidden job." Ask for a referral to another employer. Employers are impressed by applicants who demonstrate initiative and confidence. If you project confidence and competence, you greatly increase your chances of convincing others of your potential.

Don't Be Afraid to Reapply

If you don't get a job with your preferred employer now, don't give up. Opportunities can develop later. If an opening comes up in the future, you have the advantage of being known by the employer because a known applicant saves valuable time in recruiting a new employee. Besides, you never know how close to being hired you were. You might be at the top of the list the next time an opening occurs.

Don't Vent on Facebook!

So you found a great company, you got an interview, and you did your absolute best but still didn't get the job. Rule 1—don't take it personally! And whatever you do, don't air your disappointments on a social networking site.

When you're frustrated, it's only natural to turn to your social network for moral support, but it's best to keep your venting local and off the computer. What airs on Facebook doesn't always stay on Facebook—or on Twitter or YouTube or anywhere else online. Keep your negative comments to yourself.

Don't assume that just because you didn't get the job the company didn't like you. Perhaps you weren't right for the position, but who's to say you won't be a perfect match for the next opening? Keep your options open and your bridges intact. Leaving things on a positive note shows professionalism and an optimistic outlook—traits that employers appreciate. Here are some steps to take after an unsuccessful interview:

- Write a positive Facebook status update about your experience, mention how you'd like to be considered for future opportunities, and tag the company in the text.
- Send out tweets commending the company on a great interview process.
- Write a note of thanks to everyone who interviewed you. If you don't have their email addresses, search for them on LinkedIn and Facebook.

Keeping your name in front of the employer can put you first in line for the next opening. One way you can do this is by calling the interviewer every couple of months just to check in. Keep the phone call brief and polite. Your purpose is to keep your name at the top of the list of applicants.

Be Persistent

Be persistent in pursuing your preferred job. Stay focused on your goal and consider all of the factors that may affect the status of the position. Changes in business conditions may affect the status of your target job. Consider how these changes may also present new opportunities to you as a job seeker.

Many organizations and businesses keep applications in their active file for a specific period of time. If you are interested in a position with a particular company, find out the organization's policy for keeping applications active. You may need to call a prospective employer periodically to keep your application active and to remind the organization that you are interested in new job openings.

Stay Informed

Once a month at your computer or at the library, read the local business journals. Know what's happening in your community and look for networking opportunities.

> **COMPLETE** **CAREER ACTION 13-1**
>
> Internet Research on Handling Job Search Rejection, p. 275

> **COMPLETE** **CAREER ACTION 13-2**
>
> Action Plans for Improving Your Job Search Campaign, p. 275

drbimages/iStockphoto.com

WATCH OUT!

It Isn't Always about You

An application for a job can go flat for reasons you cannot control.

- The company may implement a hiring freeze before the position is filled, or the decision maker may decide that the department doesn't need to fill the position.

- The hiring committee may be told to give preference to current employees and local applicants, or they already know who the "best candidate" is.

- For political reasons, the person who interviewed you may want to defer to the candidate that another member of the committee recommends.

- The last job search may have backfired, and the hiring committee may decide that none of the candidates is a perfect fit.

- The hiring committee may decide, or be told, to postpone the job search. Overall, fewer jobs are filled in May and June, at the close of the current fiscal year.

- The committee may get applications from overqualified applicants and decide to redefine the job responsibilities.

Chapter Checklist

Underline each action you are already taking and circle the actions you need to work on.

- Take concrete action to recharge my motivation and improve my chances of getting interviews. [1]

- Improve my interview performance so that I get job offers. [2]

- Ask each interviewer to evaluate my performance so that I can identify any areas that need improvement. [3]

- Ask for referrals to other departments or organizations. [3]

- Reapply at a later date and call back periodically to check the organization's hiring status. [3]

Critical-Thinking Questions

1. Which strategies will you use to improve your chances of getting an interview? [1]

2. What specific steps will you take to improve your interview performance? [2]

3. Why shouldn't you abandon your efforts to obtain a job if you get a rejection notice after an interview? [2]

3. What can you gain from seeking an evaluation of your interview performance from an interviewer who did not hire you? [3]

4. If all of your efforts fail to result in a job offer, what last request should you make of an interviewer? [3]

Want access to career resources, study tools, activities, and job information links? Get started at www.cengage.com/career/yourcareer.

TRIAL RUN

The search for a new job is challenging and often frustrating. This activity may help you put things into perspective and renew your energy.

Take written notes during each part of the activity.

The activity starts in the present day. Jot down words and phrases that describe the general business climate in the country and your community and the key issues in your career field and in your own career.

Think back five years and repeat the activity. Break into teams of people with related career interests. Take notes during the discussion. Reflect on the changes in your career field. How many of the changes were deliberately planned for and implemented? How many changes were unexpected? How did the larger business environment affect your industry? What things that seemed small five years ago turned out to have big consequences? What big things turned out not to be so big after all?

In teams or as a class, project ahead five years. Take notes during the discussion. What changes do you predict in the general business environment and in your career fields? Where do you expect the most changes? How confident are you about these predictions? What are the implications of these changes for the public and for the people working in the field? If what you expect and what you hope for are far apart, what can you start doing to bring them closer together?

Think about these discussions for a few days and reflect on your own professional life five years ago and five years from now. Write yourself a letter to be opened in five years:

* Describe the circumstances leading to this letter: this assignment, your work situation today, your current plans, recent setbacks, etc.

* Record your predictions about your situation in five years.

* List helpful actions and "attitude adjustments" you have decided today to take. Be specific about your plans so that in five years, you can judge how well you succeeded.

* Include anything else in your letter that you believe you will enjoy reading in five years or that you believe will be helpful to reflect on.

Put the letter where you will find it or give it to someone who can mail it to you.

CAREER ACTION

13-1 Internet Research on Handling Job Search Rejection ⬚1 ⬚2 ⬚3

Search the Internet for additional tips on persevering after being rejected for a job. Use the search phrase *job search persistence rejection* or go to job club sites and blogs you bookmarked in earlier research. Summarize your findings and file your research in your Career Management Files Tracker.

CAREER ACTION

13-2 Action Plans for Improving Your Job Search Campaign ⬚3

Review your complete job search campaign thoroughly. Answer the following questions in detail. As necessary, include specific action plans you will take to improve the effectiveness of your job search. Check off each item as you complete the related actions.

1. After reviewing my self-analysis activities in the Career Actions from Chapters 2 and 3, have I overlooked anything important that supports my job target? (List the items and describe any needed research or improvement.)

2. Have I checked with my support network members to find out whether they have any new job leads? (List them here and follow up immediately.)

3. Could my resume be improved or tailored to a new job target? How could it be improved? Who could do a good job of helping me with it?

4. Should I make additional telephone calls/personal visits or write additional letters to prospective employers? (List details on a separate sheet of paper and begin following up today. Don't put off these actions.)

5. Could my cover letters be improved? How could they be strengthened? Who can give me advice?

6. Have I followed up on the cover letters and resumes I sent and on all job leads? Have I followed up on every interview? (List any follow-up needed in these areas.)

7. Have I done thorough research on my current job leads—enough to talk intelligently and persuasively about how I would fit in with the organization? (List any research that must be completed.)

8. Have I tried every possible job source? (Refer to the list of suggested job sources in Chapter 5. List any you could use now.)

9. Should I reapply with any employers? If so, when?

10. Did I follow up on interviews thoroughly? What else can I do?

11. Have I scheduled my job search on my daily and weekly calendars?

For Your Career Management Files Tracker

File your completed Career Action worksheets in your Career Management Files Tracker.

CA 13-1   Internet tips for handing job search rejection

CA 13-2   Action plans for improving your job search campaign

Outcomes

1 Develop strategies for adjusting successfully to a new job.

2 Develop good work habits.

3 Explain attitudes and actions needed to work effectively with coworkers.

4 Describe actions you can take to manage your entire career.

© Photographer/Image Source

Take Charge of Your Career

OVERVIEW Chapter 14 has guidelines for adjusting to and succeeding in a new job. Techniques are included for developing successful interpersonal skills, achieving top work efficiency, mastering new responsibilities, and learning how to prepare for a successful job performance evaluation. Once you master your job and are performing at your peak, you will likely be interested in working toward career development and advancement opportunities. This chapter also provides clear guidelines for earning a promotion and achieving career growth throughout your working life.

akva/Shutterstock.com

JUMP START
Your Successful Career

Congratulations on reaching the final chapter in *Your Career: How to Make It Happen!* One of the strongest messages in *Your Career* is that *you* are in charge of the success of your career search. On the job, you are in charge of the satisfaction you gain from your career. For this activity, talk to two or three older members of your personal support network. Ask each person the same questions:

- What part of your career has brought you the most satisfaction and pride? Was it related to money or to "a job well done"?
- What was your best "career move"? Did you recognize it as a positive change at the time?
- What do know now that you wish you had known on the first day of work? What mistakes do you see the younger people you work with making?

Reflect on how you can apply this wisdom to your own career. Share your reflections with a classmate. Did you hear the same things or different things?

Outcome 1 Start Your Successful Career Immediately

All workers who start new jobs have one challenge in common: adjusting to the new workplace and the new job. This adjustment includes learning to perform specific tasks, learning how your job relates to the business as a whole, learning to work with others, and understanding the formal and informal rules and ways of doing things. Mastering these elements take time and effort and training assistance from your employer.

Don't expect to achieve top efficiency overnight. It doesn't happen. Experiencing some anxiety while trying to learn so much new information and so many new procedures is normal. Maintaining enthusiasm, an eagerness to learn, and a positive attitude will help you adjust successfully.

Starting a new job is an important personal and professional step that helps shape your lifetime career. Successful careers are developed through planning and determination to succeed. You will achieve peak success by being persistent and by accumulating skills, knowledge, and experience.

Your employer will want you to succeed, and your coworkers will help you get off to a good start. The following techniques will help you adjust to a new job and achieve a successful lifetime career.

Maintain a Positive Attitude: *The Most Important Success Factor*

Employers hire and promote employees who have positive attitudes and who demonstrate enthusiasm. Employees who appear defensive, negative, or uninterested are not promoted and may eventually be terminated. Two employees with equal job skills but vastly different attitudes will develop widely different career paths. The one with a strong, positive attitude will progress steadily, while the one with a negative attitude will stagnate.

Approach new colleagues and superiors (and tasks) with the attitude that you will do your best and that you expect the best from them, while being patient with their constraints. People most often live up to the expectations others have of them.

And remember: It's easy to be cheerful and upbeat when things are going well. An employee who can remain positive when things are difficult is a valuable employee indeed.

Maintain a Positive, Professional, Competent Image

Your coworkers will perceive the image you project as a reflection of the quality of work you do. Your image projects from three sources: your inner confidence, your outward appearance, and your verbal and nonverbal communication. Review and practice the tips on self-esteem, appearance, and communication skills from Chapters 1 and 8. Maintain the professional appearance you had in your job interviews, but dress appropriately for your job duties and organization.

If you project an unsure attitude through your speech, appearance, and actions, you will be perceived as a tentative, unsure worker—even if your work is excellent. Purposely think, speak, dress, and act positively. This projects career-building confidence and competence.

Projecting a positive, professional, and competent image gives you a competitive edge. For example, if you make an error, your professional image may influence people to view the error as a part of learning rather than a sign of incompetence. Successful people act positively, practicing the success strategies presented in Chapter 1 until they become habits.

Copy the habits of successful people: think of yourself, see yourself, and present yourself as a winner.

Ask for the Information You Need to Do Your Job

During a job interview, you learn general information about the position and the job duties. To perform the work, you need more detailed information about your job duties, your department, and the work processes your job is part of. Make sure you know what is expected of you—do not risk doing the wrong work really well. If you are not given this information, do the following:

- Ask for a job description. A job description typically identifies the specific duties and responsibilities of the job, the skills and competencies required, the equipment and tools to be used, the expected outcomes and contributions to the organization, and the relationship of the position to other positions in the company.

- Ask about any training you will receive. Your employer expects you to have the basic knowledge and skills you need to do your job, but you may need additional training for certain tasks.

- Ask how and when your job performance will be evaluated. See "Prepare for Your Performance Evaluation" on page 284.

- Ask who you should go to with questions.

Most organizations have a written **employee handbook** that covers policies and procedures such as work hours, the probationary period for new employees, pay and benefits, and rules about using company equipment and email. Learn the rules and follow them.

Respect Your Organization

In return for offering you a job and salary, the employer expects your support. Show your support at work by serving your employer's needs and interests. Show your support outside work by speaking well of the company and its personnel, products, and services. Speaking negatively about an organization harms its reputation and may result in your being fired. Never post negative remarks about your employer online.

Learn about Your Organization

Learn as much as you can about your company and its leaders. Read your company's annual report if it has one. Read the company website

Expect that adjusting to your new job will take some time. Be alert, listen, and stay positive. Look, speak, and act professionally.

thoroughly and search the Internet for information about the company's history and for news stories about the company.

Learn about your company's industry and its main competitors. Research the competitors' products or services and try to understand why customers might buy them instead of your company's offerings.

Embrace your employer's values and goals. Most places of business have a mission statement that includes their goals and values. Read the mission statement and think about it. How are the larger organization's goals and values reflected in your department? If there are gaps, what do you think accounts for them? How can you apply the mission statement to your own position?

Guard Company Information

By accepting employment, you agree to join your employer's team and help your company succeed. Divulging confidential company information could undermine the ability of your employer to compete in the marketplace. Therefore, you have a moral and legal obligation to protect internal company information. You are also obligated to protect information about the businesses and individuals your employer does business with, such as customers and suppliers.

Depending on your position, you may have access to private and sensitive information about individual employees (such as salaries and promotions) or about management decisions (such as the downsizing of a division or department). Never share information you learn through your job with your coworkers.

While breaches of confidentiality are sometimes intentional, they can also occur through ignorance and carelessness. Do not leave confidential documents on your desk or walk away from your computer without

closing a confidential document. Make sure you know the rules in your department and follow standard procedures for storing and releasing confidential information. Be especially careful about email messages, which can be forwarded without your permission or knowledge.

When you are hired, you may be required to sign a nondisclosure agreement that defines the type of information that may not be shared with outsiders and the penalties for violating the agreement. Employers dismiss and often sue employees who are found to have leaked confidential information.

Pay Attention to the Corporate Culture

Every organization has a unique personality and culture that is expressed in many ways, from the company's mission statement to the way employees dress for work. To enhance your success, learn and adhere to the culture's values, including the expected work ethic and the customs and rules for interacting with coworkers and customers. For example, if you are given a laptop computer, do not assume that you can take it out of the office. If you are hired in November, do not decorate your cubicle with turkeys and cornucopias until you see what others are doing (and maybe not even then). Many of the elements that make up "how things are done" are not spelled out. Observe your coworkers and ask a trusted coworker for advice.

Community involvement is another aspect of corporate culture. If your employer sponsors volunteer or community service activities, get involved. Participation provides many benefits, including expanding your network of contacts, developing leadership skills, and demonstrating your support for the employer's goals and related activities.

To be an effective employee (and for your own advantage), you should also be **aware of organizational politics**. Every organization has formal and informal politics, which are affected by changes in personnel. Learn who is respected—or even feared. These people often influence office politics greatly and are usually powerful within the organization. Learn to deal with them successfully. Note, however, that first impressions are not always accurate. Take time to observe and learn office politics. Avoid affiliating with "complainers" who are not in harmony with your employer's philosophy.

Know Your Internal Customers

You may work in a department where you do not interact with the people or organizations that keep your company in business by buying its goods or services. Nevertheless, you have internal customers, the people or groups that depend on your department (or on you) to help them get their jobs done.

If you work in the marketing department, for example, the product development group is your customer because it depends on you to develop effective marketing campaigns. Get to know who your internal customers are, what their needs are, and how they depend on you or your group; then go out of your way to provide great service.

COMPLETE | **CAREER ACTION 14-1**

Internet Research on Workplace Success Tips, p. 299

Outcome 2 # Develop Good Work Habits

If you try to work without planning and organizing, you are doing yourself a great disservice. Motivate yourself to develop these critical self-management skills.

Show Up for Work Every Day

Go to work every day. Absenteeism causes work inefficiency, disruption of workflow, and lower productivity. It also places stress on workers who must cover for the absent employee, causing resentment and frustration. If you must be absent because of a severe illness, a serious emergency, or an unavoidable problem, let your employer know as soon as possible. Chronic absenteeism is not tolerated by employers and is an eventual ticket out the door. Patterns of questionable excuses raise questions in the employer's mind.

Be punctual and dependable. Be on time for work at the start of the day and after breaks. Be punctual for meetings. Those who make an effort to be punctual will not appreciate your being late. Being on time also means finishing projects and assignments when they are due.

Plan How You Will Use Your Time

Use some type of planner to organize your workweeks: a spiral-bound planner, the planner in your email program or some other planner on your computer, or a planner app on your smartphone. Record appointments, meetings, assignments, deadlines, and reminders. Enter important tasks and dates as soon as you learn of them so that you don't forget to enter them later. Consider using one color for work obligations and another color for personal obligations.

Block off time to work on larger projects and longer-term assignments so that you don't end up having to do them all at once and miss deadlines for your ongoing work. For example, if you are giving a presentation at a meeting on Thursday, block off time to work on the presentation on Monday, Tuesday, and Wednesday.

At the beginning or end of the day, take five or ten minutes to plan the day's work. On paper or online, make a list of the things you need to do that day. There are many ways to organize to-do lists (and many templates online). For example:

- Put the most important tasks at the top of the list (tasks that need immediate attention or completion).

- List the tasks as you think of them and then label them A (most important tasks), B (tasks to do after you complete the A tasks), and C (tasks with no specific deadline).

- Under the most important tasks, list the smaller steps you need to do to accomplish the tasks.

Beside each task, write the deadline for completing it and the amount of time you think it will take. Be realistic about time requirement, especially when you are new on the job, and ask your supervisor or a coworker for advice.

Don't Procrastinate

Small tasks and diversions can be appealing when you have a difficult or unpleasant task to complete. Like most people, however, you already know that **procrastinating**—putting off doing something that you need to do—provides only a temporary feeling of relief. Try these techniques to overcome procrastination:

- Break tasks into smaller steps that seem more manageable.

- Tell someone else about your deadline and ask that person to check up on you.

- Set a length of time to work on the task so that you can at least get started. You may find yourself working longer than you expected.

- Tell yourself how much the "future you" will be glad you did your work on time.

- Make a contract with yourself that includes a reward for completing the dreaded task.

Keep Your Work Area Neat

Your work area, like your appearance and demeanor, sends signals to your supervisor and your coworkers about your professionalism. Arrange your work area for efficiency and comfort and clear your desk of clutter. Place the items you use frequently, such as your stapler and notebook, within easy reach.

If neatness doesn't come naturally to you, straighten your work area at the end of the day. At the very least, clear out the clutter and organize your work space at the end of the week. Throw away unnecessary or outdated items and shred sensitive documents that you no longer need.

Manage Your Time

StockLite/Shutterstock.com

Managing your time effectively is one of the keys to becoming an efficient worker and an effective employee.

First, determine your priorities and plan your work around them. Ask your supervisor and coworkers what tasks are most vital to the successful operation of your department. Prioritize your work based on their answers.

Do your most important daily tasks first to avoid overlooking vital tasks during rush work periods. Reassess your priorities as new tasks are assigned and periodically review them with your team or supervisor.

Group similar tasks and complete them in one block of time. This focuses your attention and enhances task performance. For example, schedule one block of time to prepare documents and another to place phone calls.

Control Email and Papers

Piles of documents and long lists of email messages can accumulate quickly. Try these strategies to keep things under control:

- Act on documents (paper and email) at once if they require immediate action or if you have the time.

- If it isn't your responsibility, forward the document to someone who can handle it.

- If you don't need it, throw it away or delete it.

- Use email folders to sort messages by project, sender, or some other method.

Outcome 3 Succeed with Your Coworkers

The ability to interact well with supervisors, coworkers, suppliers, customers, and others is a critical skill in every workplace. Organizations care about the relationships among people because people are their most important resource. Wherever you work, you will not be successful unless you can get along with your coworkers.

Develop a Good Relationship with Your Supervisor

A good working relationship with your supervisor is essential because you need your supervisor's advice, help, and general understanding to do your work. Depending on your job, you may have day-to-day personal contact with your supervisor or only occasional direct contact. When you are first hired, however, you can usually count on spending time together. Do not act flustered if you don't understand everything that is being explained about your job. Things that are unclear will become apparent as you learn more about your job and work with your new coworkers.

Your supervisor's key responsibility is to ensure that his or her group produces the assigned amount of work on time and within acceptable levels of quality. If you get a new assignment that will mean not meeting your deadlines for other work, ask your supervisor which work should be completed first. If your supervisor gives you the new assignment, make it clear that you will have to postpone completing the other work.

Before you approach your supervisor about a problem, demonstrate your initiative by thinking of possible solutions. Offer your own ideas, but don't press for your opinion or ideas if other people have information that you didn't. Always do your best work to support the final decision, no matter whose idea it was.

If you find a faster way to do your work—without cutting corners or having a negative effect on someone else's work—try it on a small level and tell your supervisor about it afterwards.

Find out what your supervisor needs to meet the group's or department's goals and do what you can to provide it. Regularly using your initiative to meet your supervisor's needs is a definite career booster.

Ask for Feedback and Accept Criticism

Asking your supervisor for feedback about your performance demonstrates initiative and professionalism. Periodically ask your supervisor directly whether your performance is meeting expectations or if you need to improve. Ask for specific recommendations for improvement as necessary.

Because you are human, you will make an occasional mistake. The challenge is to learn from your mistakes and accept criticism maturely. When you work for someone else, you agree to perform according to that person's standards. Because your employer pays your salary, he or she has the right to criticize your performance or behavior if it doesn't meet established standards.

If the criticism is deserved, don't deny fault. Don't react defensively or blame others. Accept the criticism professionally and make improvements. To learn from your mistakes, ask for suggestions about how you can improve the situation. If you don't think the criticism is justified, tactfully present evidence that supports your opinion.

If your employer or supervisor continually criticizes you unfairly, particularly in front of others, request a meeting to discuss the reason for this behavior. If the criticism continues even though you make the recommended improvements, consider seeking a position in another department or looking for a new employer.

COMPLETE **CAREER ACTION 14-2**

Job Performance Evaluation, p. 299

Develop Good Relationships with Your Coworkers

The way you relate to the people you work with will influence your career success as much as the quality of your job performance—no matter how skilled or educated you are. Studies repeatedly verify that job failure is most frequently the result of poor interpersonal skills (behavior and attitude), not lack of skill.

- **Get to know your coworkers.** Be friendly and approachable; do not get a reputation as a loner.

- **Respect diversity.** Do not exclude anyone or treat anyone differently because of factors such as race, gender, religion, or physical ability.

- **Be tactful.** The world's most successful people have these qualities in common: they are tactful, diplomatic, courteous, and helpful in dealing with other people.

- **Treat people the way you want to be treated.** Help others accomplish their assignments, compliment them on work well done, critique their work tactfully only when necessary, and listen to what they have to say. This behavior encourages others to treat you the same way.

- **Listen to what your supervisors and coworkers tell you.** Pay attention to what is happening in the organization and learn from the people you work with.

- **Check your own work** so that no one else has to correct it. Meet your deadlines and deliver outstanding work.

- **Offer to help a coworker who needs help** meeting a deadline, provided your own workload is under control, of course.

Prepare for Your Performance Evaluation

MichaelDeLeon/iStockphoto.com

Learn how and when you will be evaluated on your job performance so that you know where to focus your efforts to achieve a good evaluation. This will also help you avoid overlooking an area that is important to your employer.

Find out how heavily the employer weighs each performance area so that you can concentrate on the most important ones. If you don't receive this information with your other employment documents, ask your supervisor to explain the evaluation process.

If your employer uses an informal method of job evaluation, ask what is considered good job performance and what criteria are used in determining promotions or raises. This will provide you with guidelines for your successful performance. As you become more knowledgeable about your job, show initiative by setting your own goals and deadlines for improving performance and growing in the job.

- **Stay out of office politics.** Don't take sides when coworkers disagree about something that is not directly related to *your* work.

- **Do your share of the work.** Don't make excuses or complain about your workload.

- **Maintain stable emotions** in the workplace, leaving your personal problems at home.

- **Respect the need for silence in the workplace.** Turn off your cell phone and conduct conversations in a private place, not over the tops of cubicles or while standing in front of someone's cubicle.

- **Don't look for problems or hold grudges.**

- **Avoid the office grapevine.** Gossip is not harmless; misinformation and half-truths can damage a person's reputation and career. Develop a reputation for being discreet and courteous: your coworkers will respect you, and it's a good business decision.

- **Don't look for new best friends at work.** Don't join a clique that may divide you from the rest of the department. Don't share information about yourself that can be used against you if circumstances change. Remember: work is work, and home is home.

When you need help with a project or are in line for a promotion, your reputation for working well with others will more likely be rewarded. Treat everyone (your employer, your peers, the custodian, etc.) with respect.

Be a Good Communicator

Good communication skills are important for career success. Effective verbal communication, listening, and written communication can improve your productivity and enhance your interactions with coworkers and managers.

Use Excellent Phone Manners

Phone manners are important, especially in a customer service economy. Greet callers pleasantly and promptly, listen carefully, and answer their questions patiently and thoroughly. Check your voice mail messages frequently and leave brief, specific, and clear messages for others. Return calls promptly.

Be a Good Listener

Wikipedia defines **active listening** as a "communication technique that requires the listener to understand, interpret, and evaluate what (s)he hears." It is listening with the goal of understanding what the speaker intends and is a powerful tool for gaining information and solving problems. In a conversation, give the other person your full attention. Focus on what is being said, look directly at the other person, and do not interrupt. Ask questions to show the other person that you want to understand. A good rule of thumb is to listen twice as much as you talk.

Recognize That People Have Different Communication Styles

Even in the same culture, people have different communication styles. They process information differently, approach problems differently, want information given to them differently, and socialize differently. Learning the different styles of the people you deal with and adapting your style accordingly can be an important tool in resolving disputes and avoiding conflicts in the workplace.

Use Email Appropriately

Email is the most widely used form of communication in the workplace. Make your email messages businesslike and brief and use informative subject lines. (For reasons of confidentiality, some organizations have a policy against using a client's name in the subject line.)

The email messages you write at work are not private and can be legally monitored by your employer. Network managers have full access to network data, including email messages. Even if both the sender and receiver delete a message, it still exists on the sending and receiving servers.

The best way to keep every job you will hold over your working life is to do your best work all the time.

Don't use email to handle serious issues or difficult problems that are best resolved in person. Never send an email that discusses negative information about your organization or department, sensitive or personal information, or information that you would not want to be shared with anyone other than the person you are writing to. The receiver can forward your message without getting your permission. Likewise, don't forward an email without getting the writer's permission. Continue to use your personal email for communications with friends and family.

Do Your Part on Teams

It is rare for a worker in any job to do everything alone. Most tasks are completed and many goals are reached through cooperation with and support from others.

When you work on a group project or are assigned to a team, know what your role is and understand your assignments. Do not let yourself fade into the background, expecting other team members to carry the weight without you. You are accountable for your share of the responsibility, your share of the work, and your share of the credit for what the team accomplishes.

Working in teams is a great way to learn from others and is a great opportunity to build relationships and promote your professional image.

Demonstrate Your Maturity

Be responsible for your actions:

- Perform at your best level and expect the same from those you supervise.

- Be aware of your strengths and weaknesses. Capitalize on your strengths and make an effort to improve your areas of weakness.

- Be self-reliant and self-disciplined.

- Show your maturity by thinking like a manager, acting like a leader, and being an example to others.

 ## Manage Your Career

Work takes up a large portion of the average adult's time. You may change jobs or even career fields (by your choice or, unfortunately in today's business climate, by someone else's choice). Today more than ever "Keep interested in your own career, however humble; it is a real possession in the changing fortunes of time."[1]

Be Smart about Money

Many goals—a home, a car, an education— require both personal effort and money. Managing money well is also essential for landing a job and achieving career success. In fact, many employers routinely run credit checks when screening job applicants.

Employers often will not hire applicants if their credit reports show a history of poor money management, such as making late payments or defaulting on school loans or other lines of credit.

Learn about Your Benefits

Take the time to learn about employee benefits and take full advantage of those that can save you money. Enroll in benefit programs at the start of your employment and update your benefit selections during your company's annual benefit enrollment period. You may be able to pay for additional benefits at group rates.

In addition to insurance programs, some employers offer flexible spending accounts that allow you to set aside pretax income to

[1]"Desiderata (poem)." Max Ehrmann, 1927.

pay for medical expenses and dependent care. These accounts can lower the amount of your income that is subject to tax. Some employers offer similar accounts for things such as mass transit fares and monthly parking fees.

Some employers offer personalized benefit plans. Employees can use their accounts for a wide range of benefits, such as disability insurance, child care, long-term care insurance, elder-care services, family-care leave of absence, and domestic partner benefits.

If your new position doesn't have all of the benefits you had hoped for, you may need to make alternative plans for health and disability insurance. These are available through professional organizations, credit unions, auto clubs, and alumni groups.

Save Money

"In the fall of 2008, America suffered a devastating economic collapse. . . . Millions of Americans lost their jobs; millions of families lost their homes; and good businesses shut down. These events cast the United States into an economic recession so deep that the country has yet to fully recover."[2]

If you are fortunate to have a job, you owe it to yourself and to the people who depend on you to *get into the habit of saving money*. No matter how little, save money out of every paycheck you earn.

Small savings add up. For a week or two, keep track of (1) how much you spend on food and (2) where you spend this money. Then make some of these changes and see how much you can save: eat dinner at home more often, make your own coffee, take your lunch to work twice a week, stay away from vending machines, and/or fill plastic water bottles with

[2]Wall Street and the Financial Crisis: Anatomy of a Financial Collapse. Majority And Minority Staff Report, Permanent Subcommittee On Investigations, United States Senate. April 13, 2011.

Who Needs Disability Insurance?

Blazej Lyjak/Shutterstock.com

Disability insurance is designed to replace all or part of your income if you cannot work or, because you are disabled, can earn only a reduced income.

More Americans are underinsured for disability than for any other basic form of insurance. As every reader knows, people can—and do—become disabled at any time in their lives, no matter how healthy they are and how carefully they live. You cannot ensure that you will not be in the intersection when another driver runs a red light. You cannot be sure that you will never eat a contaminated piece of food or drink a contaminated glass of water. You cannot go back and remodel your genetic heritage.

At age 25, you have a 44% chance, before you retire, of being disabled for three months or more. Health insurance, workers' compensation, and Social Security are not substitutes for disability insurance.

If your employer offers disability insurance, get covered. In addition:

- Establish a healthy lifestyle when you are young and stick to it. Think of it as an insurance premium that you pay in time and effort instead of dollars.

- Be careful with high-risk activities. Reduce your risk by wearing recommended safety equipment and following proper safety practices.

filtered water from your kitchen sink. The product website, www.cengage.com/career/yourcareer, has links to sites with more savings tips.

Plan for Your Retirement Now

It is *never* too early to start saving for retirement, so take advantage of any savings plans that your employer offers.

Many large companies offer tax-deferred savings plans—known as 401(k) or 403(b) plans—and will contribute to your retirement savings if you participate in the company-sponsored plan through payroll deductions.

Because you save your own money and contributions from your employer, this is one of the best ways to save for retirement. Depending on your savings plan, the amount you put aside can reduce your taxable income, the gains aren't taxed until you retire, and you may draw from the plan to pay for your education or buy a home.

You should also get investment and retirement savings advice from a financial planner or an investment banker who can help you establish an individual retirement account (IRA) if needed.

Expect Changes in Your Company and Industry

Your working life—the period of time in your life when you work—will last about 55 years, and maybe longer. Over the course of your working life, changes will occur in the organizations you work for, in society, in your industry, and in every industry. The U.S. economy may take a generation to recover fully from the Great Recession that began in 2008, and a stable economy is likely to be very different from the prerecession economy in the first decade of this century. You may even witness a geological change: The U.S. Geological Survey puts the odds of a magnitude 7 earthquake striking California within the next 30 years at 60%. (Good things will happen too, of course.) Keep an open, flexible attitude toward changes

at work. Don't make yourself obsolete through stubborn resistance; you may miss an open door to a career development opportunity.

Be Flexible and Accept Changes

Expect differences (some major) between the way your employer conducts business and the methods you learned in school or on another job. While schools often teach theories, employers interpret and apply theories and techniques (often developing their own) to accomplish specific work goals and tasks. Changes in technology make some textbook theories obsolete. Personalities also influence work methods.

A process that may seem inefficient or that is different from the method used in your previous job may serve a purpose that is not immediately apparent to you. Projecting a know-it-all attitude to your supervisor and coworkers is a sure way to alienate yourself, perhaps permanently. If you think a technique could be improved, request a meeting with your supervisor to clarify the reasons for using it. Asking thoughtful questions is a good strategy for opening the discussion.

Stay Up to Date

Continually update your skills and knowledge through education and training. You are living in an economy that is based increasingly on knowledge and service and less on manufacturing and goods.

In the late 1990s, for example, enormous wealth was created by ideas—many of which were applied to software and processes that increased productivity. Innovation (new ways of doing things) was the key.

Just as companies invested in new factories and machines during the Industrial Age, investment in employees with knowledge and information is the key in today's Information Age. That is why it's important for you to invest money and time in your ongoing training, education, and learning.

Earn Your Advancement or Promotion

If you like your company and want to advance in your career there, find out what it take takes to get promoted and take steps to help ensure that the person in the next cubicle doesn't get "your" promotion.

- **Demonstrate in your work habits that you are mature enough to handle new responsibilities.** Be professional, hardworking, and accurate in performing your job. This sets a positive example for your coworkers. Employers value and look for these qualities when retaining and promoting people.

- **Tell your supervisor that you are willing to take on new responsibilities.**

- **Do high-quality work.** Do the best possible job and achieve the highest possible quantity and quality of work.

- **Don't complain or criticize.** Instead, offer creative yet practical suggestions for improving procedures, saving money, and exploring better ways of doing things.

- **Be professional.** Think, act, speak, and dress professionally. If you want a promotion, act as though you already fit the part.

- **Learn about the new responsibilities you would have.** That way, your supervisor will know that you are ready to be promoted because you understand the duties of the new position and can be trusted to become productive in that position quickly. If the position will require new software skills, learn them on your own time. The Internet provides many free resources for learning how to use software.

- **Find a mentor.** A mentor is someone inside or outside your organization who can advise and coach you—someone who is respected and knowledgeable in your field. Seek advice from mentors who are experienced in the areas you need to improve. Don't limit yourself to just one mentor. Look for people who are sensitive to your concerns, who help you

MAKE IT A HABIT

Be a Lifelong Learner

Rapidly changing technology and a global economy have created a fast-changing world. Jobs and careers will continue to evolve. To have a successful career and distinguish yourself from the pack, you must keep your skills up to date and be prepared to learn new skills quickly. In short, you must make learning a lifelong pursuit.

There are many ways to continue learning and avoid being left behind. For example:

- Finish your college degree if you haven't already done so.
- Keep your licenses and certifications up to date. Expand you options by getting new certifications for your profession.
- Take continuing education courses.
- Use the resources of your professional association or industry trade group. Join the local chapter and attend meetings, subscribe to newsletters, and read blogs.
- Use free online training resources for software and for business topics such as teamwork and marketing.
- Follow industry experts on Twitter. Join LinkedIn groups that relate to your career field.

Your commitment to education and training is critical to your career success.

Goodluz/Shutterstock.com

"**Always display** the qualities that your employer perceived in you when you were hired. Make your employer glad that he or she chose *you*."

learn new skills, and/or who take time to explain organizational dynamics. Strive to meet your mentors' expectations for your performance.

- **Develop expertise.** Identify your greatest working strengths and interests and build on them. Take advantage of all training in these areas. Become known for your special expertise. This will help focus your career in a direction that best suits you and will expand your career opportunities.

- **Expand your knowledge and skills.** Stay current in your job and industry knowledge.

- **Get involved in professional groups, training, and education.** Tell your supervisor about meetings you attend and mention something you learned.

- **Increase your organizational awareness.** Learn all phases of the organization, its goals, and how each job is designed to meet the overall goals.

- **Increase your visibility.** Get involved in organizational committees and cross-team projects in which you can excel. Show extra initiative and demonstrate leadership. Develop your speaking abilities.

- **Show initiative.** Personal initiative is a major factor affecting your supervisor's opinion of your suitability for taking on more responsibility and being promoted. When you finish your assigned duties, don't sit and wait for more work to be assigned. Find an appropriate task to perform on your own, notify your supervisor that you are ready for another assignment, or ask how you can help someone else. Think creatively about better ways to do your job. Then research and plan how to implement your ideas.

- **Take risks.** Don't be afraid to take risks or to fail. Although success is rewarded, no one is perfect. Take appropriate, measured risks when necessary and have a back-up plan you can use when things don't go as you intended. Learn from your mistakes and don't repeat them.

- **Suggest ways to improve work procedures.** There is a right time, place, and method for presenting your ideas or suggestions to your supervisor. Learn by observing how others present their ideas. Explain (and show) how your idea can improve a problem area (a cheaper vendor for office supplies, for example) and offer it as a suggestion for consideration. Do not try to bulldoze your ideas through.

- **Use subtle self-promotion techniques.** Sometimes it's not enough to perform well; you must also make your superiors aware of your achievements—without bragging. Focus on your experience, not on yourself. Whenever you talk with coworkers and managers, be positive and enthusiastic about your job and your projects. Speak with confidence about your experience and accomplishments, but avoid making too many "I" statements.

Even if you know you don't want to stay at your current company, observe the people who have positions above you.

COMPLETE   **CAREER ACTION 14-3**

Research Success Tips for Your Career Field, p. 302

Know the Difference between a Job and a Career

A job involves performing a designated set of responsibilities and duties for a specific employer. A career encompasses a family of jobs. Your career is your life's work. Thus, *high school history teacher for Washington High School* is a job and *teaching* is a career. Similarly, *evening wear salesclerk* for the *After Five Store* is a job and *retail sales* is a career.

Many people don't understand the difference between a job and a career. As a result, they spend a great deal of time and money changing careers when they only need to change jobs. In other cases, people change jobs repeatedly and continue to be dissatisfied because they're not in the right career.

Most people change jobs at least eight times during their working lives. With changes in technology and in people's values and interests, it's also common for people to change careers at least once during their lifetime. If you realize that your current employment situation is no longer satisfying, consider whether the dissatisfaction is with your career or with the specific job. If you're unhappy with your supervisor but enjoy your work, for example, you may need to change jobs. But this doesn't mean you need to change careers. If you don't enjoy the type of work you do, however, you may want to consider a career change.

Think Carefully before Changing Jobs

You may want to consider a job change if:

- Your current employer can't offer you job growth or advancement.
- A poor economy requires layoffs or an entire class of jobs is being shipped overseas in an offshoring trend.
- You want to move to a new location.
- Your department is dissolved.
- Your philosophy and values conflict with those of your current employer.
- You want a new challenge.

Keep Your Career on Track with Social Networking

Building a career is not just something you do between jobs. It should be something you think about even when you're happy in your work. It's important to keep your skills sharp, to stay up to date in industry advances, and to keep yourself relevant in the field. Social networking sites are ideal for ongoing professional development because they are free or low-cost and require little investment of time. There's really no excuse not to take charge of your career online!

- Keep your LinkedIn profile updated and check in regularly to expand your network as you meet people in your line of work. Request recommendations from coworkers who can attest to your proficiency and professionalism and join groups that relate to your career field.
- Install an RSS reader (Rich Site Summary or Really Simple Syndication) on your computer and subscribe to the RSS feeds of top industry blogs. Don't be afraid to comment on articles that interest you and share your own knowledge.
- Do periodic searches on Twitter using industry-specific keywords. Respond to and retweet interesting tweets you find. Share articles you've discovered using Twitter and establish yourself as a knowledgeable professional.

Never Quit Your Job before You Have a New One

If possible, complete your job change while you are still employed. Because being employed is current proof that you do a job satisfactorily, you're considered more employable when you're currently working. As a mountain-climbing instructor says to students, "Never let loose of your support before you have hold of another one."

Don't Rush into a Job Change without Adequate Planning

Give any change of job serious thought and planning. A job may look good, but without proper research, you could find yourself in a situation that is as bad as or worse than your current one. Evaluate your current job by asking yourself, "Is there room for advancement, or are other important opportunities available?" If the answer is no and you will not be happy staying in your current position, you have strong grounds for considering a new employer. If the answer is yes, there may be advantages to staying with your current employer.

Know the Advantages of Staying with Your Current Employer

Seeking advancement or growth with your current employer can offer many advantages, including the following:

- Staying is less risky because you are already established and don't need to repeat the process of adjusting to new surroundings and people.

- Your reputation for job stability is better if you stay rather than move frequently from one employer to another.

- In outsourcing and off shoring situations, some employers recognize the value of keeping their best employees. They may offer you retraining opportunities and help you transition out of a vulnerable position.

- You won't lose accumulated benefits such as vacation time, retirement, and profit sharing.

- If your current job offers important benefits such as healthcare coverage and life insurance, it can be risky to give them up. With

4X6/iStockphoto.com

WATCH OUT!

Think Like a Free Agent

An employer and an employee are partners in a contract that must work for both parties. A job may be temporary, so think about your options and be prepared to take the next step in your career. As Robin McCraw (page 99) says, "I've learned over my career that something will always change. Even though I didn't expect this change, or welcome it or want it, it's a fact of life now. A person who can adapt to and manage change is a valuable employee."

Being able to adapt to change is also a valuable life skill. If you lose your job and cannot find a full-time position, you may need to consider a series of part-time jobs until you find full-time employment. One of your achievements in this course is your Career Portfolio. You may also need to develop a "portfolio career"—a career made up of a variety of jobs and activities that capitalize on your strengths and provide an acceptable level of income. These may include part-time jobs, temporary jobs, contract work, maybe even a hobby that that you can turn into a home-based business.

Keep an open mind—and keep your ears open for new opportunities. Maintain your network and use your resume as a sales tool to highlight your relevant skills and successes—not just your jobs. Stay up to date in your fields and activities and take pride in the new skills you acquire.

today's rising cost of benefits, some employers are finding it too expensive to provide extensive coverage. When considering a job change, always consider benefits in conjunction with rewards and compensation.

Know What You Can Gain by Changing Employers

Changing employers can also offer many advantages, including the following:

- You increase your job interest by becoming involved with new challenges, surroundings, and people.

- A job change may result in quicker advancement than you could achieve by seeking a promotion in your current organization.

- You gain knowledge, broaden your experience, and increase your support network, expanding your career growth opportunities.

- You start with a clean slate as you develop your reputation for good job performance.

Think Very Carefully about Changing Careers

If after thorough consideration you decide that you aren't happy in your work and that a change to another job in the same field would not bring satisfaction, you may want to consider a career change. Ask yourself the following questions:

- **Have I changed positions several times only to find that I'm still unhappy?** Repeated changes of employment that don't improve your job satisfaction may indicate a career problem, not a job problem.

- **Are my problems the result of personality or philosophical conflicts with my supervisor or coworkers?** If so, it's likely that you need a new employer rather than a new career. The exception occurs when the types of people usually found in your career field,

regardless of the organization, don't fit your personality or philosophy.

- **Am I unhappy with the work environment?** If you don't like working at a desk, for example, decide whether this is common to your career field or only to your job. Would you prefer outdoor work? You may want to look at other careers if your career doesn't provide the opportunity for the type of work you want. Is your problem with the work environment common to the career or only to some jobs in the career field?

- **Am I constrained in expressing my values?** Again, is this a function of your job or your career?

- **Is my position interesting?** What are your interests? Are you unable to satisfy them in your career or just in your current job?

- **Am I frustrated that I'm not using my skills and abilities?** Is this a job-related or career-related problem?

Even if you determine that your unhappiness is related to your career rather than your current job, you still have to weigh the pros and cons of making a career change. Rarely can you just jump into another career without making sacrifices, such as taking a lower salary. You need to evaluate the advantages and disadvantages and decide whether you're gaining more than you're losing.

Reassess Your Situation

First, determine what alternative careers fit your interests and abilities. Study the options to decide which career you think is the best fit. Apply the strategies in Chapters 2 and 3. Then after you have selected an alternative career, find out what additional education or training you need, how long it takes to prepare for the field, and what it will cost. Also determine whether the education or training is available nearby and whether you can get the necessary skills while continuing your current job or if you need to return to school and/or relocate.

Be Realistic

What are the job opportunities in the new field? Are the jobs in a desirable location, and will the pay meet your requirements? Be aware that when you change careers, you often have to start over at the entry-level salary.

What kind of risk taker are you? Are you willing to give up the security of your current position and career and take a chance? Do you expect to be significantly more satisfied in the new career? In the final analysis, decide whether the probable advantages of a new opportunity sufficiently outweigh the disadvantages and whether you are willing to assume any risk involved.

You must also be prepared to discuss your decision persuasively with prospective employers who may question whether you will be happy with such a career change. It is important to convey to employers that you have considered and planned for this change carefully and that you believe the advantages outweigh the disadvantages.

Resign Professionally

Resigning professionally is good career insurance. Make every effort to leave your current employer with good feelings; do not leave in anger or with hostility no matter how dissatisfied you might be. Throughout your career, references from your past employers will be requested each time you seek a new job. For this important reason, you should leave a job gracefully, pleasantly, and professionally.

Follow these guidelines to ensure that your resignation is accompanied by feelings of goodwill and a willingness by your employer to give you a positive reference.

- Find out how your current employer typically reacts when learning that someone is looking for a new position. Does your employer become upset and fire that person or try to make it difficult for him or her to find new employment? Does your employer respond positively by offering to support the person in finding new employment? Or, even better,

does your employer provide positive inducements (such as pay raises or promotions) to keep the person in the organization? If so, you need to consider whether you're willing to accept a pay increase or promotion and stay.

- If your current employer responds positively to people leaving, it's advantageous to discuss your plans immediately. The employer may provide you with references, helpful suggestions, or even a better opportunity where you are.

- If your current employer resents losing employees and even fires those who seek other opportunities, do not give notice that you are planning to leave until you have another firm offer. You don't want to jeopardize your current position. Remember that you are more employable when you are currently employed.

- Do your current job to the best of your ability through your last day on the job. You're most likely to be remembered by how well you performed at the end of your employment. This can greatly influence the quality of future references from your current employer.

- Update your career portfolio before you leave. If appropriate, request letters of recommendation from your supervisors. Assemble samples of your work and documentation of your achievements that are pertinent and exemplary.

- Plan for an orderly and efficient transition of your responsibilities to the person taking your place. If you are asked to help train your replacement, be as thorough as possible, taking care to explain your duties clearly and completely.

- Give your current employer at least two weeks' written notice before you leave your job. This is common courtesy and is important in maintaining good standing with your employer. Giving less notice is considered unprofessional. You should submit a formal letter of resignation. See the sample letter in Figure 14-1 on page 296.

COMPLETE **CAREER ACTION 14-4**

Write a Letter of Resignation, p. 303

Be Ready to Activate Your Job Search

You can lose your job at any time through no fault of your own. You must be ready to start looking for a new position immediately.

Keep Excellent Records of Every Job You Hold

Keep your resume up to date so that you can hit the ground running. When Robin McCraw (page 99) lost her job in a company-wide layoff of 8,000 employees, a job she had done so well for 12 years, she spent several weeks writing her resume before she thought she could start looking for jobs. When she didn't get any "hits," she took more time revising her resume until she was satisfied that it conveyed her accomplishments and all the skills she had acquired. Create an entry for your current position and use the keywords in your job description in the list of job duties. Keep your list of accomplishments up to date. If you are promoted, update your resume with your new title and responsibilities.

Don't put your Career Management Files Tracker on the back shelf of a closet. Add documents from each job you hold, such as your job description and performance evaluations. Print copies of emails commending your work and forward them to your personal email account.

Continue adding to your Career Portfolio. If a layoff is imminent, ask your supervisor for a letter of recommendation. Ask your supervisor and coworkers to post recommendations on LinkedIn and offer to do the same. Throughout your career, add records of all of your work-related achievements: samples of exemplary work, letters of recognition for a job well done, and other documents that support your good job performance and achievements. Evidence of your career accomplishments will be especially important if you are part of a group layoff, when many people with similar skills will be applying for the same jobs. You must be able to show prospective employers hard evidence of your accomplishments if you want to, or are forced to, find a new position.

Maintain Your Network

Networking is not a job search activity to be discontinued once you get a job. When you get a job, send a thank-you note to all of the members of your network who helped you or expressed interest in your job search. Tell them about your new position.

To achieve the greatest levels of career success, stay in touch with your contacts so that you are ready the next time you want to pursue a career goal. Staying networked pays off. When you need important information or the time comes to seek a new job, you'll be leagues ahead of the job seekers who don't stay networked. Follow the advice on page 291 about using social media to keep your career on track. Continue to network online through LinkedIn and Twitter and post positive comments about your employer.

Make a Great Career for Yourself!

Do you remember the advice in Chapter 11 to "make up your mind to have a good time and *then* go to the party"? Make up your mind to take the advice in the title of this book: make *your* career happen. You've done a great deal of work in the activities in *Your Career: How to Make It Happen*. The advice and cautions you have learned and the documents you have created can help you stay ahead of the competition throughout your career. (Think how much easier it will be to write a cover letter using the drafts you wrote in Chapter 7.)

Bookmark the product website and *Career Transitions* and use their many resources. Follow trends in your career field and continue your subscriptions to career-related newsletters (file them in an email folder so that you'll have them when you need them). Times change, so stay current with the best advice about job searches and new trends in careers and job searches. Save the work you've done in this class: this book, your Career Portfolio and Career Management Files Tracker, and your assignments and career documents—you'll be glad you did.

Marjorie Margolis

3236 South Everett Road   •   Cabin Creek, WV 25035

(304) 555-8515   •   Margolis.Marjorie@email.com   •   linkedin.com/in/MarjorieMargolis

March 17, 20—

Godshalk & Lake LLC
1414 Cromwell Avenue
Charleston, WV 25302

Dear Ms. Ackerman:

This letter is to serve notice that I will be leaving Godshalk & Lake LLC on March 31.
I have taken a position as a service manager with Morgan/Brown & Company in Ashland,
Kentucky.

I have truly enjoyed working for Godshalk & Lake and view my employment here as a
valuable experience and an opportunity for professional development. Thank you for
your guidance and assistance during the past three years; I sincerely appreciate it.

Best wishes for your continued success.

Sincerely,

Marjorie Margolis

Marjorie Margolis

Figure 14-1 Sample Resignation Letter

Chapter Checklist

Underline each action you are already taking and circle the actions you need to work on.

- Focus on these goals to adjust successfully to a new job: keeping a positive attitude; projecting a professional, competent image; and being a good team player. [1]

- Learn about and respect my employer and keep company information confidential. [1]

- Show up for work every day and be dependable and punctual. [2]

- Develop and practice good work habits and do my best work the first time. [2]

- Develop and maintain good relationships with supervisors and coworkers. [3]

- Expect changes in the workplace to occur and be flexible and adaptable when faced with changes. [4]

- Take steps to become—and be seen as—promotable. [4]

- Stay in contact with network members and add to my network. [4]

- Keep good records of job duties and accomplishments in every position and be prepared to begin a job search quickly and efficiently. [4]

Critical-Thinking Questions

1. What is the most common cause of job failure? Why is this the case? [1]

2. What five things can you do to master a new job? [1, 2]

3. Why is it important to know how your performance will be evaluated? [3]

4. Why is it essential to adapt to change? How can you demonstrate that you are flexible and adaptable? [4]

5. Once you have mastered a new job, what specific actions can you take to increase your professional development and make yourself promotable? [4]

6. What additional training or course work could you take to increase your knowledge and skills? [4]

7. What growth-oriented responsibilities are you interested in pursuing? [4]

8. What actions can you take in your current job to prepare for a promotion and increase your visibility? [4]

Want access to career resources, study tools, activities, and job information links? Get started at www.cengage.com/career/yourcareer.

How do you measure up to the traits that executives, supervisors, and business owners said that they most admired in new workers?

Trait	Description	Recent situation where you showed (or should have shown) this trait
Willing to go the extra mile	Stays a little late or does a little more to see a project through to the end	
Flexible	Can relate to different personalities of clients and coworkers	
Kind	Is a generally nice person who does not talk about coworkers, bosses, or clients	
Poised	Presents himself or herself confidently and is at ease with others	
Cooperative	Pitches in and works as a team player	
Enthusiastic	Comes to work with a smile, is full of energy and ideas	
Honest	Tells the truth, does not cover up mistakes	
Loyal	Is concerned for the organization's welfare	
Disciplined	Keeps his or her work and priorities in order	
Conscientious	Is thorough and hardworking	
Dependable	Arrives on time, misses as few days as possible, meets deadlines, keeps his or her word	

CAREER ACTION 14-1 Internet Research on Workplace Success Tips [1]

Search the Internet and/or *Career Transitions* for articles related to the topics in this chapter. Some keywords to use in your search include *career advancement, promotion, time management, performance evaluation, adapt to change,* and *mentor/mentoring.* Write a summary of two articles that are useful to you and file them in your Career Management Files Tracker.

CAREER ACTION 14-2 Job Performance Evaluation [3]

Career Action 14-2 is a sample job performance rating form that is representative of the forms used by many organizations. In the left column, rate your job performance in your current job or past work experience, in volunteer or internship work, or in another significant task-oriented activity (O = Outstanding, V = Very good, G = Good, A = Acceptable, U = Unacceptable). On the lines below each item, give one or two examples of your performance. Circle the items you rated acceptable or unacceptable; make these your targets for improvement.

Rating　　　**Performance or Behavioral Category**

_____ **ABILITY TO ACQUIRE AND USE INFORMATION AND FOLLOW INSTRUCTIONS** (Uses initiative in acquiring, interpreting, and following instructions and using references)

List specific examples: _____

_____

_____ **INTERPERSONAL SKILLS** (Is tactful, understanding, and efficient when dealing with people)

List specific examples: _____

_____

_____ **BASIC SKILLS** (Is proficient in reading, writing, mathematics, listening, and verbal and nonverbal communication)

List specific examples: _____

_____

_____ **JOB SKILLS** (Demonstrates command of required knowledge and skills)

List specific examples: _____

_____

_____ **THINKING/PROBLEM-SOLVING SKILLS** (Generates new ideas, makes decisions, solves problems, and reasons logically)

List specific examples: _____

_____

_____ **ABILITY TO COOPERATE WITH OTHERS** (Works well with team members and under supervision, exercises leadership, and works well with people of diverse backgrounds)

List specific examples: _____

_____

_____ **QUANTITY OF WORK** (Does required amount of work)

List specific examples: _____

_____

_____ **QUALITY OF WORK** (Does neat, accurate, complete, and efficient work)

List specific examples: _____

_____

_____ **GOOD WORK HABITS** (Maintains good attendance and punctuality, is dependable, and follows safety/work procedures)

List specific examples: _____

_____

_____ **ATTITUDE** (Demonstrates enthusiasm, interest, and motivation)

List specific examples: _____

_____

_____ **TECHNOLOGY** (Works well with technology—tools, computers, and procedures)

List specific examples: _____

_____

_____ **PERSONAL QUALITIES** (Demonstrates responsibility, initiative, self-confidence, integrity, and honesty; practices good self-management; sets and maintains goals; exhibits self-motivation; and is cooperative)

List specific examples: _____

_____

Overall Evaluation of Performance and Behavior

Review the rating code (Outstanding, Very good, Good, Acceptable, or Unacceptable) you placed next to each category of your Job Performance Evaluation on the previous pages. Place a check mark below next to the rating you recorded most frequently.

_____ Outstanding   _____ Very good   _____ Good

_____ Acceptable   _____ Unacceptable

Employee's Short-Term Goals (List your short-term job or career goals here.)

_____

_____

_____

Employee's Long-Term Goals (List your long-term job or career goals here.)

_____

_____

_____

Suggestions for Improving Performance or Behavior (List the steps you can take to improve your work performance or behavior.)

_____

_____

_____

General Comments about Employee's Job Performance (Add any other appropriate comments to describe the quality of your work performance.)

_____

_____

_____

Signature of Supervisor (This is where your job supervisor would sign your performance evaluation.)

_____

_____

_____

CAREER ACTION

14-3   Research Success Tips for Your Career Field [4]

Arrange meetings with knowledgeable people in your field to learn (a) how the job performance of employees is evaluated, (b) what techniques help ensure success on the job, (c) how employees can earn promotions, and (d) what methods are recommended for making a job change. Use the following questionnaire, adding pertinent questions that are relevant to your field. Or design and use your own questionnaire.

1. What advice would you give a new employee (in a position similar to the one you are seeking) to help him or her adjust quickly to the job, the company, and the people the employee would interact with?

2. What are the most important things to learn about your company when starting employment there?

3. What advice would you give a new employee to help ensure the highest degree of job success?

4. How does communication affect productivity and success on the job in your company?

5. Does your organization encourage risk taking? If so, in what ways?

6. What criteria do you use to evaluate the performance of an employee? Do you have a job performance evaluation form I could review?

7. What advice would you offer employees to help them increase their visibility?

8. How can an employee earn a promotion here?

9. If an employee must leave your company, what steps do you prefer the employee take? How much notice do you expect? Do you prefer that the employee help train the replacement? Do you expect a letter of resignation?

CAREER ACTION   14-4   Write a Letter of Resignation [4]

Review Figure 14-1 on page 296. Then prepare a letter of resignation for a position you currently hold or have held. File your completed letter in your Career Management Files Tracker.

For Your Career Management Files Tracker

File your completed Career Action worksheets in your Career Management Files Tracker.

CA 14-1   Internet tips about workplace success

CA 14-2   Job performance evaluations

CA 14-3   Success tips for your career field

CA 14-4   Resignation letter

Using Social Media in Your Job Search

OVERVIEW The Appendix has guidelines and advice for using social media to your advantage in your job search and your career. For more information about this important topic, see the following features:

Contents

Introduction to Social Media and Social Networking

In the early days of surfing the Web, most of the sites you visited talked to you. They offered information, advice, news updates, recipes, weather reports, etc., but there was no talking back. Email was pretty much "it" for two-way communication in the first generation— Web 1.0—where the Internet was a place to find, not exchange, information. The ubiquitous "shopping cart" symbolizes perhaps the major innovation of the first generation of the Web.

Then something shifted. People began commenting on blogs, forums went up where people exchanged information, and chat rooms became popular. This was social media in its earliest form, the user-centered Web 2.0, with "virtual communities" of people who talk to each other and collaborate and who develop and share their own content.

Social media differs from "standard media" (newspapers, magazines, books, television) because you can communicate too. Sure, you may yell at the TV when your favorite team

---

Social Media Glossary

Blogs: Websites with self-published posts listed in reverse chronological order. Blog posts are usually tagged with keywords, are available as RSS feeds, and often allow reader comments.

Connect: The act of requesting admittance into an individual's LinkedIn social network. A user who is accepted is a **connection**.

Feed: The delivery of frequently updated content, usually summaries of longer entries, from sites that create the content. Users install the RSS reader and subscribe to feeds that interest them, such as feeds that post job listings in the healthcare industry. (RSS is the most widely used tool for publishing Web feeds.)

Follow: To sign up to receive the tweets of another Twitter user. A person who signs up to receive your tweets is your **follower**.

Friends: On social networking sites, contacts whose profile you link to in your profile. Adding a contact is referred to as **friending**, and removing someone is referred to as **unfriending**.

Hashtag: Indicated by a #, a tag used in Twitter to organize and group tweets on similar subjects; similar to keywords used to find content through search engines. (Twitter usernames start with @.) See *tags*.

Influencer: A subject matter expert who is vocal in an online community and is respected for his or her opinion; therefore, he or she has the capacity to shape others' opinions.

Like: Functionality that allows users of a site such as Facebook to recommend content or demonstrate agreement with commentary. Recommendations are shared with the social network.

Online presence: (1) Whether you show up when someone does a search on your name. (2) Whether you use tools that show that you are available for contact via social media.

Post: An item on a blog or another online forum.

Retweet: To forward a user's tweet; a tweet that is forwarded. A retweet looks like this: RT *@tweetersname*: tweet you are retweeting.

Tags: Keywords attached to an item of content so that users can find the item easily through search engines. See *hashtag*.

loses a big game, but no one other than your unfortunate neighbor is going to hear you. Social media—Web 2.0—has opened up a new avenue for people to express themselves. Now when your favorite team loses, you can rant on Facebook, Twitter about it, write a blog post, post a video log, or exchange views with other fans on a sports forum. However you choose to engage online, the Web is now a place where people connect with other people. Web 2.0 emphasizes self-publishing, collaboration, and interactive information sharing.

Social media has become one of the most rapidly growing industries in the United States. Facebook, YouTube, Twitter, LinkedIn, Tumblr—a decade ago none of these names existed. Today you would be hard-pressed to find an Internet user who hasn't at least heard of one of these monoliths of social media networking.

Facebook alone now reaches about 73% of the total U.S. Internet population each month! Millions log in daily to each of these social media networks (and countless others) to share, search, learn, laugh, and do business. That also means a huge resource of knowledge, experience, and networking is free at your fingertips and is useful at all stages of the career ladder.

Whether you are new to the workforce or a seasoned veteran interested in expanding your business connections, networking with social media can be a useful tool in shaping your career.

Don't be afraid to dive in!

Learn from Companies How to Market Yourself

Outcome 2

Few, if any, people have million dollar coffers to fund their own advertising campaigns, much less additional funds to research what works and what doesn't. But companies do, and there are lessons to be learned from their successes and failures.

There has been a great deal of discussion about how to use social media as a marketing tool. In the early days, when everyone was learning what social networking sites could do, the tendency was to use them to convey a message. This is how traditional marketing campaigns worked. You watched a commercial on TV or saw an ad in a magazine, and the message was a one-way street. Companies quickly learned that simply broadcasting their message on social media channels was not very effective. The most successful social media campaigns capitalized on community engagement.

In 2010, Forbes.com compiled a list of "Best-Ever Social Media Campaigns." On the list was the Blendtec's funny "Will it Blend?" video series on YouTube, which boasted phenomenal views and boosted sales of blenders by more than 700%. Burger King's Subservient Chicken, who took orders from Web surfers to do silly things like dance or do push-ups, was another standout, giving Burger King a viral boost from its target demographic, young people. (A blog post, a video, an image, a joke, a marketing campaign, a song, etc., "goes viral" when it is rapidly shared across the globe via email, retweeting, and other online means. Companies aim for viral marketing, but social network communities and other users ultimately determine what content goes viral—another example of the power of social networking in the Web 2.0 world.)

The best-ever list included many other examples of creative outreach using different social media outlets and tools, but all of the marketing campaigns had one thing in common—they engaged their audience and created buzz (the online equivalent of word of mouth).

Every successful marketing initiative starts with identifying a target audience and setting a goal. As a job seeker using social media to market yourself, the tactic remains sound. If you're looking for a job in the nursing industry,

Social media: The tools and platforms people use to publish, converse, and share content online. **Social networking sites:** Online places where users can create a profile for themselves and then socialize with others using social media tools.

it won't do you much good to hang out on a motorcycle forum (as interesting as that may be). Don't abandon your hobbies, but while you are searching for a job, focus your efforts where you will reap the most rewards.

If you're looking for a job as a chef, find foodie forums and join groups on LinkedIn and Facebook where other foodies interact. You can do something clever (for example, filming yourself making a five-star meal and posting it on YouTube), but don't rely on gimmicks to market yourself. You need to put yourself in front of people. You don't see multibillion dollar companies being passive wallflowers on their social media networks. They aggressively engage their market to make an impression so that people will purchase their products or services. That's your job as well, except that the product or service you're offering is you, a valuable future employee.

Listen, speak up, and engage in the online communities you belong to.

Establish Your Online Presence

Outcome 3

The first step in using social networking in your job search is to become part of a network. Millions of college students already network socially using Facebook, Twitter, FourSquare, YouTube, and other popular sites. You may be one of them, in which case you're halfway there! Start with the network you have and build on it while keeping your career-building goals in mind.

Other networking sites such as LinkedIn and NetworkingforProfessionals.com are targeted specifically to job seekers and people interested in building a professional network. So if you don't already have a profile, look into building one. LinkedIn in particular is growing by leaps and bounds, is free, and offers many benefits to job seekers.

Because each networking site has its own protocols and requirements, take the online tours and follow instructions and guidelines carefully whenever you join a new network. No matter what networks you join, use the following strategies for effective online networking:

- **Share information about yourself.** The more your network knows about your career goals, the more they will be able to help you. Provide information about your education, career goals, current and past jobs, values, and interests and update your career information regularly so that it is current.

- **Be tasteful and professional.** Remember that much of what you post online is accessible to the public, and employers regularly check these sites for networking purposes and for checking up on possible candidates. An employer who visits your Facebook site or Twitter feed and finds unprofessional or tasteless content or photos or negative remarks about a previous employer is unlikely to hire you. Avoid potential embarrassment and lost opportunities by using good taste in online networks.

- **Be polite and businesslike in your communications.** Nearly everything you say online is accessible by others, and your comments will contribute to others' impressions of you. Make sure your posts and messages are well written and free of errors. Use abbreviations and texting language only when you are certain your network will understand them.

- **Follow the rules and respect members' preferences.** For example, do not repeatedly try to connect to members whose profiles indicate that they do not want to be introduced to new contacts at this time.

- **Share resources.** People will be more likely to connect with you if they think they will get something in return. A college student could be perceived as having little to offer an experienced professional. Show the network that this is not the case by reading and learning what topics are interesting to your network. Help people connect to other people in your network and send links to articles and information that will be useful to the network.

- **Join network groups that share your common interests and goals.** LinkedIn and Facebook are particularly valuable for this. Search networking sites for groups that have your interests, skills, and job goals and sign up to receive their emails and updates.

Participate in conversation threads and let people know who you are and what you have to offer. This is not the time to be shy.

- **Look for high-quality contacts.** Tens of thousands, even millions, of members in different social networks make it difficult to find those members who can help you. Use the search features of the site to find people you know, people who are connected to your school or place of employment, and people who are active in the industry in which you are interested. Try to find active, well-established connections by looking for members with many friends/connections and many hits on their pages. You also can try to connect with people who pay for premium memberships on networking sites. These people are likely to be active networkers and will be more interested in connecting with you.

- **Be careful whom you connect with.** Always read members' information and postings before connecting with them. You do not want to be associated with anyone who has negative, unprofessional, or offensive content or photos in his or her profile.

Using social networking sites does not involve leaving email behind, of course. Follow the advice in the book to use a professional email address—ideally, one that matches the full name on your resumes and cover letters, such as Caroline. Watson@email.com. Consider using a professional signature on your job-related emails. Here's a good example of a college junior's signature:

> "Learn from yesterday, live for today, hope for tomorrow." —Albert Einstein
>
> Caroline Watson
> Gervelis Law Firm: Intern Summer 2011
> Miami University Undergraduate 2012
> English Literature/History
> Pre-Law

If you haven't done so, create a free email address for your job search and create your LinkedIn account. If your name is already taken, add a number (your graduation date, for instance) or consider using a descriptor of your job goal or career field such as the one Sheree Long uses in Figure 6.10 on page 128: linkedin. com/in/sheree.aama to indicate that she is certified by the American Association of Medical Assistants.

Outcome 4 Research People and Companies

Social media sites are at their best when they are used to communicate and network with others, but their usefulness for conducting background research shouldn't be understated.

It hasn't always been easy to research a company. Company websites offer some information, but it's usually spun to reflect positively on the organization and may not be updated on a regular basis. Social media has changed all of that. Whether you've already secured an interview or are checking out a company for employment potential, social networking sites are an excellent tool for finding the data.

LinkedIn is particularly useful for this type of research. In the LinkedIn search box, you have the option of changing the drop-down menu and searching for a specific company. On the first page, you can learn if you are connected with anyone at the company, who the new hires are, if there are any new job listings or position changes in the company, how many employees the company has, when the company was founded, and a map showing the company's location. A link in the right sidebar takes you to statistical information about the organization, including a breakdown of years of experience most of the employees have, where most of them went to college, how many have advanced degrees, how long they have been employed, and more data (most of which is offered in comparison with the average statistics in similar companies). With all of this information, you can get a fairly good idea of the company you are hoping will hire you.

LinkedIn is also excellent for researching company employees. Not sure to whom to address your cover letter? If you look through the employees listed with the company on

LinkedIn, you may very well find the right person. You can also see if anyone you know is employed there and, if so, can learn a little about his or her background and interests.

Facebook and Twitter are the best resources for getting an idea of the company's values and the issues it's currently facing. Company blogs are also useful. Read the most recent status updates, tweets, and posts and read what others are saying about the company. Although organizations can spin information on their own site and blog, they can't control what others say about them on other outlets. Facebook and Twitter can also be good places to learn about upcoming job openings.

What was once a time-consuming task that required a great deal of legwork and many phone calls has been made relatively easy with social networking sites. Take advantage of the readily available information to become informed about the companies that have captured your attention so that you are ready for your interview.

Outcome 5 — Maintain Your Social Network after Your Job Search

So you signed up for social media accounts, you built your network, you enjoy engaging with people, and you even found a job. Now what?

Networking with social media tools isn't something you do just between jobs. It's an ongoing opportunity to build and maintain a thriving professional network. Keep your profiles up to date and check periodically to see what others are up to in your network. If others are now job hunting, help them as you were helped—this applies to your in-person networks too, of course.

Resist the urge to add people to your network to boost your numbers. Be selective. Anthropological studies suggest that people can maintain a stable relationship with no more than 150 people—in person and online. Beyond that it's hard to keep up and interactions become diluted and shallow. Keep your network at a sustainable number.

One of the most important things to keep in mind after the job hunt is over is that people are still watching what you post. As you become friendly with people, it's tempting to treat your social networks with a more cavalier attitude. There have been many incidences over the last few years of people posting crude, obscene, and privileged information on social media accounts—and ending up unemployed. Do yourself a favor by keeping the following guidelines in mind:

- **Don't trash your boss or complain about your job online.** Many people have found themselves unemployed after this infraction. Even if you haven't "friended" your boss, you never know who in your network has, and your post will almost certainly get back to your employer.

- **Don't release nonpublic information** you learn on the job or through any of your accounts. An EMT lost his job after tweeting about a call he went out on. Even though he didn't use the patient's name, the tweet was detailed enough that it constituted a violation of the patient's privacy and resulted in the EMT's termination.

- **Don't post offensive photos or comments** that will reflect poorly on your organization. Your employer has a right to protect the company's name and reputation.

Don't abandon your social networks after you've been hired, but be smart about engaging with them. Don't say anything on a social networking site that you wouldn't say to an auditorium of 500 people because that is, in effect, what you're doing. Keep your comments professional.

Over and over, research shows that people who use multiple resources to find job leads *find jobs faster*. Harness the power of social networking in your job search.

To boost your confidence and your know-how, read or reread the social networking features listed on page 304. You can find these features in one document at www.cengage.com/career/yourcareer.

GLOSSARY

A

action verbs in a resume and cover letter, concrete verbs and phrases that reflect an employer's requirements (for example, *build*, *prepare,* and *test*).

active listening a communication technique that requires the listener to understand, interpret, and evaluate what he or she hears; listening with the goal of understanding what the speaker intends.

assertive behavior the ability to express oneself and to stand up for one's point of view without disrespecting others.

B

behavioral interview an inteview technique in which the interviewer asks questions aimed at getting the applicant to provide specific examples of how he or she has success-fully used the skills required for the target job.

board interview see *panel interview.*

business ethics the application of ethical principles in a business environment.

business etiquette expected professional behavior in the workplace based on courtesy, manners, and customs.

C

campus interview an interview generally scheduled through a school's career center.

career compentencies the skills and traits that employers look for during job interviews and expect employees to demonstrate on the job.

career information survey a meeting in which a job seeker interviews a contact about his or her job or career; the job seeker's goal is to develop networking contacts and learn about a job or career.

Career Management Files Tracker a three-ring binder for collecting, organizing, and updating career development and job search information; used to store completed Career Action worksheets, self-assessments, skills and experience invento-ries, draft resumes and cover letters, and job search aids.

Career Portfolio an organized collection of documents and other items that demonstrate a person's skills, abilities, achievements, experience, and qualifications.

career target a job that is ideal for a person right now; it suits the person's qualifications and interests, matches his or her ideal salary and work environment, and provides a challenging and interesting work situation. See also *contin-gency job target* and *stretch job target.*

character questions interview questions asked to learn about the applicant's personal attributes, such as integrity, personality, attitudes, and motivation.

chronological the most traditional resume format; used to showcase work experience, skills, and a career progression that are directly related to the job target.

code of ethics an official document that provides written guidelines for an organization's employees and vendors to follow; based on specific ethical standards and values.

combination a resume format that uses the best features of the chronological and skills-based organizations to emphasize the match between the job seeker's skills and a position's requirements.

computer-based interviews time-based interviews in which applicants log on to a password-protected website with instructions on how to complete the interview; typi-cally consist of 50 to 100 multiple-choice and true/false questions.

contingency job target a job that is a backup plan; a person could easily get this job because he or she is overqualified or has a contact. See also *career target* and *stretch job target.*

cover letter a letter of inquiry or introduction that introduces a job seeker to a prospective employer.

E

employee handbook a written handbook that covers an organization's policies and procedures such as work hours, the probationary period for new employees, pay and benefits, and rules about using company equipment and email.

employment application a form with a set of questions used to collect information about a job applicant's skills, qualifications, and experience.

ethics guidelines or accepted behavior about what is right or wrong.

F

functional resume see *skills-based.*

G

gatekeeper the administrative support person, receptionist, or human resources staff member who must screen all job applicants.

general information questions interview questions asked to obtain factual information.

H

hidden job market job openings that are not published and that a job seeker must uncover; studies show that 80 to 85 percent of job openings are hidden.

I

informational interview see *career information survey.*

J

job application see *employment application.*

job club a group of job seekers who meet regularly to share experiences and advice, set goals, and offer encouragement.

job reference a person who can and will vouch for someone's capabilities, skills, and sustainability for a job. See also *references.*

job search network the network of people who can help a person with job leads and contacts.

job-specific skills skills and technical abilities that relate to a specific job.

K

keywords in a resume, terms that represent the job qualifications a company has programmed the resume scanning software to search for; also used in cover letters.

L

long-term goal a goal that is expected to be achieved over a long period of time. Compare with *short-term goal.*

M

master resume the generic version of a resume that a job seeker uses for networking and distributes at job fairs.

N

networking developing relationships with people who can help in forming job search strategies and in finding strong job leads.

O

Objective in a resume, a concise statement of the job seeker's immediate employment goals.

P

panel interview an interview in which the job applicant speaks with more than one person at a time.

performance how an employee carries out work assignments.

personal career inventory the information a person compiles about himself or herself through the Career Action assignments; an important resource when preparing resumes, cover letters, and job applications and when preparing for interviews throughout a job search.

personal support system the group of people who can motivate, advise, and encourage someone during his or her job search and throughout his or her career (for example, family, friends, instructors, and career counselors).

personality test a pre-employment test used to determine whether a job applicant's personal and behavioral preferences are well matched to the work involved.

plain text cover letter a text file (.txt) version of a cover letter that has no formatting (no bold, no tables, no bullets, etc.) and is used as the source file for the cover letter in online applications.

plain text resume a text file (.txt) version of a resume that has no formatting (no bold, no tables, no bullets, etc.) and is used as the source file for online applications.

positive behavior purposely acting with energy and enthusiasm.

positive self-talk purposely giving oneself positive reinforcement, motivation, and recognition.

positive self-visualization purposely forming a mental picture of one's successful performance and recalling the image frequently.

positive thinking making a conscious effort to be optimistic and to anticipate positive outcomes.

power verbs see *action verbs.*

power words see *action verbs.*

print cover letter a cover letter that is formatted like a standard business letter and is designed to be delivered by regular mail, delivered in person, or attached to an email or online application.

print resume a printed, word-processed resume designed to be visually appealing and delivered by regular mail, delivered in person, or attached to an email or online application.

proactive approach a focus on solving problems, taking positive actions, and taking responsibility for one's actions. Compare with *reactive approach.*

procrastinating putting off doing something that needs to be done.

productivity the effectiveness of an employee's work.

Profile in a resume, a brief statement that describes the job seeker by stating his or her most relevant experience and qualifications.

ualifications in a resume, a bulleted list of skills that high-lights why the job seeker is the ideal candidate for the job.

R

reactive approach a focus on problems and on avoiding difficult situations. Compare with *proactive approach.*

references people who are willing to vouch for a person's qualifications and recommend that person to prospective employers.

resume a brief one- or two-page document that details a job applicant's qualifications for a particular job or job target.

S

screening interview an interview used to identify qualified applicants for the next level of interviews and to screen out applicants who do not have the basic qualifications for the job.

self-esteem belief in one's abilities and worth.

short-term goal a goal that is expected to be achieved in the near future; an individual step in a series of steps needed to achieve a long-term goal. Compare with *long-term goal.*

skills test a pre-employment test used to test the skills needed for a job.

skills-based a resume format that emphasizes skills related to the job target; used when a job seeker lacks formal work experience that is directly related to the job target.

Social media The tools and platforms people use to publish, converse, and share content online.

Social networking sites Online places where users can create a profile for themselves and then socialize with others using social media tools.

stress questions interview questions asked to determine how the job applicant performs under pressure and whether he or she is good at making decisions, solving problems, and thinking under stress.

stretch job target the hard-to-get "dream job" a person would like to have in the near future; the job might be in a competitive organization or field that does not hire many candidates, it might offer exceptional salary and benefits, or it might offer a desirable location. See also *career target* and *contingency job target.*

structured interview a formal interview technique often used by professional interviewers; the interviewer typically asks a predetermined set of questions to obtain factual information and ensure fairness.

T

team interview an interview given by a group of three to five employees; the applicant meets individually with each person; after the interview, the team members meet to discuss the applicant's performance.

transferable competencies abilities that can be applied in more than one work environment; the basic skills and attitudes that are important for all types of work.

U

unstructured interview an interview approach generally taken by people who are not professionally trained in interviewing; is more formal and conversational in tone than a structured interview approach.

V

values deeply held beliefs about the importance of different personal qualities and traits.

W

web resume a resume formatted in HTML so that it can be posted on the Internet as a web document.

Work Experience in a resume, the section that lists the job seeker's employment history; jobs are listed in chronological order starting with the most recent job.

INDEX